The
Old
World
Roots

THE BROKEN STONES

THE BROKEN STONES

Written by
HERBERT L. MINSHALL
Paintings and sketches by the author

Commissioned by
HELEN K. COPLEY

Edited by
RICHARD F. POURADE

A COPLEY BOOK

PREVIOUS COPLEY BOOKS

Library of Congress Cataloging in Publication Data

Minshall, Herbert I.   1912-
    The Broken Stones

    Bibliography: p.
    Includes index.
    1.Paleo-Indians — North America. 2. Paleo-
lithic period — North America. 3. North America —
Antiquities. 4. Indians — Origin. 5. San Diego,
Calif. — Antiquities. I. Title.
E77.9.M56   970'.01   76-22630
ISBN 0-913938-17-3

Dedication

The Broken Stones is dedicated to all the adventurers who undertake the long journey into man's distant past in a search that can never end.

Helen K. Copley

CONTENTS

A Foreword

The Broken Stones peels back some of the story of man in America, back beyond the longest racial memory.

In canyons almost in the heart of the City of San Diego there have been found broken stones that bear the marks of having been worked by unknown hands far in the distant past.

And in the same region, along the coastline facing the Pacific, and in the dry deserts to the east, bones of long-dead humans are yielding tentative dates as far back as 48,000 years.

But beyond the dates being attributed to the bones lie the broken stones. Are they 75,000 years old? Or 100,000? Or even more?

Were they surely shaped by man? As tools and weapons? Yes, says a new breed of anthropologists, both amateur and academic, who are shaking the foundations of a scholarly discipline.

They are not really amateurs but avocationists. Their presence in anthropology is not new. Some of the great archaeological discoveries, for example, have been made by them, as merchants, lawyers, physicians, engravers.

This book is the product of an avocationist, an artist by training, who pulls together all that has been learned or suggested by other amateurs as well as experts, including his own discoveries, in the region with which he has made himself familiar.

To them the broken stones are beginning to speak — and they speak of the presence of man on the American Continent many, many thousands of years before he shaped the first bow and arrow.

Not all those who work in anthropology are ready to accept all the findings nor all the conclusions. Not yet, anyway. Sorrow often has been the lot of those who moved too fast.

But as science develops and tests new dating techniques, the challenges and the questions grow weaker.

The Broken Stones tells — if the stones speak the truth — how man could have arrived in America from Asia long before the last ice sheets cut off passage down the continent for hundreds of centuries.

And that was a long time ago.

RICHARD F. POURADE

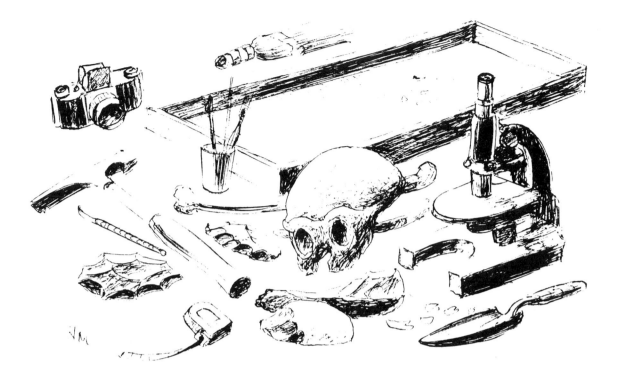

Memory and the Glacial Past

Man is surely the only animal for whom yesterday has meaning. Our fellow creatures are curious enough about the world of here and now, but we alone among the travelers are preoccupied with where we came from and when and how. And not only the recent yesterdays intrigue us; we peer with fascination far back into our primordial beginnings and try to retrace our steps throughout the long journey.

Most humans' view of the past extends backward through several realms of diminishing intensity. Primary are the recalled periods of one's own lifetime, events and sensations often relived with poignant clarity. I can know at will the haunting sounds and odors of childhood: distant train whistles in the night; the clip-clop of horse-drawn milk carts in the pre-dawn streets; the warm aroma of fresh loaves baking in the kitchen; the damp, slightly sour smell of a wooden icebox in the summertime.

At quite a different level are what might be called family recollections, happenings and conditions not experienced directly but known by constant retelling from one generation to another until they seem almost to have been part of one's own life. Beyond this stage of vicarious but personal experience and stretching far back into an increasingly vague dimness are all those kaleidoscopic visions of the past acquired from reading, from school lectures and television documentaries, historical movies, old paintings and engravings — a mélange of impressions which may seem quite vivid but probably bear small resemblance to reality. Thus I can sail with Christopher Columbus and see with surging joy and excitement the long blue smudge along the dawn horizon that is Santo Domingo rising from the violet sea beyond the stubby bowsprit and the frayed, salt-stained mainsail. I hear the hoarse "Gracias" of the crew and smell the rank odors of a wooden vessel too small and too long at sea. But this is largely my own fantasy and only memory in the broadest sense, a reordering of possibly valid fragments into a pattern of my own choosing.

Before the inscribing of clay tablets at Ninevah and Sumer the record of human memory is mute. Only the vaguest hints of human experience have been left for us to build on, yet the cities of Sumer rose above the plain only yesterday in the vast sweep of the human past. Stretching back as long as 3,000,000 years by present reckoning is the shadowy line of human evolution, of forms increasingly primitive as they march backward but still clearly kin of ours, back in time to a point so distant as to be invisible to us now.

Most of this slow creep of time has been designated the Pleistocene Epoch. It ended about 10,000 years ago and the remaining period including the present is called the Holocene; together they form the Quaternary. The Pleistocene was an age of alternating glacial cycles and more temperate interglacial stages in the Northern Hemisphere. In North America the last four of these glacial advances have been named and roughly dated, although Pleistocene chronology is a matter of some disagreement and tends to change as new information becomes available.

The most recent glacial cycle, the Wisconsin, is thought to have begun about 70,000 years before the present. A period of great fluctuations, as many as four separate advances of the ice have been identified. These substages have been named the Iowan, the Tazewell, the Cary and the Mankato. They were separated by interstadials of somewhat milder climate; the first one, the Altonian, may have lasted as long as 20,000 years during which the glacial capping across Canada, called the Laurentide Ice Sheet, melted enough to produce a broad corridor from the Beaufort Sea to the unglaciated south. By about 10,000 years ago the Wisconsin was in full and rapid retreat but one more minor substage, the Cochrane, has been suggested.

At the height of the glacial advances the continental ice cap in the northern latitudes was more than a mile thick and hundreds of miles wide from north to south. On the highlands of the Northern Cordillera, the Rockies and the Sierra Nevadas huge montane glaciers accumulated, grinding out valleys and resculpturing the land as at Yosemite in California. It seems certain that in these times survival in the glaciated lands by humans and most other creatures would have been impossible.

South of the glaciers in such periods the climate was much cooler and wetter than now. Many areas that we see as barren deserts would have been green, watered and stocked with grazing game. The beds and shorelines of ancient lakes are scattered today throughout the Great Basin and the southern deserts, clear testimony of a more pluvial time. Great Salt Lake is the vestigial remnant of an enormous body of water called Lake Bonneville that covered vast stretches of Utah, Nevada and Idaho during Wisconsin time and undoubtedly during earlier glacial advances.

The long, generally warmer and drier period that preceded the Wisconsin, from about 125,000 to 70,000 years ago, is called the third interglacial or Sangamon. Like the glacial periods, the interglacials, and the warmer periods within glacial cycles called interstadials, were not uniform in temperature but varied considerably over the millennia. Nevertheless, mammals including man could have moved rather freely over the entire continent in these milder times, slowly and gradually dispersing over favorable terrain.

The Illinoian or third glacial advance began about 175,000 years ago and was interrupted by the Ohe interstadial from 150,000 to 140,000, its second phase retreating at the start of the Sangamon. These are extremely tentative and general dates since exact information is increasingly lacking as one moves backward in time. Later movements of continental ice tend to obliterate the earlier glacial till, the rubble left by melting ice, as though a giant bulldozer had moved across the land, and only peripheral moraines may be left as evidence.

In dating glacial events core borings of ocean sediments have been extremely helpful. Successive layers reveal changes in climate reflected by temperature changes in the sea environment, recorded by the presence of minute fossilized shellfish species whose temperature preferences are known and whose ages can be determined by radiometric measure.

Two earlier ice advances have been identified, the Kansan and the Nebraskan, and before them others are presumed to have occurred during the earliest and longest Pleistocene phase called the Villafranchian, but these are only guessed at and are still shrouded in mystery. They probably played no part in Man's evolution since hominids at such early stages of development were almost certainly creatures of the warm tropics.

The mechanism by which these great glacial cycles were triggered is not known precisely. It was once thought that some kind of solar shift allowed less heat energy to reach the earth, thus cooling world climates and increasing snowfall to amounts greater than the summer melt-off. The solar theories have generally been abandoned today in favor of changes in the atmosphere that either block heat energy from reaching the earth, or allow a greater reflection of light from the earth's surface and thus a loss of heat energy back to space. The latter effect would of course be progressively intensified as more and more of the earth's land surfaces remained covered with highly reflective snow and ice.

The Pleistocene was also a period of vigorous volcanic activity and orogeny, or mountain building. Volcanic ash in large amounts in the upper atmosphere may well have been the agent precipitating a glacial cycle. If so, some scientists believe, modern air pollution on a worldwide basis may eventually have the same effect, but no climatic changes of decisive significance have yet been observed.

The presence of man in the Pleistocene world is marked by a few scattered remnants of fossil bone, but more widely and almost universally by the stone tools he left behind. These deliberately broken stones, called artifacts, reveal the slow, ages-long human progress from tool-users of sharp stone fragments in their natural form; through the earliest manufacture of simple choppers called pebble tools, water-worn stones purposely sharpened by striking off flakes from the end or side; through more carefully fashioned chopping tools flaked from both sides and given a thinner, sinuous edge; through symmetrical handaxes and finally stone projectile points of exquisite workmanship.

Over the millennia of the distant human past, despite the dramatic events of fire and ice and towering ranges rising ever higher into the sky, the tiny span of a human lifetime would have encompassed few if any changes in the familiar world whether that world were tundra, grassy savannah, forest meadows or rich, fecund marsh and sea coast. For most ancient people a lifetime was less than forty years and the world no more than perhaps twenty miles across. At night the same stars blazed and burned above their heads as I see lighting the clear night sky above my own.

•   •   •   •   •   •

One day I found by chance a fragment from that human past; a chipped stone tool of mahogany brown quartzite, heavy and massive, polished by time but clearly showing the telltale marks where each flake had been methodically struck away, the typical small batter-marks produced by smashing the marrow bones of long-vanished creatures. It seemed to me so ancient as to make the fluted spearpoints of Paleo-Indian mammoth hunters seem recent by comparison. I felt a strange sensation almost akin to reverence, as though I had been shown a glimpse of God's mysterious process. I longed to know the maker of this worn chopping tool and when and how he lived, what thoughts troubled or exalted him, and above all what succession of events led his ancestors here to my peaceful canyon surrounded by the city.

Now I know only a little more; something far short of certainty but beyond idle speculation. Out of black darkness he has emerged into a dim half-light, a shadowy figure slowly coming into focus, primitive in action and appearance but already towering above his fellow creatures.

The First Glimpse at San Diego

The year was 1947. Heat waves shimmered over the dry, sandy bed of the San Diego River and the scattered cottonwoods and sycamores along its margins. In their deep shade cattle drowsed, and a few widely-spaced ponds nourished red-winged blackbirds, tules and spicy skunk cabbage. Just south of the river bottom a narrow black-topped road ran up Mission Valley beside green fields of corn and alfalfa and sunbaked stretches fallow and redolent with dove weed. The road served the dairies, truck farms and isolated homes that occupied this rural enclave surrounded by the city; in places it curved around the projecting shoulders of the terrace that buttressed the steep south wall.

About five miles up the valley from the sea Texas Street climbed up a lateral canyon to the densely-settled mesa top, and a few hundred yards west of the intersection a large borrow pit had been cut into the terrace by a sand and gravel firm. Here an almost vertical series of cutbanks displayed in cross section the successive layers of silts, clays and cobbles that composed them.

The pit was deserted now except for a lone visitor who had noticed it from the valley road, parked his car and was scrambling up the steep banks like a squirrel, examining with minute attention the soils and gravels. As he poked and probed at the face of the cliff and studied the rock specimens weathering out he felt a growing excitement, almost a feeling of awe.

To the casual, untrained eye there was nothing unusual to be seen in the exposure. A careful observer might have noticed a surprising amount of broken rock in some of the strata and areas in which all of the rock fragments had turned red, violet or salmon pink, but this would probably have been attributed to oxidation or brush fires. Even most archaeologists might have passed it by. No weathered bone protruded from the cliff, no flaked spearpoints, no bits of pottery nor beads nor recognizable stone tools of any kind. But some of the broken stones had characteristics that made them seem odd and out of place.

These stones were of porphyry and quartzite, common materials in the stream gravels of the region. But they had been transformed from the original cobble shapes into elongate objects of polygonal cross section, as a potato might appear if lengthwise slabs had been removed all around, leaving little or no skin. Some were apparently snapped-off sections, others were quite irregular but seemed related and a few were so symmetrical as to defy rational explanation. To almost anyone else on earth the broken stones might have been dismissed as meaningless, but the searching, inquisitive mind of the man who

Section of the south wall of the borrow pit near Texas Street as it appeared about 1950. Charcoal taken from an exposed hearth to the right of the gully and just below the top of the lowest bench proved to be beyond the range of radiocarbon dating at that time, or more than 35,000 years old, as expected, since the soils of the terrace are at least of the Third Interglacial age.

examined them on that warm summer day worried the problem like a dog with a bone.

Dr. George Francis Carter, then in his mid-thirties, was chairman of the Isaiah Bowman Department of Geography at Johns Hopkins University. He was also trained and experienced in another field, having been for several years curator of archaeology at the San Diego Museum of Man, and was particularly well grounded in the prehistoric cultures of the region. A slim, redhaired young man with a disarmingly unpretentious manner, Carter had returned to his native San Diego to do field research on the Pleistocene marine terraces along the Southern and Baja California coasts, a project for which he had a grant-in-aid from Johns Hopkins University for the summer of 1947. But his first and primary enthusiasm was for archaeology, and he had been excited by finds of artifacts and hearths at levels along the coast which suggested much earlier dates for La Jollan shell middens than had previously been proposed.

The La Jollan people lived along the coast of Southern and Baja California in prehistoric times and had disappeared before the arrival of the first European explorers in the region. Although their culture had been studied for over twenty years and was well represented by artifacts, food refuse and human skeletal remains, its maximum age had generally been placed at about 7,000 years. But Carter's analysis of Pleistocene events and particularly the sea level changes called *eustasis*, brought about by the periodic accumulation and subsequent melting of vast amounts of ice on the land during the glacial cycles, had convinced him that the earliest horizons of this culture dated well back into the last major glacial advance, the Wisconsin, which ended about 10,000 years ago.

The terraces that Carter studied were of two kinds. When the sea level was lowered in relation to the land, either because of eustatic forces or the slow uplift of the landmass itself, benches were cut by wave action and then abandoned as the sea level subsided even more. A few miles inland in the valleys running down to the sea, terraces were left along the bases of the valley walls as streams cut down through ancient flood plains and valley fill in response to the lower sea level.

River terraces of the latter kind can hardly be younger than the end of the last interglacial, for the sea is not thought to have been substantially higher than the present level since the onset of the Wisconsin ice some 70,000 years ago, so that anything found solidly in place in these ancient flood plain remnants must be that old or older. The terrace at Texas Street was such a flood plain; its silts would have required many millennia to accumulate, and scattered through a layer of clay and silt forty feet thick lay the strangely broken stones.

As Carter pondered the puzzle of how they might have been formed he became increasingly convinced that only human activity could have been responsible. He returned several times in the summers that followed, and in 1950 came back for more field research, this time supported by the Wenner-Gren Foundation. As commercial work in the gravel pit had progressed, new surfaces had been exposed in the terrace formation. Careful examination disclosed more broken rock and fire-reddened streaks but also some basin-shaped areas containing burned earth, charcoal and bits of charred bone and shell. More of the same polyhedral stone specimens were found and Carter deduced that they were discarded cores from which functional stone blades had been struck.

Next Page
An early view of the terrace at Texas Street, San Diego. This aerial photograph, taken before gravel pit operations exposed a cross section of valley fill near the center, shows the terrace structure at the foot of the valley wall, with a large gully cutting through it. The road up the valley curves around the terrace; just beyond it Texas Street can be seen intersecting the valley road and running up to the mesa on the right. On the left can be seen the dry bed of the San Diego River.

Experimenting with cobbles of similar material was unsuccessful until the work piece was set on a stone anvil and struck with a steel hammer. By this method long blades or flakes running the length of the core could be extracted, sometimes being detached from the anvil end of the core rather than the end struck by the hammer. It appeared that this technique of bipolar flaking — so-called because both ends or poles of the axial core simultaneously received the hammer blow and anvil resistance or counterblow — could explain the unique shape of the collected specimens, and also might explain the mystery of why so many of the flake scars were lacking the usual percussion marks normally expected on examples of human workmanship.

Even in those first optimistic years Carter realized that opposition to his announcement of interglacial man at Texas Street would be formidable. He began to accumulate supporting evidence. In addition to what seemed to him clear proof of human activity at the site he needed to demonstrate beyond question its antiquity. All other apparently very ancient sites in the Americas known to him at that time lacked any means of positive dating except the implications of primitive, crude stone tools, extinct animal bones and

Hearth in the terrace at Texas Street, San Diego. This basin-shaped feature was exposed in the wall of the gully cutting through the interglacial deposits, and photographed during George F. Carter's early investigation in the early 1950's. The clays at the base were described as "burned pink," and the overlying dark stratum contained bits of what was later determined to be charcoal. This was one of a series of hearths found at this level by Carter; some contained bits of burned bone and marine shell.

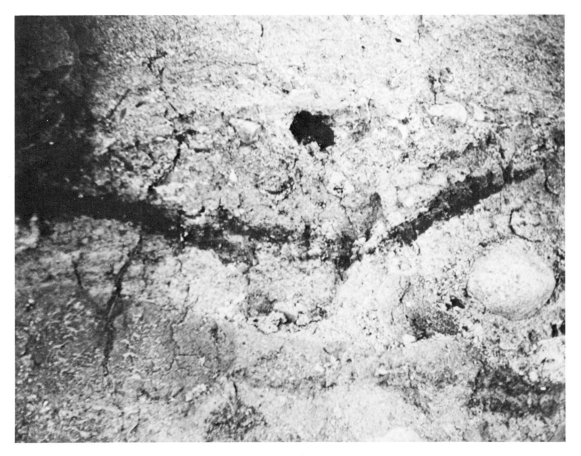

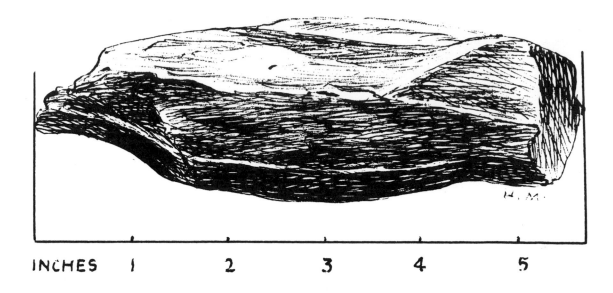

INCHES   1   2   3   4   5

A typical polyhedral bipolar core. Such cores are said to be "exhausted" when the striking platform at the right end becomes so small that no more long blades can be conveniently removed. Experiment has shown that the more slender the core becomes, the greater grows the danger of smashing the fingers holding the core in position on the anvil.

evidence of climatic change. Here the situation was far different since the stone specimens were in a geological formation clearly attributable to a high sea level, far higher than was believed to have occurred since the last interglacial about 70,000 years ago. His studies of the local terraces and the dating and effects of sea level changes here and around the world in response to the glacial and interglacial timetable had given him an unusual insight into the problem.

In addition, the soils themselves could be analyzed, and significant indications of age and weathering in changing climates could be revealed in support of their interglacial origin. Such things as maturity of the development of soil horizons, soil acidity, accu-

Some of the original specimens identified as artifacts by George F. Carter during his investigation of the Texas Street site at San Diego in the 1950's. All are of quartzite except the piece at right center which is porphyry. The small irregular specimens in the top row are typical of the so-called "Carterfacts," a designation coined by a skeptical critic. Careful examination of them, however, reveals evidence of bipolar flaking, a technique practically unknown at the time of their discovery. The two large pieces in the center row appear to be tools, although both are strongly abraded, possibly by the blowing sand and dust expectable in a dry interglacial climate. The larger piece on the left is thought to be a maul for bipolar flaking, while the porphyry specimen on the right would be classified as a bifacially-worked chopping tool. The three specimens in the bottom row are elongate cores from which slender blades or flakes have apparently been extracted by the bipolar method. The piece in the upper right may be a snapped-off remnant of such a core.

mulation of salts, grain sizes, clod formation and structure, and contained pollens all contributed to the determination of relative antiquity.

Since the origin of the terrace was being attributed to lowering of sea level by accumulation of glacial ice after a high sea level period of valley filling and not to upward movement of the land, the stability of the landform would have to be established. Critics would be quick to suggest that Southern California is noted for its instability, and that local subterranean forces might have thrust up the land here far more recently than was being proposed. But every examination of the perfectly horizontal strata attributed to the Pleistocene, and overlying more ancient tilted formations in the vicinity, indicated tectonic stability here for at least two million years. While a slow regional uplift might have occurred this could not account for a sea level change of sixty feet in the last 100,000 years.

As the results of his investigations were gathered together and organized, Carter began to publish them in various professional journals. He eagerly escorted visiting scholars over the site at Texas Street, explaining his theories, pointing out the hearth features and the obvious origin of the terrace, demonstrating the lithic specimens and the theory of bipolar flaking, showing that in comparable areas there were neither the vast quantities of burned and broken rock nor the uniquely broken stones he identified as artifacts. His guests nodded politely, behavior he mistakenly took for complete agreement, but he was later surprised to read articles by some of these same affable visitors in which his claims were described as inconclusive or completely unfounded.

There was only one solution — work harder and produce a report so complete, detailed and documented as to leave no basis for disagreement. In 1953-54 Carter obtained a Guggenheim Fellowship and a partial sabbatical from Johns Hopkins to continue his research, and in 1955 Wenner-Gren provided grant-in-aid of publication. In 1957 *Pleistocene Man at San Diego* was published by the Johns Hopkins Press. The reaction of anthropologists throughout the country, with the exception of a few supporters, was a bitter disappointment to Carter. Despite his painstaking care in assembling and presenting his evidence, the book was greeted with skepticism and disbelief by many of the most influential scholars.

Skepticism of Carter's claims was not unreasonable; in fact it was perfectly expectable. In summary, the three principal bases for doubt were: the unfamiliar and therefore questionable stone specimens being offered as evidence of human activity; the identification of the concentrated zones of burned earth, red and broken rock and charcoal as "hearths" and not simply the residue of brush fires; and finally, and to some the most compelling, attribution of the landform in which the evidence lay to an interglacial high sea level and not to a more recent elevation of the earth's surface there by tectonic activity, the Southern California region being supposedly highly prone to earth movement and faulting. In this latter controversy Carter was to be solidly supported in the following decade by California Institute of Technology geologist C. R. Allen and others, who agreed with him that no substantial deformation had occurred in the San Diego Block for over a million years, saying in effect "Carter was right."

• • • • • •

George Carter and I grew up together in the same neighborhood of San Diego in a district called Mission Hills, on the mesa above Mission Valley and only a mile or so from Texas Street. We were good friends, a couple of skinny kids who liked the same things. We tramped the river bottom and the hills beyond hunting doves and rabbits, huddled shivering in duck blinds together and knew the primeval, gasping excitement of having pintails begin to circle our decoys. We sailed with the Sea Scouts and we also shared another compelling interest that, like hunting and sailing, stayed with us all our lives. We discovered archaeology.

When George was a young boy his father had shown him places in the hills where Indian arrowheads of obsidian and quartz could be found scattered in the topsoils. When we were in our early teens George found an arrowhead in a flower bed in his front yard and traced the topsoil to a borrow pit across the valley within easy walking distance. We located the spot and were enchanted to discover that it had been a campsite of the Diegueños, the Indians that the Spaniards found inhabiting the region when they first arrived in Southern California. We collected a number of artifacts, mostly projectile points and stone knives but also a clay pipe and an arrow straightener, and took them to the San Diego Museum of Man where we encountered Malcolm Rogers, now considered to have been the dean of archaeologists in this region.

From Rogers, a trim, leathery man with piercing blue eyes, we quickly acquired both a lifelong enthusiasm for delving into the past and a firm respect for professional methodology. We prowled promising territory endless hours, noting and collecting, and learned a great deal about the peoples who had drifted through our corner of the world. We developed what might be called "archaeologists' stoop" from always walking with our eyes fixed hopefully on the ground.

George Carter decided early to make archaeology his life work, and upon graduation from high school he attended the local state college for a year, then transferred to the University of California at Berkeley and took his Bachelor of Science degree with a major in anthropology. He was appointed curator of archaeology at the San Diego Museum of Man at a modest salary.

My choice was different since from childhood I had known I would be an artist when I grew up. I worked part time as an apprentice commercial artist even in high school, and after graduation was employed full time. But adventure called and I left to enter the California Maritime Academy and then to follow the sea for two years. Forced ashore by the shipping strikes of the mid-thirties, I worked a year at the Museum of Man during the California Pacific International Exposition and renewed my earlier enthusiasm, going on field trips with Malcolm Rogers and Carter to the Colorado River Desert. But soon I was back in the commercial art business and George was at the University of California working for his doctorate in geography, a field which he felt offered a solid grounding in earth sciences and would be useful in solving the problems of American antiquity.

After World War II and naval service I was back at college, having decided to abandon the ulcer-breeding world of advertising art and become an art teacher. Carter served as an analyst in the Latin American Division of the Office of Strategic Services during the war, and taught at Johns Hopkins for over twenty years. In 1975 he was teaching at Texas Agriculture and Mining University where he held the title of Distinguished Professor.

During his work at Texas Street and the La Jolla sites we saw each other occasionally, but I was too involved with trying to become a successful art teacher to follow his work closely until his book was published in 1957. The book's negative reception was incomprehensible to me then. I recall one of those biting critiques to which *Time* magazine was partial, a piece which dismissed Carter's claims as verging on the preposterous. I read many more balanced judgments in professional journals, articles which pointed out the likelihood that the broken stones could be attributed to natural causes, and the burned areas and so-called hearths to brush fires.

It is highly important to recognize the role that skepticism plays in the scientific process. Science attempts to be a body of fact, not a collection of beliefs, opinions and theories. The latter play a part in the search for truth but they do not establish it. Skepticism and critical argument are absolutely essential elements of the testing process, and disagreeable as they may be at times, they force the scholar to prove his theories with the best evidence he can muster.

In the field of American antiquity it has been the practice to proceed with extreme caution. Prudent scientists have reserved their judgment on the question of man's earliest appearance in the Western Hemisphere, assuming relative recency of arrival until irrefutable evidence is offered to the contrary. Dates had been moved backward slowly, particularly before the development of radiocarbon dating.

Radiocarbon dating is a method of deducing the age of organic and previously living material developed by Williard F. Libby and associates at the University of Chicago in 1944. It utilizes the fact that radioactive isotopes of carbon, called Carbon 14, are produced in the atmosphere through the bombardment of nitrogen particles by cosmic rays, and are absorbed into the tissues of all living organisms throughout life. Upon the death of the organism the Carbon 14 slowly decays and disappears at a constant and known rate. Thus formerly living matter such as charcoal, wood, shell and in some cases bone can be reduced in the laboratory to pure carbon and the percentage of Carbon 14 remaining can be measured, permitting scientists to determine the approximate number of years that have passed since the organism ceased to live. Ages up to 70,000 years are theoretically possible to determine but in practice after about 40,000 years such small amounts of Carbon 14 remain that measurement is not feasible in most laboratories.

But unfortunately radiocarbon dating has had many limitations, requiring suitable organic material in sufficient quantities and subject to contamination. Dates have frequently been questioned. Many respected anthropologists have felt that to be valid, evidence of great antiquity should include not only indisputable stone artifacts but human skeletal remains of a clearly primitive type, preferably overlain stratigraphically by material from a universally recognized and accepted culture. Since it is not known with any certainty how long the modern form of man, *Homo sapiens*, has been in existence, this ideal situation may never be encountered. In 1957 when Carter's book came out the generally accepted age for man in the Western Hemisphere was probably about 15,000 years. Although obtaining a concensus from all anthropologists would be difficult if not impossible, in 1970 the figure might still have been less than 30,000.

These ages have been established by the finding of clearly recognizable artifacts, primarily stone projectile points, in geological contexts that could be dated with some assurance or in clear association with the bones of extinct mammals such as giant bison and mammoths that are believed to have become extinct late in the Pleistocene. In more recent years radiocarbon dating has been utilized effectively, being applied to organic materials found with obviously man-made implements. But as the artifacts get cruder and less familiar in their march backward through time, their identification as the work of man falls increasingly into the realm of opinion.

Scholars of American antiquity will vigorously attack any purported evidence if there is an area open to question, but few professional or avocational archaeologists doubt that the age of man in America will continue to be extended backward in time. The question is how far. Many have encountered evidence themselves which seemed to suggest far greater antiquity than could be proven, but have been reluctant to publish the data because they felt the evidence was inconclusive. Others have felt that all such data should be published and shared with other workers in the field as important contributions to the advancement of knowledge, even though conclusive proof could not be offered.

Regardless of his inner feelings of frustration and chagrin, Carter responded to the criticism of his findings with redoubled efforts to convince the people he respected and admired. He sent samples of the artifacts around for inspection and lost some of the best ones in the process. He wrote articles attempting to refute the arguments of the most insistent critics. He corresponded with scholars all over the world, and particularly with those in America who had seen their own claims for very early man questioned.

A few prominent anthropologists published views in support of Texas Street: John

14

Witthold of the University of Pennsylvania; Sherwood Gagliano of the University of Louisiana; Luther Cressman of the University of Oregon; Thomas E. Lee, publisher of the Anthropological Journal of Canada, and Ruth D. Simpson of the Southwest Museum in Los Angeles. The vast majority of Carter's peers simply remained unconvinced.

At last George Carter decided that only time and the inevitable new discoveries would prove him right, and he gave up the active struggle and turned to other matters. But a few years later a series of developments in Southern California began to reinforce and throw new light on the limited testimony of the broken stones and hearths at Texas Street, and he found himself actively engaged in the search again.

A Few More Lonely Voices

From the towering Brooks Range in Alaska to the Sacramento Mountains of southern New Mexico, a chain of ranges stretches almost unbroken for nearly 3,000 miles down the western spine of the continent of North America. Only in southern Wyoming does the rugged barrier subside; here the central High Plains gradually rise and merge with even higher and more barren rolling prairie, and the Continental Divide is invisible to the eye. The drainage of the North Platte runs east to the Atlantic via the Missouri, while only a few miles to the west the Green River gathers its creeks and forks to augment the Colorado.

Across this sunburnt land with its scanty grass and stunted sage, its flat-topped buttes and mesas, the Black's Fork River has cut a winding valley to the Green. Rising in Utah's Uinta Range, the stream runs north and east, a gentle flow in summer and fall but covering its flood plain in spring freshet when deep snows melt on the high mountains to the south. Bordering the gravels and sand bars and scoured out flats of the present level are eroded terraces and benches, the remnants of older flood plains. Flat-topped and with relatively gentle slopes, their upper surfaces are paved with gravels formed and deposited far back in the Pleistocene, before the slowly rising land and down-cutting of the stream left them high and dry.

This great rift in the mountain chain has always been, and is today, a broad avenue of easy passage between the High Plains and the Great Basin. Long trains of freight cars are hauled over the deceptively tilted slopes, and huge diesel rigs roar endlessly along the interstate freeway past occasional pronghorns grazing unconcernedly on the meager forage beyond the fences.

A century and more ago the canvas-topped Conestoga wagons went creaking and lurching by in choking clouds of alkali-bitter dust. Before that bearded men in streaked and greasy buckskins rode over the prairie swells leading strings of ponies, eager to trap beaver along the creeks and sloughs of the Green.

Indians used the land for passage over the centuries. Ute raiding parties, bright in paint and feathers, scouted carefully through the draws, avoiding the skyline and seeking Shoshone horse herds lightly guarded. Far back in the past their predecessors dwelt in the Valley of Black's Fork in a more pluvial time; a time when the grass grew tall and berries and fish and game abounded. And even these ancient Paleo-Indian people could look back in time and surmise that earlier men had been there long before them, for stone tools lay on the higher terraces so worn and polished by time and weather and so crude in their workmanship that they could only be attributed to far more primitive human inhabitants.

In 1932 these tools drew the attention of Edison Lohr and Harold Dunning, two Colorado men who were interested in archaeology. They showed samples of the artifacts to Dr. E. B. Renaud, a professor of anthropology at the University of Denver and Director of the Archaeological Survey of the High Western Plains which was jointly sponsored by the University of Denver and the University of Wyoming. Dr. Renaud was immediately interested, and organized a field expedition to Black's Fork for the summer of 1932.

Renaud was born and educated in France, where he studied under the great European anthropologist Abbé Henri Breuil. He knew thoroughly the paleolithic stone work of the Old World and had become reasonably familiar with the Paleo-Indian traditions of the American West as they were understood at that time. In 1932 few archaeologists had encountered any of the early non-projectile point sites that have since been discovered, with their pebble tools, simple chopping tools and scrapers occasionally associated with the bones of long-extinct animals. In 1975 many such sites were known, among them the Lively Complex of Alabama, Tule Springs in Nevada, Los Encinos in New Mexico, the valley of the Little Colorado in Arizona, Manly Terrace in Death Valley, California, and the sites presented in this book.

Renaud's party spent a week, despite extremely difficult conditions under the scorching midsummer sun, examining and collecting from surface sites in the vicinity of Black's Fork between the towns of Lyman on the west and Granger to the east. In the first part of the Seventh Report of the Archaeological Survey of the High Plains, published in January, 1933, by the Department of Anthropology of the University of Denver, Dr. Renaud reported the presence of a certain number of early paleolithic implements among the Wyoming specimens and presented the following conclusions:

"... Therefore, the presence of early and late Chellean and early Acheulian coups-de-poing together with early Clactonian flakes is perfectly consistent and would suggest a cultural complex in America similar to that in Europe, and also a possible very great antiquity for these artifacts from our S-W Wyoming sites as well as for the rest of the industry associated with them. This typological resemblance between Old and New World implements is striking and may be very significant. However, only a systematic geological and paleontological study of the sites could, together with the archaeological diagnosis here presented, reveal the true age of this lithic industry."

To the bewilderment of Dr. Renaud, this statement according to one of his later reports was "harshly criticized by one of the irreconcilable opponents of the antiquity of man in America, who had seen neither the site nor the specimens. After such subjective and unfair criticism, the best course to pursue was to do more extensive exploration, to collect more numerous specimens, to study them more closely, and to compare them directly with Old World artifacts of well-authenticated origin and established age and culture, and to obtain the expert opinions of qualified scientists not prejudiced on the subject of the antiquity of man in the New World."

Dr. Renaud and the Archaeological Survey did all of these things. Three expeditions were sent to the area, thousands of artifacts were gathered, classified and studied, and some were taken to France and England for direct comparison with similar industries from Europe and Africa. In the opinion of experts abroad, the Black's Fork tools did indeed represent a similar and parallel development in the New World.

The Black's Fork river valley near Lyman, Wyoming. This view from a terrace high above the present flood plain of the river looks toward an even higher and more ancient terrace on the skyline, a remnant of a gravel-strewn flood plain believed to have been formed no later than the end of the Illinoian glacial advance some 125,000 years ago, and possibly much earlier. Lodged among the gravels on these highest terraces are water-worn stone artifacts of crude and primitive workmanship and resembling Asian specimens of recognized great antiquity. As one stair-steps down increasingly younger terraces to the modern flood plain, the growing sophistication of the tools keeps pace, although specimens of all ages may be found on the higher ground, since the area has for scores of millennia been a source of excellent stone readily available to human inhabitants.

In the Tenth Report of the Archaeological Survey of the High Western Plains, published in January of 1938, Dr. Renaud offered the following letter from Reginald A. Smith of the Department of British and Mediaeval Antiquities of the British Museum in London, 17 September 1937:

"I was much interested to see some of your finds on the banks of the Green River, Wyoming (Black's Fork Culture), and must congratulate you on opening the door for palaeolithic man in America, as some of the specimens looked exactly like specimens from the Egyptian desert, and both in shape and condition conformed to palaeolithic standards. Such finds are common in Egypt and are accepted as palaeolithic though found on the surface, and I look forward to another controversy like that about the Trenton Gravel finds. You have all my sympathy."

Dr. Renaud had this to say about the letter:

"I personally appreciate the final sentence of Mr. R. A. Smith's letter... for he knows well the obstinate and relentless opposition one will encounter on the part of the too numerous American scientists. ... Happily, European scientists, whose predecessors have gone through this distressing phase, and who have seen specimens and collections come to their laboratories and museums from far away districts of Africa and Asia, are much more open minded and ready to welcome evidence of the antiquity of man in America, an antiquity harmonizing with already accepted proofs of its existence in many parts of the Old World."

Renaud was decorated by the French Government for his significant contribution to the science of anthropology. But in America the reception of Renaud's interpretation of the Black's Fork material as evidence of great antiquity was, and continued to be for forty years, one of general skepticism. American archaeologists did not deny that the majority of the specimens were artifacts, but they were widely considered to be merely the cast-off blanks and discards of relatively recent people attracted to the sites because of their suitability as quarry workshops. Flakes and chips of stone littered the ground in places, lending credence to such a theory.

The matter of age also plagued Renaud and his colleagues, for the pieces were found on the surface almost entirely; they could not be dated by geological stratigraphy, and

This shows the terrace profile of two sites at Black's Fork basin, about five miles northeast of Lyman, Wyoming.

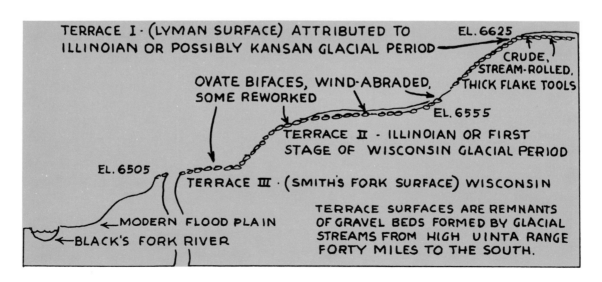

TERRACE I · (LYMAN SURFACE) ATTRIBUTED TO   EL. 6625
ILLINOIAN OR POSSIBLY KANSAN GLACIAL PERIOD
CRUDE,
STREAM-ROLLED,
THICK FLAKE TOOLS
OVATE BIFACES, WIND-ABRADED,
SOME REWORKED
EL. 6555
TERRACE II - ILLINOIAN OR FIRST
STAGE OF WISCONSIN GLACIAL PERIOD
EL. 6505
TERRACE III · (SMITH'S FORK SURFACE) WISCONSIN
TERRACE SURFACES ARE REMNANTS
OF GRAVEL BEDS FORMED BY GLACIAL
MODERN FLOOD PLAIN   STREAMS FROM HIGH UINTA RANGE
BLACK'S FORK RIVER   FORTY MILES TO THE SOUTH.

specimens of vastly differing ages were obviously present, particularly on the higher benches. Later examination has disclosed artifacts covered by soils and in association with charcoal which was dated by radiocarbon measure at 6,000 years, but of course this only dated those artifacts recovered from the same level of exposure and not the thousands of others from different levels and localities.

In 1938, Dr. E. H. Stephens, a professor of geology at the Colorado School of Mines, visited the site at Black's Fork and attempted to date the terraces and the stone industries found on them. In brief his opinion was that the tops of the highest terraces above the present flood plain and the older valley floor represented surfaces formed during the Illinoian glacial period, about 175,000 to 125,000 years ago, or possibly even earlier. On these terraces two kinds of artifacts were found. One group showed moderately polished surfaces attributable to wind and dust abrasion and was presumed to be much younger than the other group, which was heavily stream-abraded. But Stephens' report is contradictory. On Page 16 of the Archaeological Survey of the High Western Plains, Twelfth Report, published in March of 1940, he stated:

"All of these weathered and abraded artifacts were found in material lying on surfaces above the valley train of the Smith's Fork glacial stage (which he attributed to the Wisconsin, the most recent glacial advance) and thus must have been worn by streams earlier than that stage."

But in his conclusion on the following page Stephens reported:

"In all the specimens examined the wear was by wind abrasion thus eliminating the possibility of dating them by determining the time of the abrasion as might be done if the weathering was by water action."

It was this last statement, inexplicable and contradictory in view of the preceding remarks and the fact that many clearly water-worn specimens were reported by Renaud from the highest surfaces, which was quoted by critics questioning the antiquity of the sites. But because of its importance in establishing the antiquity of the culture, the geological history of the terraces needs to be understood.

The entire region has been slowly rising throughout the Pleistocene. The rivers have been continuously excavating their valleys to compensate for this slow elevation. In periods when vast glacial accumulations of ice were melting on the higher mountains, enormous rivers swept across the plain, depositing gravel beds sometimes miles across. During more arid interglacials the narrower river channels gradually cut down through the wider glacial flood plain, leaving remnants in the form of flat-topped, gravel-strewn terraces flanking the river valleys. Erosion further reduced the terraces until they appeared as buttes or ridges above the modern flood plain, but could still be dated by their relative heights, the highest being the oldest.

In dating the artifacts found on them, the reasoning is that stream abrasion exhibited by the specimens could only have occurred when the gravel bed containing them was the surface of an active stream. As soon as the river cut down to a lower level and abandoned the terrace top all possibility of further stream abrasion vanished.

The theory that they might have been redeposited on the higher terraces seems untenable. In their worn and rounded state the specimens would have been useless as tools, and ample fresh lithic material was clearly available to man. No other agency could have moved them to a higher elevation.

The question of wind-and-sand erosion versus stream abrasion of stone specimens is an interesting one. There is no question that wind-driven sand or silt over long periods of time could remove a thin outer layer, blur the sharp edges and leave a polished surface resembling melted wax. But such a process has two limitations that are completely different from water action on stones in a stream bed.

Wind-driven sand strikes all exposed surfaces equally. The result will be that all facets of an artifact will remain faintly discernible except in the most exceptional circumstances, since the same amount of material is removed from all parts. The original crisply-defined character of the piece is thus softened or almost obliterated, but rarely transformed to a different and unrecognizable shape. And of course the unexposed surfaces resting on or fixed in the soil will remain immune from this treatment, unless one visualizes some unexplained force other than flowing water turning over all the stones like nest eggs to expose them equally.

On the other hand, the stream rolls the pieces over to get at all sides eventually, and pecks down the edges and protrusions first, so that in time the artifact may again be returned to smooth cobble form, with the edges and flake-scar margins entirely erased. Such rounded edges are the most noticeable characteristic of stream-rolled artifacts.

This situation so intrigued me that I visited the Black's Fork sites in the fall of 1974. I had been told that one of the richest areas, and the easiest to find, was in the vicinity of the municipal rubbish dump of the town of Lyman, Wyoming. I drove out over a frightfully pot-holed road on a day of brilliant sunshine and fresh prairie wind. Well below me and about a mile to the north the Black's Fork River wound through its lowered valley, glimpses of bright blue against the bronze of the cutbanks. Hawks wheeled overhead, and the distant blur of the Uinta Range showed above the south horizon. The ancient terraces stood on the plain as isolated buttes or hills, their flat tops suggesting man-made structures like the pyramids of the Maya.

As I reached the rubbish dump the landscape was covered with smoking heaps of rags, tin cans, old cars and parts of cars, bottles and broken glass — a Twentieth Century midden in the making. I drove just beyond and off the road, and as I stepped out of the car I saw on the ground at my feet an almost perfect ovate biface of light grey quartzite and about five inches long, the kind of symmetrical tool that Renaud called a coup-de-poing, and that reminded him of the tools called Acheulian in Europe and considered extremely ancient there. This was an absolutely incredible experience!

Artifacts from the terraces of Black's Fork near the town of Lyman, Wyoming. Specimens in the top and center rows are from the highest terrace surfaces while the pieces in the bottom row are from the lower terrace II. The three artifacts in the top row are cleaver-like tools made on flat, elongate cobbles. The examples at top left and top center appear to have been heavily stream-abraded, which would be evidence of extremely early human presence since no active stream could have existed on the terrace surface for well over 120,000 years. The dark color of these three tools is also highly significant since they are made of light colored quartzite like the fresher piece in the center of the bottom row. The small dark spot on the latter represents the cortex or highly altered outer rind of the original cobble. As can be seen, the flake scars on the specimens in the upper row have actually achieved the same degree of color and texture as the cortex, the result of an incredibly long period of weathering. The specimens have been tilted to show their edges, in some cases rounded and ground down by stream abrasion almost to the point of obliterating the once-crisp flake scars. In the center row left is a tool called a skreblo *in Siberia. This piece has been flaked far back in the past, weathered over a long period of time and then picked up by later people and resharpened, a not uncommon practice on quarry sites. In the center is a crude chopper; at right is a smaller and heavily abraded skreblo. The bottom row includes an elongate biface of chert, also resharpened by later folk, a relatively fresh ovate biface showing evidence of use on its edges, and a small biface of green chert which has been weathered and wind-polished to a beautiful silky mahogany-colored surface. Many of the tools at Black's Fork have received this rich, glossy polish.*

I gathered up my knapsack and geology pick and headed for the top of the terrace, for my primary interest was in establishing to my own satisfaction the antiquity of the site. The whole area had obviously been used as a series of quarry workshops over extremely extended periods of time, for the slopes were littered with flakes and what is called debitage, the chipping waste produced by flaking rock into tools and weapons.

The principal materials, as Renaud had reported, were quartzites of various colors, cherts and some jasper. These had become lodged in the fixed mosaic called desert pavement as the finer materials had been gradually eroded away by the action of wind and runoff of snow melt and rain. Unbroken cobbles and finer gravels, fragments and artifacts had all acquired a silky polish and a rich color from sun and long exposure to dust as fine as talc. The dust was carried by winds described by one Wyoming rancher as causing the sage hens to lay the same egg as many as three times if they faced away from it. The terrace tops had sandy soils on them and some areas were sprinkled with many small rock fragments and pebbles, suggesting that only a shallow layer lay over the Pleistocene gravels. Near the edges or crests of the benches the desert pavement took over, and it was in these zones that the artifacts were found, as well as on the upper parts of the slopes.

Here on the terrace both kinds of specimens were seen. Seven pieces were collected that had clearly been stream-rolled and abraded, and were considered to have been flaked by man before being water-worn and battered. These were all of quartzite which had acquired a rich grey-brown patina that gave an impression of vast antiquity. Three were backed side scrapers of which two had been deliberately backed by the removal of flakes, and the third was backed by the pebble cortex. The other four were crude choppers made by sharpening large split cobbles or thick flakes by removing flakes along one or both edges. On these tools the flake scars were visible only as rather blurred indentations or scallops in the edges of the stones, of a size that would seem to rule out their having been made by stream battering, but without any visible cones of percussion or sharp edges remaining.

It seemed obvious to me in examining these pieces that the scars must at one time

24

have been sharp and distinct, and that the specimens had been functional tools. I could think of no way that they could have displayed such an appearance except to have had originally sharp facets ground down to the blurred profiles they now exhibited by having been rolled and battered for long periods in a stream. If Stephens' dating was correct, that stream could not have existed since the retreat of the Illinoian ice 125,000 years ago.

No controversy existed about the human origin of the fresher artifacts collected but they were of course undatable. They were ovate and elongate bifaces of large size, some being seven inches long; two concave scrapers of the kind called spokeshaves and possibly used to dress down wooden spear shafts; some small scrapers made on flakes; choppers and hammer stones. Eighteen of these unrolled specimens were collected, but the number was only limited by careful restriction to those needed for an adequate scientific sample.

One pointed biface made of chert showed two distinct sets of flake scars, some extremely weathered and some quite fresh, showing that the artifact was picked up and resharpened for use perhaps many centuries after having been lost or discarded by its original maker.

One small bifacial scraper made of jasper and polished by centuries of wind-scour was as beautiful as a piece of fine jewelry, reminding one of the jade pieces ancient Chinese Mandarins handed down from one generation to the next, to be enjoyed simply for the sensual pleasure of holding them in the hands and responding to their silky smoothness. Other pieces were in delicate colors of green, pink or gold, so that the collection was extremely handsome as well as meaningful.

The findings of Renaud and the members of his survey indicated that the complex he designated as the Black's Fork culture extended for many miles up and down the valley and peripheral regions as well. There were more than thirty miles of fairly rich sites and outlying areas where the culture could be found in less generous proportions. Unless I stumbled by chance upon an exceptionally rich concentration the numbers of artifacts still on the sites must have been staggering, and must have been the result of many millennia, perhaps scores of millennia, of human activity. Renaud collected over 4,000 pieces which he classified as artifacts; I collected two dozen and examined a great many more in an area of less than two acres and in a matter of a few hours.

In closing his Twelfth Report of 1940, Renaud offered these modest conclusions:

"Unhappily, the actual age of the various cultures found in the Black's Fork Basin ... cannot be scientifically established and proved beyond doubt because of the complete lack of palaeontological material and the absence of sites where the artifacts could be dug out of known geological formations or seen in stratification. This unfortunate circumstance cannot be held against the archaeologist, most desirous to find such sites for his own satisfaction as much as to answer the questions of others. Systematic field work and prolonged search for this ideal combination of evidence by the archaeologist and even with the kind assistance of expert geologists, so far has been fruitless. The study of the terraces of the main sites, and of the artifacts collected on them does not furnish conclusive proof, only arguments obtained by deduction, and for which the elements have been given in preceding chapters.

"Five years of painstaking work in the field and in the laboratory, the physical appearance of the artifacts and their typology, their close resemblance with Early and Middle Paleolithic cultures of the Old World repeatedly acknowledged by expert European scientists, and observed by placing side by side our American specimens and those from Europe and Africa, the presence of numerous coup-de-poing-like implements, the extensive use of Clactonian flaking, together with a Pebble Industry so similar with those of East Africa and Southwest Asia: all these considerations confirm me in the belief that our lithic industries of the Black's Fork Basin, and in particular the Typical Culture, represent an important chapter in the study of the stone age cultures of North America and a significant contribution to their knowledge."

SHEGUIANDAH, ONTARIO

Set in the sparkling blue waters of Lake Huron, Manitoulin Island lies close along the northern shore. Named for Manitou, the benevolent Creator revered by Indians of the region, it has had a history of successive drownings and rebirths throughout the Pleistocene, by water and by glacial ice. A limited record of those advancing and reshaping ice sheets and the subsequent green, submerging seas of ice-melt is revealed in the soils and gravels that now cover the scoured dolomite bedrock. But the record is fragmentary and confused, for ice fronts and storm-driven waves have cut and ground away much of the evidence.

In the northeastern part of the island the shore is indented by Sheguiandah Bay; above it on a slope is the small village of Sheguiandah. Just beyond the village pale knobs of quartzite thrust up through the mantle of dark soils, and here humans have come for millennia, when the island was exposed and ice-free, to avail themselves of the stone, excellent for chipping into tools and weapons, just as people did far to the west at Black's Fork, Wyoming. But this is a completely different setting with a cool, moist climate and a generous forest environment mostly lumbered off into pasture now.

In the summer of 1951 the site was discovered by Thomas E. Lee, a young archaeologist on the staff of the National Museum of Canada in Ottawa. At the time of the discovery Lee was struck by the profusion of chipping waste in the vicinity of the quartzite outcrops, and by the numbers of artifacts he found on the surface nearby. He could not have guessed then the enormous richness of the site, nor known of the underlying geological evidence of extreme antiquity suggested by the presence of glacial till, the unsorted rubble left on the surface when thick layers of ice retreat. Certainly he could have had no hint of the bitter controversy, frustrations and personal misfortunes that were to follow his investigation of the lower strata there.

In the four years following Lee's discovery, careful and extensive investigations were carried out by the National Museum of Canada, under his direction. Large surface collections were made from the twenty-six-acre hilltop; these consisted of relatively recent and familiar types of stone artifacts including well-developed projectile points. Excavations in the habitation or midden area exposed at least five separate and distinct tool assemblages, with two of the lower horizons occurring in glacial till. Well below the till deposits other quartzite flakes and finished artifacts were found. Ancient quartzite quarries were located under as much as five feet of chipping waste; flakes and fragments accumulated over generations of human activity. Several peat bogs or swamps on the site were excavated, and artifacts suggesting very primitive culture levels were found beneath thick layers of peat.

The investigations at Sheguiandah were carried out with the greatest care and attention to minute detail. Within what appeared to be the occupied zone, an area of 1,250 square feet was excavated and examined literally inch by inch. A small test pit was also dug to bedrock for geological study. In the swamps, hollows in the terrain which lacked drainage, four hundred square feet of trenches were opened in the hope of finding preserved organic material that might be dated. The peat from the lowest level of its occurrence was tested by radiocarbon analysis and found to be over 9,000 years old, thus giving a minimum date for the artifacts found below it. Pollen recovered from the peat layers was carefully studied to determine past climates and environments. Geological studies were particularly extensive, and scientists of various disciplines visited the site and offered their opinions on the age of the deposits.

The different strata exposed by excavation in the habitation area were clearly defined, as were the different culture levels as expressed by the artifacts found in them. On the surface were scattered traces of a known recent Indian culture called Point Peninsula. No pottery was seen. From the surface to a depth averaging six inches the soil was humus and contained large bifacial tools, scrapers, blades and gravers. The next layer averaging approximately one inch in thickness had drills and projectile points and was composed of a fine, buff-colored soil thought to have been wind-carried, deposited prior to the development of forest cover on the knoll.

The next two layers averaged ten and nineteen inches respectively and were clearly deposited at different times with an interval of unknown duration between them. Both were composed of completely unsorted materials ranging from clay to boulder size and were typical of glacial till. The upper one contained large, thin, secondary-flaked bifaces, usually broken, with scrapers and utilized flakes showing wear. The artifacts in the lower layer of till were quite different: small, crude bifaces and a few scrapers, suggesting an earlier and more primitive culture horizon.

Below the bands of glacial till was a thin sorted layer of sand interpreted by geologists as having been deposited by meltwater "right off the ice." A large notched biface, two scrapers and some flakes of quartzite were found in this zone, and unlike the worn flakes in the overlying unsorted deposits, these were sharp-edged. The fine, sorted layer lay over and between large boulders which completely paved the habitation area about thirty inches below the surface. Below the boulders were grey silty clays which produced a large broken biface tool, several battered objects believed to have been bifaces, and some flakes. The clay layers continued down to bedrock at about eighty-six inches.

It was the lower levels in the habitation area, with their crude bifaces and lack of projectile points, that indicated to Lee great antiquity for man and became the subject of controversy. Dr. John T. Sanford of the Department of Geology, Wayne State University, Detroit, Michigan, who had made a study of sedimentation and stratification, made many visits to the site during the years when it was being excavated. On the basis of repeated examinations and research, he published in 1957 his opinion that the artifacts dated back at least to the early Wisconsin glacial period and perhaps to the Sangamon interglacial, which would be 60,000 to 80,000 years ago. In 1971 he revised this position as follows:

"The glacio-fluvial materials underlying tills at the habitation area certainly must be as old as early Wisconsin in age, and the artifacts in the lower till layer, and probably those in the uppermost certainly date from early rather than late Wisconsin time. Evidence demonstrating the appearance of humans in the Western Hemisphere, at least so far back as early Wisconsin, and probably in Sangamon time, appears to be convincing. A Sangamon age for the earliest artifacts at Sheguiandah would appear more logical than an early Wisconsin date, at this latitude."

During the four years that the site was being excavated it was well publicized, and scores of geologists were attracted to it. Visits by archaeologists were more rare; only about half a dozen made brief inspections. As the implications of great antiquity began to become apparent there were increasing expressions of skepticism from archaeologists in the United States and Canada.

In 1955 the work at Sheguiandah was abruptly halted by the director of the National Museum of Canada. Lee was ordered to modify his claims of great antiquity for the site, claims which were causing the museum administration embarrassment. Lee could hardly comply, and he was forced to resign from his position. When he tried to publish the results of his investigations and his interpretation of the evidence, he found his manuscripts rejected by professional journals.

The controversy was based on two areas of disagreement. One was the acceptance of the artifacts as finished tools of a very primitive and thus early culture, as opposed to roughed-out quarry blanks intended to be worked at leisure somewhere else into more

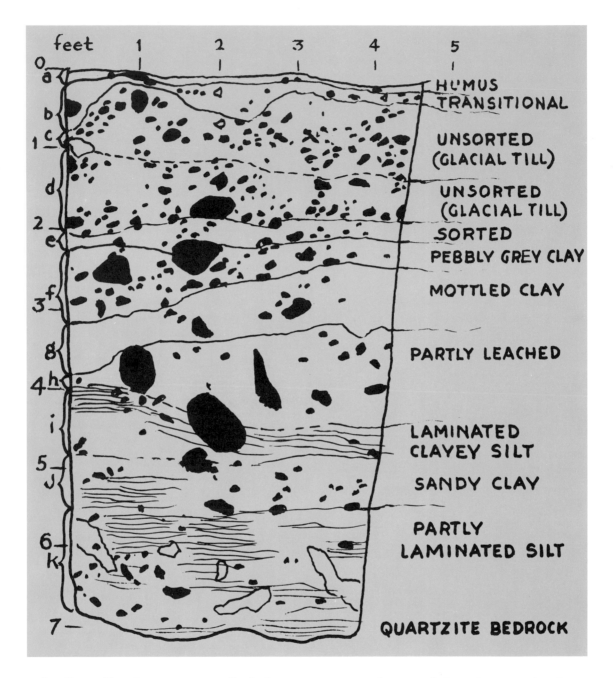

Sketch profile of a test pit in the habitation area at Sheguiandah in Ontario. Artifacts of at least five cultures and periods occur from the surface to the layer marked "f" at thirty inches, in or beneath glacial deposits from "c" to "f." (From a drawing by Thomas E. Lee.)

sophisticated tools and weapons. The other was the designation of the two layers as glacial till representing separate stages of the Wisconsin, as opposed to deposition by some other unspecified agency without age significance. If one accepted the layers as glacial till the first premise became immaterial; the specimens needed only to be recognized as

28

the work of man. Even if one accepted the glacial till but claimed the artifacts were somehow inserted in it later, how could the broken biface far below in the clay under the paving of quartzite boulders be explained?

Most geologists agreed that two types of deposition could account for the kind of unsorted deposits seen at Sheguiandah; mud flows and glacial action. While critics were inclined to attribute the layers to recent mud flows, to others, such an explanation could not be supported in view of the terrain. While there was slightly higher land to the north, the slope was less than five per cent, not enough for significant downslope movement of soils and gravel and particularly the large boulders in the layers, and low, sharp transverse ridges of bedrock lay squarely across the path of any such proposed downslope movement. A mud flow cannot occur unless the soils are suitable to produce mud, while the porous sand, gravels and boulders in the disputed layers could not even hold water. Added to this, the area of deposition, if it could be said to slope at all, was a reverse slope, so that the argument would seem to be untenable.

On the other hand, the conglomerates looked exactly like glacial till and even contained small patches of clean sand that could only have been deposited as frozen sand lumps. Sanford and many other geologists stated that the deposits would definitely have been called glacial till had it not been for the presence of artifacts within them. The reasoning was that if man had not arrived in the New World that early, the deposits could not be attributed to glacial action.

The rubble called till was picked up originally by ice. The leading edge of the glacial ice sheet, which was actually highly compressed snow, was forced to move laterally by its own weight as pancake batter spreads on a griddle. The moving ice and contained rubble scoured the land like a bulldozer, scraping everything movable before it, enveloping and incorporating in its own awesome mass particles from silts to giant boulders. When it finally melted all that unsorted material was simply left behind as a layer of sediment on the land. Thus the artifacts that were in the till at Sheguiandah might have been carried some distance before being deposited at the site. Nevertheless it was clear to some archaeologists that they must have been flaked by man at some period before the ice advanced.

Judging from specimens illustrated in Lee's papers and reports, the artifacts resembled the stone work found on many other very early sites in Asia, Europe and North America. There were large coarsely-flaked bifaces similar to those collected from the high terraces at Black's Fork, except that the Sheguiandah quartzites, since they had been deeply buried, lacked the rich, velvety polish produced by blowing dust on the Wyoming surface finds. The battered objects found by Lee in the clay layer beneath the glacial till might well be comparable to the stream-battered bifaces found by me on the highest levels above the Black's Fork River and which I attributed to the Illinoian glacial retreat some 125,000 years ago. Also taken from the deposits at Sheguiandah were quartzite cores similar to those found by Carter at Texas Street and interpreted by him as evidence of an anvil-supported bipolar flaking industry dating from the Sangamon interglacial that followed the Illinoian.

Lee, despite his setbacks, continued to play an active and vigorous role in his profession, as a professor in the Centre d'Études Nordiques at the Université Laval in Quebec and as an editor and publisher of the Anthropological Journal of Canada. He has done a great deal of field work in the Arctic, seeking out evidence of the earliest pre-Columbian Nordic incursions north and east of Hudson Bay along the bleak shores across from Greenland. His Journal has been particularly hospitable to imaginative but unknown scholars of American antiquity. But his discovery and findings at Sheguiandah, which he believed should have been hailed as a landmark in American archaeology, brought him only frustration and bitterness. His experience was not unique to archaeology, as the work of others had demonstrated through the years.

CALICO, CALIFORNIA

The Mojave Desert embraces some of the most desolate and beautiful lands on earth. Set in the southwest corner of the Great Basin, it is a rugged mixture of lavender and gold ranges splashed with the shifting blue patches of cloud shadows; broad shimmering flats and dry lakes often transformed by the quicksilver magic of mirages; high mesas jumbled with house-sized granite boulders and Joshua trees. In winter it is sometimes dusted with snow, producing an effect incredibly rich and jewel-like with the strong, bold colors of varnished rock and cactus set off by glittering white skeins and patterns. Deep in midsummer the Mojave broods sullenly under a pale, hot sky; its details blurred and wavering in the haze.

Only a few miles from the bustling highways that cross it the high desert has a timeless quality one cannot fail to notice, an immensity of both space and time. In the thin air of its westerly ranges the bristlecone pines, those strange twisted relics of the past, cling stubbornly to life, the oldest living things on earth. Far below on the terraced shores of long-vanished lakes and rivers lie the discarded stone tools of ancient men, people who dwelt there in another time when cool waters sparkled under a milder sun.

That was a totally different world. Willows and tules spread emerald margins around the shores and sheltered mallard and teal, herons waded watchfully in the shallows, and on the slopes small bands of horse and camel grazed. The clamor of geese and swans and the shrill trumpeting of mastodons and mammoths were often on the wind that rippled

Top
Artifacts from Sheguiandah, Manitoulin Island, Ontario, Canada. In the upper right are six small chert scrapers from the more recent or post-glacial levels. Here, as at Black's Fork in Wyoming, the later pieces are usually of the finer-grained materials like chert, while the most ancient tools are generally of quartzite where available. The remainder of the specimens shown are from layers of glacial rubble or till deposited during the last glacial cycle, the Wisconsin, which ended about 10,000 years ago. Such deposits do not represent the time of man's inhabitance, which must have been before the formation of the glacial ice, which picked up and then, centuries and even millennia later, deposited the till when the glacier finally retreated. The artifacts from the glacial till are all of quartzite except the tool in the lower left, which is slate. In the center of the bottom row are two elongate bipolar-flaked cores similar in appearance to specimens from Texas Street and other sites in Southern California.

Bottom
A rock arrangement believed to be the remains of a hearth at the Calico site near Barstow, California. This feature at the bottom of Master Pit II more than twenty feet below the surface of the alluvial fan was interpreted by the investigators to be the result of human activity. The nine large stones on the left, placed into a C-shape or open-sided oval, seemed to have been carefully selected for size and shape, carried to the site and assembled so that their smaller ends pointed in and down, a configuration that was difficult to attribute to coincidence. Smaller stones had been placed in the interstices to reinforce the structure. Although no charcoal was preserved, the human origin of the feature was supported by the finding of stone specimens identified as artifacts in its vicinity. Its function as a fireplace was verified by testing the magnetism in one of the large stones; the results revealed that the smaller inner end of the stone had been subjected to much higher heating than the outer portion, expectable if a hot fire had once burned at the center of the basin. The removed stone was found to be heat-reddened on it's underside.

Bristlecone pines, the oldest living things on earth.

the seas of grass. On the higher elevations were groves of piñon trees bountiful with nuts in season, and juniper thickets sheltered peccary, deer and ground sloth.

But now, barren and eroded, the Calico Mountains stand in the folds of their burnt brown foothills, wearing the pattern of contrasting earth tones that reminded prospectors of calico cloth some hundred years ago. They sprawl east and west near Barstow, California, parallel to and overlooking the Mojave River, an ephemeral desert watercourse which rises in the San Bernardino Mountains to the west, and which once spread over the land here to form ancient Lake Manix and its extension, Coyote Lake, to the northeast.

In their time lakes of the Great Basin provided fish, frogs and crawfish, mussels, succulent lily roots, and waterfowl, and they attracted larger game of many kinds. On the nearby slopes and alluvial fans generous supplies of fine-grained rock for flaking offered the raw materials for tools, while wood for fires and weapons was plentiful. It would seem that the area provided, during the pluvial periods of the Pleistocene and probably well into the intervening interglacials, a rich habitat for man.

As the region was slowly uplifted throughout the Quaternary, and as lakes appeared and flourished in the pluvial cycles only to vanish into dust for millennia in the arid desert interims, new watercourses cut down through the ancient floodplains leaving remnants as terraces stairstepping up from them. The highest are of course the most ancient as at Black's Fork, Wyoming. On these now barren terraces soils were gently eroded away by wind and water leaving the heavier materials on the surface and concentrating

32

them into a fixed mosaic known as desert pavement. Here in rich profusion lie the lost
and discarded artifacts of countless generations of hunters and gatherers whose distant
ancestors drifted into the Great Basin in the remote past and found traces of even more
ancient men scattered among the broken stones of the quarry workshops on the Calico
outwash fans.

In the 1950's Ruth De Ette Simpson, an archaeologist then on the staff of the Southwest Museum of Los Angeles, began a series of surveys of the Lower Mojave Basin and
became particularly interested in the surfaces of the ancient Lake Manix beaches. Some
of the artifacts she collected seemed to her far older than the dates usually assigned to
these cultures, then thought to have maximum ages of no more than a few thousand years.
But on the bases of geological association, weathering, amounts of desert varnish and
patination, the surface changes on rock caused by long exposure and chemical action,
and finally the primitive nature of the tools, she deduced that those on the highest
beaches actually dated well into the Wisconsin. Radiocarbon dating of shoreline tufa
later bore out her first judgment.

Her exploration of the surface of an old dissected alluvial fan disclosed an abundance of ancient-appearing stone artifacts, and a few specimens that were even cruder in
appearance that she felt could only be classified as lower paleolithic stone tools. Finally in an abandoned miner's cut more of these latter specimens were actually found in
place below the surface, but in gravels of a secondary deposit which gave no indication
of their age. From 1958 to 1963 many of the large crude tools, among them ovate bifaces
similar to specimens from Black's Fork, were collected from the surface. Ruth Simpson
designated this moderately old surface assemblage as the Lake Manix Industry. No name
had been given in 1975 to the older assemblage seldom seen on the surface.

In 1963 the late Dr. Louis S. B. Leakey of Nairobi, Africa, visited the Calico site.

The Calico site near Barstow, California. Beneath the protective roofing, two large pits or shafts have been excavated through the soils of a dissected alluvial fan at the foot of the Calico Mountains. The pits extend down to the mudstones of the Miocene formed over 25,000,000 years ago. Other control shafts were also dug around the periphery of the site. The low-lying basin in the background was once, in a time of more humid climate, Lake Manix, a large freshwater lake which could have provided food for generations of early humans in the vicinity. Traces of such early inhabitants in the form of what were believed to be artifacts led to extensive investigations carried out by the San Bernardino County Museum under the direction of Ruth De Ette Simpson, with the collaboration and advice of the late Louis S. B. Leakey of Nairobi, Kenya. This inhospitable landscape of barren desert pavement was, during the pluvial periods of the Pleistocene Epoch, a far different and more inviting land, with grass and grazing game on the lower slopes and piñon and juniper on the hillsides. Never glaciated, such regions did have cooler climates and more abundant rainfall than at present, and would have offered in such periods a highly suitable environment for primitive man.

Few anthropologists on earth had more familiarity with very ancient man and his tool industries, and Leakey was excited by what he saw. He felt that the oldest specimens were artifacts and unquestionably represented a level of culture and a human occupation of far greater antiquity than most American anthropologists had been willing to accept, and he proposed that a major investigation of the site be undertaken.

Since the gravels in which the cruder specimens were found could not be dated and could represent almost any age, Leakey believed that excavation on a ridge of the fan remnant would, if artifacts were found at a lower level, hold more promise of being datable geologically. Because of his considerable prestige he was able to obtain funding from the National Geographic Society, later augmented by his own foundation, the University Museum of the University of Pennsylvania and the Wilkie Foundation as well as private donations. Ruth Simpson transferred to the staff of the San Bernardino County Museum as county archaeologist, and the latter museum became the sponsoring institution.

Excavations were begun in the fall of 1964 and continued from mid-fall to mid-spring for six seasons, after which work was continued on a less concentrated basis primarily by volunteer service of former crew members. During that time two extraordinarily impressive shafts or pits were dug down through the alluvial strata of the fan to the underlying mudstones of Miocene age. Several control pits were also dug nearby to study the landform structure, and these also showed that the specimens identified as artifacts by the investigators did not occur indiscriminately throughout the fan. The work was directed by Miss Simpson with the advice of Dr. Leakey, who visited the site about twice a year.

Digging was done by both paid employes and volunteers, each worker being responsible for a five-foot square which he carefully and painstakingly excavated with small hand tools and brushes. All soil was screened and as specimens of interest were located in the pits their exact positions were recorded vertically and horizontally from a common datum point, and they were measured and photographed *in situ* before removal. Specimens were then sent to a field laboratory on the site for cleaning and preliminary examination, and if considered to be significant artifacts by the investigators, they were sent to the San Bernardino County Museum. Casts were made of the more impressive specimens, both to safeguard the originals and permit wider study.

Hundreds of specimens that the investigators believed were artifacts were recovered from the pits. Most were found grouped in clusters at two levels in the pits, at about seven feet below the surface and at about twelve feet, and they also appeared to be grouped horizontally into somewhat concentrated areas, although a few were distributed at random throughout the excavated spaces. Thousands of unmodified fragments, cobbles, and small boulders were also found, so that the specimens believed to be the result of human activity constituted only a small proportion of the whole assortment.

Also exposed at about the twenty-four foot level was an intriguing feature designated a hearth by the investigators, although no charcoal nor visible evidence of heating could be seen. Composed of a group of stones arranged to form an oval basin dipping down toward its center, it had nine large cobbles in groups of three with nine smaller rocks in between, the whole snugly arranged side by side. The nine larger stones were all similar in size and shape; they were about seven inches long and had thicker ends on the outside and smaller ends pointing in and slightly down. The interior of the basin thus formed was about fourteen by twenty inches.

To many observers the arrangement had a convincingly man-made appearance. It looked just like a carefully constructed hearth. The matched cobbles would have required considerable effort to locate and assemble, and the odds on their being so grouped by natural accident or coincidence in view of the extremely unsorted conglomerate around them seemed at the time to be astronomical.

One of the chalcedony cobbles from the hearth was removed and tested for magnetism and found to have its particles aligned to magnetic north. High heating destroys the residual magnetism in such specimens, the iron particles are then slowly realigned again. Thus if the hearth cobbles' magnetism were found to be aligned with magnetic north this would suggest that they had been heated in the position in which they were found. Furthermore, it was possible to determine in the laboratory that the end of the hearth rock that had been nearest to the center of the fire circle had been heated six times as much as the end away from the center. Lending additional credence to the identification of the feature as a hearth was the fact that when the test cobble was removed from the matrix it was found to be distinctly reddened on its underside, indicating it had rested on and in a bed of coals when heated, rather than having been burned over by a brush fire. The latter case would be expected to have produced maximum heat-staining on the upper surface of the cobble, and this can be verified by examining recently burned-over terrain.

Since the whole area was considered to have been a quarry workshop where excellent stone, mostly chalcedony with some chert and jasper, was available, the finding throughout the pits of unmodified cobbles and fragments as well as what were identified as flakes, exhausted cores, discards and finished tools, seemed perfectly expectable to the investigators. In fact one might anticipate finding a very small proportion of functional tools exhibiting use wear in such a situation. The most likely place to find the latter would have been in the vicinity of the hearth, since it would seem to represent a place of relatively permanent habitation to have justified such a carefully structured feature. It was at about this level in Master Pit II that some of the most impressive specimens were exposed, including at least two bifacially flaked pieces that were almost identical to quartzite specimens collected by the author at Black's Fork.

The flaked stones considered by Simpson and Leakey to be finished and used tools were nevertheless quite crude. As at other very early sites in both Africa and East Asia they resembled and were identified as choppers, chopping tools and scrapers. Many were included in which much of the original cortex or skin of the cobble remained and only one side or the end had been flaked and sharpened. Such pieces were found at Olduvai

A schematic section of the Calico site near Barstow, California.

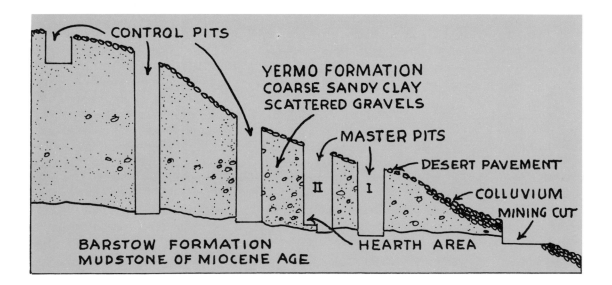

Gorge in Africa by Leakey and considered by him to be the earliest examples of human tool-making. Also included were large flaked stones resembling anvils and the same elongated polyhedral cores as Carter had found at Texas Street and identified as the results of a bipolar flaking industry for the extraction of long stone blades.

Also included in the Calico assemblage were heavy triangular pieces at first identified as small pointed anvils, but which could have been used as heavy hammers or mauls to strike away the long blades from anvil-supported cores. One such specimen that I examined displayed crushing wear on its thick end where such a pattern might have been expected if repeated stone-to-stone contact had occurred.

Another noticeable feature in Calico bifaces was the striking away of flakes from alternating sides, producing a distinctly wavy or sinuous edge. This pattern has appeared repeatedly at very early sites elsewhere, and the chances of such edges being produced by any kind of random or accidental flaking by natural agencies seemed very remote. The same was true of a number of specimens that had been pointed at one end by having flakes removed all around. To produce a sharp point in this manner would have required skill and great care by human workers; if stones had been tumbled together violently enough to produce natural flaking one might suppose such a point would be the most fragile element and could hardly have survived.

Practically no organic material remained in the deposits, although some small pieces of mammoth or mastodon tusk were recovered. These were found to be beyond the range of radiocarbon dating. In 1975 the only recourse still had been to estimate the age of the deposits geologically in order to deduce when humans could have occupied the lowest levels, and estimates varied widely.

The arguments among geologists arose in regard to how long a period would have been required to produce each of the various geomorphic elements observed. The alluvial materials in the fan, called the Yermo Formation, appeared to have been deposited at least in part in the form of mud flows. Such flows carry along, as glaciers do, cobbles and even boulders of considerable size, and these varied materials are deposited in typically unsorted conglomerates. Some of the recovered specimens identified as artifacts may have been redeposited from higher up the slope by this means, while much of the "raw material," chalcedony and jasper, was thought to have been moved to the area by mud flow action. If so, it must have been during a humid cycle for only then can the earth become sufficiently saturated to flow. George Carter told me "... In all my years in the desert I have never seen (a mud flow) — or the remains of one — and I have seen a lot of desert before, during and after great rains. Mud flows in humid regions do not break rocks."

After the Yermo Formation was deposited, the fan became completely detached from the lower slopes of the Calico Mountains by faulting and strong uplift, so that it now resembled a low hill. Dissection and erosion of the now isolated fan continued, and its lower levels were cut and terraced by the fluctuating levels of Lake Manix.

Radiocarbon dating of the organic tufa along the old lake shore gave an age of about 20,000 years, but of course this part of the fan structure, although the youngest and most recently deposited, had existed long before the lake terrace was cut. Higher and older lake terraces were presumed to be beyond the range of radiocarbon dating and no effort was made to date them, since these beaches and terraces, being cut into the already formed and now inactive fan, were far younger than the buried site and could not be related to it.

The surface of the heavily eroded and weathered fan had a compact desert pavement in which the rock was all heavily varnished and patinated, both indications of considerable antiquity. It was in this surface that Ruth Simpson had found the workshop debris and artifacts prior to excavation.

Some geologists have insisted that the age of the lowest excavated levels in which the suggestions of human occupation had been exposed would have to be placed somewhere between 200,000 and 500,000 years, the presumption being that the specimens therefore could not be attributed to man. Dr. Thomas Clements, formerly a professor of geology at the University of Southern California and geological advisor for the Calico project, estimated the age at about 100,000 years.

In October of 1970 an International Conference on the Calico Project was convened, sponsored by the L. S. B. Leakey Foundation, the University Museum of the University of Pennsylvania and the San Bernardino County Museum. A large number of invited scholars from all over the world attended, as well as many of the crew members who had worked on the project throughout the years. The sessions were held at the San Bernardino County Museum with ample opportunities to visit the site. The stone specimens were laid out for inspection and the investigators, including Leakey, Simpson, Clements and Dr. Rainer Berger, a geophysicist from the University of California at Los Angeles, made presentations which were followed by discussion sessions. The purpose of the conference was not to present proofs of any kind but to offer for the first time officially an overview of project results, to define the research problems remaining and, hopefully, to gain useful opinions and advice.

It was doubtful if Dr. Leakey expected the degree of skepticism expressed by the more conservative American delegates. To him the stones exhibited were artifacts, indisputably of human manufacture, closely resembled tools he had been looking at in Africa throughout his career, and were in a context of undeniably great antiquity. To Ruth Simpson the reception of their findings by American scholars was no surprise, although a bitter disappointment. Hours were spent by delegates in offering explanations of how the rocks could conceivably have been broken by natural means to resemble human workmanship. The investigators patiently answered these arguments as best they could but few critics were convinced. The hearth feature was attributed by one scholar to a lightning strike, even though all of the fitted cobbles still had their cortex surfaces intact and were of different mineral content.

The differences of opinion expressed at the Calico Conference included the varied estimates of age for the deposits referred to earlier. These divergent views regarding the time frame represented and the question of human or non-human origin of the stone specimens have continued to be expressed in professional journals. Dr. Robert L. Stephenson, director of the Institute of Archaeology and Anthropology of the University of

Lithic specimens from the pits at Calico near Barstow, California. They have been flaked from fine-grained stone, primarily chalcedony, deposits of which outcrop nearby in the Calico Mountains above the site. Although the specimens appear to be artifacts and closely resemble pieces from recognized archaeological sites, they have been attributed by many critics to natural flaking by freshets and mud flows, since they were found in geological strata considered by some scientists to represent periods far too early for the presence of man in the Western Hemisphere. Two of the pieces are of special interest because they are practically duplicated by specimens from San Diego. The center piece in the bottom row is an ovate biface with a rather straight end showing abrasion suggestive of use wear. Extremely similar specimens with strong use wear appear in the second row, page 63, which shows artifacts from Buchanan Canyon in San Diego made of quartzite but otherwise almost identical. The Calico example in the lower right resembles a tool called a skreblo *in Siberia, it is repeated in the upper row on page 63 from Buchanan Canyon and also at left center on page 23, the specimens from Black's Fork, Wyoming. Such tools have been found frequently in paleolithic sites in both North America and Northeastern Asia.*

South Carolina and state archaeologist, stated in the Institute's Notebook in 1971:

"... I am firmly convinced that several hundred of the recovered specimens (from the pit at Calico) are chipped stone tools of extremely primitive characteristics, chipped by man at what one might call a quarry site, at least a site where raw materials were gathered and made into artifacts. ... During the Conference I argued that if these Calico specimens had been found in a known Archaic workshop site along with a few other more easily recognizable specimens such as projectile points, they would arouse but slight comment. They would be sorted into the 'junk' category of poorly made or partially made artifacts from the site and but briefly mentioned in the report. Reponses to this argument were in agreement. The individuals to whom I put this argument agreed that under those circumstances they, too, would have no hesitation in calling these specimens crudely made artifacts 'but here they are in too old a context to be artifacts.' Are we to assume that what a thing is depends upon where it is found? I think not. If a specimen is an artifact in *one* set of circumstances, it is an artifact in *any* set of circumstances. If we were to find a Coke bottle under a foot of undisturbed Crater Lake pumice, there could be no argument that it would be still a Coke bottle. The problem would be not that it is in too old a context to be a Coke bottle but to determine how it was introduced into that context."

On the other hand, Dr. Vance Haynes, a professor of geology then at Southern Methodist University, Dallas, Texas, stated in *SCIENCE* magazine in 1973 the following conclusion:

"After examining, for the sixth time, the Calico site and the specimens recovered from the lower Yermo formation, I find no evidence to alter my previous views — that is, that the evidence for artifacts remains uncompelling and that a natural origin cannot be precluded. In fact, normal natural processes are adequate to explain the origin of all the phenomena observed at the Calico site. ... There appears to be no doubt that the lower Yermo formation is of pre-Wisconsin age, but there is little chance of applying absolute age-dating techniques directly to the deposit, except for the possibility of measuring the paleomagnetic field direction if suitable sediments could be found. A reversed polarity would establish the age as more than 600,000 years, an age that would be consistent with current geological estimates."

Dr. Philip Tobias, an anthropologist from South Africa, proclaimed many of the Calico specimens to be unquestionable evidence of man's craftsmanship, but Dr. H. R. Wormington, formerly of the Denver Museum of Natural History's Department of Anthropology, has told me that she saw nothing at Calico that she considered to be the result of human activity. However, early in 1976 compelling new evidence was announced seeming to establish unequivocally the human authorship of many of the lithic specimens.

An intensive program of micro-analysis by Clay Singer, a graduate student in anthropology at the University of California at Los Angeles and an archaeological consultant, had revealed distinct and unmistakable patterns of use-wear on a large number of the Calico pieces identified as tools, providing vital evidence of rotation, crushing, polishing and scaling. The alterations of surfaces and edges, clearly visible under the microscope, were of a nature impossible of achievement by other than repeated specialized use. These laboratory examinations, coupled with the recognition of striking similarities to assemblages from other American early man sites, appeared in 1976 to confirm the presence of humans in the Mojave at a very early period. How early was still in question, but sophisticated laboratory methods of dating were in progress and were expected to eventually provide a definitive answer. Radiocarbon testing of calcium carbonate, commonly called caliche, in which some of the lithic specimens were encased, proved to be beyond the range of measure, and established at least that the age of the site and human presence was some still unknown figure but more than 50,000 years before the present.

40

The Established Early Cultures

The two clumsy wooden caravels under Juan Rodríguez Cabrillo had worked up the coast of Baja California with difficulty through September of the year 1542, suffering the contrary and often failing winds typical of the season. But after leaving the Bay of Ensenada a good breeze sprang up from the southwest, filling the lateen sails and moving the moss-grown and shell-encrusted hulls through the thick beds of golden kelp that lay offshore all along this coast. On the second night after leaving astern the islets of Todos Santos they lay at anchor close to the looming bulk of South Coronado Island, and late the following morning, running before a fresh southerly wind, they entered the almost land-locked bay at San Diego, sailing along in the lee of Point Loma to anchor just past Ballast Point in three fathoms of water near the shore.

The sky was overcast from a building storm, and to eastward a heavy pall of smoke hung over the low, treeless foreshore and the mesa beyond the bay. Smokes had been seen often over the mainland; these were the first signs Europeans were to have of the native inhabitants of the region, for the Indians burned off the brush in the fall to keep their trails open and to take advantage of game forced from cover by the fires.

The sea-worn vessels remained in the bay a week, during which time the sailors had some encounters with the natives, communicating by sign language and learning that the

people had good contact with the interior and knew of Spanish incursions in the vicinity of the Colorado River. Relations were guarded on both sides, and one attack on a shore party by bows and arrows was reported.

The naked brown people the voyagers saw on the beaches were of a Yuman-speaking group later designated Diegueños (a then association with the Franciscan mission at San Diego). These Indians are thought to have been themselves relatively recent arrivals in the region. But to the medieval minds of the seamen they had always been there on the land in the same form since the Creation, as had the antelope and deer. It was to be many generations before the origins and evolution of man were questioned, and even descriptions of these native peoples in the old journals are meager and conflicting.

But four centuries after Cabrillo's voyage, when George Carter first saw the intriguing hints of a very ancient human occupation at Texas Street, a great deal had been learned about the Diegueño, and increasing evidence was being gathered about earlier inhabitants of the San Diego area who had already vanished centuries and even millennia before the arrival of the Spaniards. The groundwork for these studies of the human past had been painstakingly laid by Malcolm Rogers of the San Diego Museum of Man.

Rogers had been trained as a mining engineer, enlisted in the Marines in World War I, tried his hand briefly at citrus ranching and then became interested in archaeology and joined, in fact practically constituted, the staff of the museum. Working alone through the early years, his interest became almost an obsession as he began to find traces of much earlier human occupations than had been previously suspected.

These ancient peoples he first identified as the Shell Midden People and the Scraper Makers. He thought the Shell Midden culture was the oldest, and might be several thousand years old, while he believed the Scraper Maker complex developed out of it. This seemed a logical conclusion, for the artifacts found in the shell middens along the coast were extremely crude, while the traces of the Scraper Maker industry included well-made small tools, usually flaked with great delicacy and precision.

The Diegueños and a group farther to the north, called the Luiseños for the mission of San Luis Rey established in their territory, he interpreted as recent arrivals of Yuman and Shoshonean origin respectively. But his real interest was in the older cultures: the Scraper Makers whom he later named San Dieguito for the site of first discovery, and the Shell Midden People that became the Littoral Culture, and finally La Jollan.

High above the Pacific on the pink and terra cotta ledges of Torrey Pines Mesa his solitary figure might have been seen probing the ancient, crumbling middens weathering out of the cliffs. Here he found the skulls and long bones of the La Jollans themselves, buried thousands of years before in the sacred flexed position with broken grinding slabs or metates placed over the remains.

In the deserts to the east, the Colorado and later the Mojave, Rogers patiently followed backward the trail of the San Dieguito people, slowly sorting out and trying to understand the origins and time of occupation of these still shadowy ancient hunters. He worked in an era when the deserts were vast empty lands stretching to the horizon without signs of human use except some strange, cleared circles in the desert pavement that he believed were made by the earliest inhabitants, and the faint trails seeming to lead nowhere.

From both the coastal middens and the dozens of inland and desert sites Rogers collected artifacts, made copious notes of his observations, and pondered over his data endless hours. Gradually his theories took form in his mind and were published in Museum Papers. His terms became generally accepted, and his notes and collections were a priceless resource upon which later students could draw. Certainly the greatest handicap his work suffered was a lack of financial support for assistants and clerical staff. Its greatest shortcoming was far too recent dating; after his death dates obtained by radiocarbon measure showed far greater antiquity for the sites and cultures he studied than Rogers had proposed for them.

I remember Malcolm Rogers from the 1930's as a soft-spoken, thoughtful man of great dignity and reserve. Although he respected the prominent figures of Southwestern archaeology he liked to do his own thinking and rarely sought the opinions or advice of others. We called him "Sabe Todo" (Know-it-all in Spanish) sometimes behind his back, but would never have dreamed of doing this to his face. He was capable of administering a humiliating tongue-lashing in a quiet, moderate tone of voice and without profanity despite his tour in the Marines, but only when it was richly deserved, as when I burned his morning bacon on a field trip to the desert.

During World War II the museum was taken over by the Navy, as were most of the buildings in Balboa Park, and Rogers worked completely on his own for the next thirteen years. He had just returned to have access to his records and collections and to prepare a major synthesis of his lifelong study of the San Dieguito and its relationships to other prehistoric cultures of the Western Hemisphere, when he was struck and killed by an automobile. His notes and manuscripts were gathered together and edited by the late Clark C. Evernham, administrative director, and Spencer Rogers, scientific director. With supplementary chapters by Richard F. Pourade, H. M. Wormington, E. L. Davis and Clark M. Brott, they were published in 1966 by Copley Books under the title, *Ancient Hunters of the Far West.*

Although there were some revisions in dating the La Jolla and San Dieguito cultures after Rogers' death in 1960, the accepted views of the three established cultures of the region had not changed substantially by 1975. Other archaeologists carried out important work in the vicinity. The original type site on San Dieguito Creek near Escondido, now called the C. W. Harris site for the owner of the property, was re-excavated and re-examined in 1958-59 by H. T. Orr and Claude Warren, archaeologists from the University of California at Los Angeles. Their results based on radiocarbon dating suggested different and somewhat earlier time frames and interpretation of Rogers' data. Both La Jolla and San Dieguito industries appeared to occur on the same sites in this locality and their relationships were unclear.

A site on Torrey Pines Mesa called the Scripps Estates site was excavated in 1959 by George Shumway, Carl Hubbs and James Moriarty, scientists of the Scripps Institution of Oceanography at La Jolla. Several La Jollan burials still containing skeletal remains and numerous artifacts as well as food refuse were exposed, and radiocarbon dates on shell ranged from about 6,700 to 7,370 years ago. A site at Agua Hedondia Lagoon, showing a mixture of La Jollan and San Dieguito type artifacts, was considered by Moriarty to be a transitional site supporting his view of greater antiquity for the San Dieguito, and was dated at over 9,000 years before the present.

Existing knowledge of the Diegueño culture was of course based on historical observation as well as archaeological research, and full-blooded Diegueños were still alive in 1975. But without a written language the records of the past were vague and often suspect, and the modern descendants knew little or nothing of their origins.

In 1769, when the Spaniards came to stay and Fray Junípero Serra began his monumental missionary work, California was densely populated compared to the rest of the continent. Perhaps only in the Valley of Mexico were there more concentrated populations in pre-Columbian times. Although the San Diego region had a more modest human settlement than areas farther north, the Diegueños had a climate and food resources to maintain themselves in comfort without any need to practice agriculture.

Although their habit of eating worms, maggots, lizards and in fact anything that moved disgusted the more fastidious Spaniards, their real staple was the acorn. This could be harvested in season and stored in large pottery ollas until needed, and oaks covered the slopes and watered draws in much of Southern California. The nuts were milled to a coarse meal in stone mortars either portable or drilled into the exposed granite bedrock ledges common to the area, after which the meal was leached in running water in the streams to remove the bitter tannic acid. This could be done either in the lightly-woven shallow baskets the women made or simply in sand basins scooped out of a stream bottom.

The flat grinding slabs called metates were used to grind finer edible seeds to a meal and thus break down the seed cases of tough cellulose and make them digestible. Metates and mortars were also used for grinding earth pigments for the body ornamentation they practiced, and for reducing dry clay to a smooth powder in pottery-making. The handstones or manos used with metates were simply flat cobbles that had been sharpened by pecking into the grinding surfaces to make them more effective.

Numerous other food resources were utilized by the Diegueño people. They ate the tender tips of agave in the spring, and may have roasted the hearts in fire pits lined with heated stones. The fruit of nopal cactus or prickly pear was eaten as it ripened. Pine nuts were used, particularly the piñones which yield large nuts that are particularly sweet and delicious and still in great demand throughout the Southwest.

Many plants were also utilized for purposes other than food. The leaves of yuccas and agaves were pulped with stone scraper planes until the tough fibers could be stripped out and spun into cordage for fishlines, girdles, sandals, nets and sewing equipment. Tule bundles were tied into flat balsas or rafts which could be paddled out onto the bay for fishing. Willow bark was carefully peeled off and utilized for the small pubic aprons worn by women. Various aromatic herbs were used as poultices and also ceremoniously smoked in small clay pipes by the males.

The sea and the bays and sloughs provided bountiful food supplies to Diegueños as they had to all previous human populations. Not only fish and crustaceans but green sea turtles, seals and nesting gulls and terns along with their eggs could be taken in season.

Game of many kinds was killed and the hides, bone, horn, tendons, intestines and suet utilized as well as the meat and marrow. Rabbits and quail were struck with bent-wood throwing cudgels skillfully sent whirling just above the ground with lethal force. These were basically the same ancient weapons developed to such an extraordinary degree as the boomerangs of the Australian aborigines. Small game was also snared and trapped, killed with hurled rocks and shot with the bow and arrow. Larger animals like deer, antelopes and occasionally bighorn sheep, were killed with arrows, spears and in fire drives.

The people lived in separate social groupings within carefully defined territorial limits, and violent skirmishes caused by territorial infringements appear to have been frequent. Individual conflicts over sexual aggressions also were reported as frequent by the early Spanish overlords. The villages or rancherías, collections of simple brush huts, were spotted around the region in convenient locations, and in a few of these where modern communities have grown up the old Diegueño names are still used, converted by the Spaniards according to what they thought they were hearing, and later sometimes Anglicized in spelling. Poway is an example, a community just to the north of San Diego.

The people themselves were variously described as large and comely, handsome, mean and furtive, lazy and indolent, depending on the experiences of those doing the describing. It is certain that they were far from pious and devout even when they paid lip service to the religious teachings of the mission fathers, who thought of them as frequently naughty children. Compared to the great theocracies of Middle America, like the Mayan and Aztec, they had relatively few religious practices, although they believed strongly in a spirit world and respected and even feared their shamans or medicine men, whom they believed capable of healing powers and less benign magic. But in the absence of threatening natural forces such as hurricanes, volcanos or even famines and plagues, they must have felt little need to maintain a priesthood trained and able to intercede for them. This is not to say that many highly ceremonial rites were not performed, but to suggest that these may have been as much social and political as they were religious, and were intended to enhance personal prestige rather than serve as prayer or supplication.

The males normally wore nothing except a girdle at the waist for suspending a quiver of arrows or other implements, a little carefully applied paint sometimes tattooed into the skin, and a string to hold their hair bunched on top. Women usually wore a pubic apron of willow bark, scraped yucca leaves or rabbit skins, let their straight black hair fall over their shoulders, also tattooed themselves and wore necklaces of olivella shells or other beads. Until the age of puberty the children ran about completely naked.

In the rare times of uncomfortably cold weather all ages and both sexes wore robes made of sewn rabbit skins, and fiber huaraches or sandals were worn by the men for extended travel over the coastal mountains to the large now-vanished freshwater Lake Cahuilla, on trading journeys or to obtain obsidian for arrowheads.

Women made simple pottery and wove very fine baskets as well as preparing the acorn meal, gathering plant foods and preparing fibers. Men made their weapons and gear, hunted, fished and trapped, and traded with other groups for prized articles unobtainable in their own region. They bore arms against intruders or neighbors guilty of real or fancied wrongs, smoked their pipes and made speeches of great wisdom.

Both sexes produced the objects appropriate to their roles. The women made manos and metates and drilled mortar holes in the rocks, manufactured the flaked stone choppers and scrapers they needed to prepare pine nuts, hides and fibers, and worked on their beads and ornaments. The men produced beautiful and delicate arrow points and knives out of obsidian and quartz, made hafted axes and the straighteners and spokeshaves necessary for the dressing down of arrows and spear shafts. They worked shell, bone and antler into such things as fish hooks, drills and knapping tools. They modeled effigies of men and animals in clay, and pecked and painted strange abstract symbols on boulders and cave walls.

When a person died his friends and relatives burned his corpse on a funeral pyre, then raked a few burnt bone fragments out of the cold ashes, placed them in a clay funerary pot and buried them respectfully with some small treasured articles of the deceased, intentionally broken: arrow shaft straighteners, clay pipes or beads.

These last primitive inhabitants had developed far beyond the paleolithic level, but their pottery and baskets and beautifully worked stone objects were really only a superficial technological advance over the older prehistoric cultures. The acorn economy permitted a denser population and more leisure time, perhaps, but basically the rich environment and the equable climate, neither harsh nor demanding, had offered humans the same advantages over scores of millennia in the past. Thus it seems improbable that after the earliest human arrivals the San Diego region lacked occupation by man for any very substantial periods of time; that is to say, more than a few centuries.

The people of the more ancient La Jolla culture, judging by the great numbers of shell middens and their depths and richness, must have occupied sites up and down the coasts of the Californias over thousands of years. Most of these locations were within sight of the sea, but a few have been found several miles from it on sites that had been used and abandoned by San Dieguito people. Several highly speculative reasons for this could be advanced. The presence of milling implements in La Jolla sites indicated a considerable reliance on stone-ground seeds, and it seemed reasonable to suppose that seasonal camps might have been made where a particularly bountiful harvest of such plant seeds was available. Usually campers settled at the most convenient location near a stream or pond, and generation after generation over many centuries appeared to have used the Harris site and others in the region. Some were San Dieguito people who were primarily hunters and others were La Jollans, mainly gatherers of plant foods and shellfish.

Abandonment of coast locations might have been due to depletion of a particular kind of shellfish locally, or it might have been a seasonal withdrawal to sunnier locations to escape cold seacoast winds and fogs. Depletion of clams from the silting up of estuaries, and of abalones, mussels and rock oysters by heavy harvesting, undoubtedly accounted for the relatively permanent abandonment of shore sites for many years, perhaps centuries at a time. Even a very modest population could have exhausted those food resources conveniently reachable from a given campsite in a few years and have been forced to move on. The dwindling sizes of the shells in some midden horizons emphasizes this cycle, and the region around San Diego may have reached the critical condition of having the available shellfish so small in size and few in number that the coast

La Jollan people on a typical site in the vicinity of San Diego about 6,000 years ago. The woman at left is grinding seeds on a sandstone slab called a metate with a handstone or mano. Abalone shells with the holes plugged with pine gum are used as receptacles. It is not known how early the weaving of simple baskets might have been practiced, but La Jollans of this period may have been using them also. The men approaching at right have been gathering mussels from the rocks below; they are carried on a mat of springy dried rockweed which will be added to the mattress or couch of rockweed upon which the woman in the foreground sits. The mussels can be opened by placing them close to the fire in the hearth. This simple shellfish and seed-grinding economy, augmented by fish and such gathered seasonal foods as pine nuts and cactus fruit, appears to have been practiced for many thousands of years along the Pacific Coast.

here became unpopulated until a new group of La Jollan people drifted in and settled on the same previously occupied campsites to exploit the now-restored shellfish resource.

The physical appearance of the La Jollans can not be known precisely, but a number of skeletons have been recovered due to their custom of interment of the dead. They were small and slender with relatively large heads, and the remains of similar types have been found in prehistoric sites on Kyushu, Japan, as well as at other locations along the Pacific Coast. Unlike most modern Indians they appear to have been non-Mongoloid and little more than five feet tall on the average. Malcolm Rogers thought that they might have resembled Australian aborigines more than Indians as we know them, and there is some skeletal basis for this view, but we have no way of determining their skin color nor the quality of hair and features like lips and noses. I saw in 1932 in the channels of Austral Chile a primitive people called the Alakaluf who were still living at a stone-age level, primarily on shellfish and steamer ducks, large flightless waterfowl indigenous to the region. They had moderately dark skins and straight black hair, were almost completely naked in the icy wind and seemed quite small and slender. They may well have been descendants of the primitive La Jollans who drifted down the coasts for millennia and finally could go no further.

Although in 1973 the oldest firm dates for La Jollan sites were those of up to 7,370 years obtained by Shumway, Hubbs and Moriarty in 1961, and about 9,000 for Moriarty's so-called transitional site at Agua Hedondia, skeletal remains found in Laguna Beach, California, were radiocarbon-dated at over 17,000 years. Charcoal presumed to be from La Jollan hearths has been dated at over 30,000 years, and Carter found a mano or handstone at Crown Point in San Diego and learned of two metates which had been found by workmen nearby, all of which were in strata suggesting to him an interglacial date.

These hints of great antiquity for the La Jollans tended to bear out Malcolm Rogers' earlier conclusions, later revised by him and others, that these slender and sedentary folk did indeed represent an older and more primitive culture than the San Dieguito, and a culture which found little need for innovations over the millennia.

The stone tool kit of the La Jollans, discussed further in Chapter VI, was simple indeed, consisting only of crudely executed choppers and scrapers in addition to the milling tools. Their gathering economy made few demands on skill in stone knapping, and their apparently peaceful natures and simple social organization made weapons almost superfluous. In late sites crude dart points are sometimes found, perhaps influenced by San Dieguito intrusions, but hunting and weaponry seem not to have occupied their

The Indian people of San Diego County called the "Diegueño" by the Spaniards were skilled craftsmen. This view of a display case in the San Diego Museum of Man shows some typical Diegueño implements of various materials, and demonstrates the people's versatility. Clockwise from upper left are a stone mortar hole pecked into granite bedrock, a tightly-woven seed basket, a seed-beater made of stems bound with fiber, a wooden digging implement, a more coarsely-woven basket, two shallow pottery bowls, a grinding slab or metate with its handstone or mano, a fiber whisk, another shallow pottery bowl with a hunting arrow laid across it, and a deeply-grooved arrow-straightener of ground stone. The arrow is tipped with a pressure-flaked obsidian point and fletched with hawk feathers. It was used with a fairly long bow made of willow wood and strung with cord either of spun fiber or animal sinew. The Diegueño made many more types of artifacts not shown, including large pottery storage ollas, flaked stone choppers, knives, scrapers and pulping planes, nets and snares of vegetable fiber, tule balsas or rafts, throwing sticks for small game, and many more.

time. A few rodent bones are sometimes found in the middens, but whether these creatures were consumed cannot be known. Fish bones are also found occasionally, species that live close to the shore like sheepshead, but even these are rare.

One of the features that Rogers found in his early examinations of midden sites was the sweathouse pit, as he identified it. These were excavated pits in the midden areas which had been lined with, or at least provided with, large cobbles which he deduced were heated in the hearth and then placed in the pits and water poured on to produce a kind of primitive sauna bath. Others have suggested these pits were simply for roasting mescal hearts, as is still being done by Indians in parts of Baja California. The relationship of La Jollans on the California coast to other midden people and seed millers elsewhere is unclear. Shell middens have been found in many parts of the Western Hemisphere where substantial supplies of shellfish were available to humans in the past. The manos and metates typical of these cultures are also widely distributed in prehistoric sites both inland and on the coast. Burials had been less common elsewhere, but the skeleton of Yuha Man, found in the extreme western fringes of the Colorado Desert and described in Chapter VII, somewhat suggested a La Jolla burial since the body appeared to have been intentionally interred and was covered by a purposely placed rock cairn. A large freshwater lake was once nearby and must have contained shellfish, but shell middens as such are lacking now in these desert regions. If they once existed the shell has been dissolved into unrecognizable forms.

It was the San Dieguito people that became the focus of Malcolm Rogers' major work. Originally encountered in 1919 near the Harris site on the banks of the San Dieguito

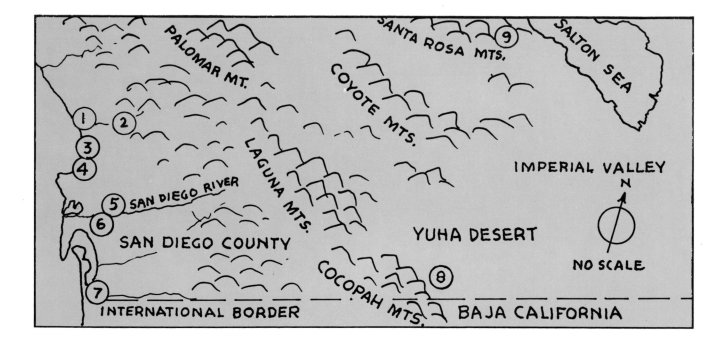

This is a sketch map of the San Diego region showing the relationship of the principal early man sites. No. 1, Del Mar site, human fossil; No. 2, the W. C. Harris site, San Dieguito and La Jollan; No. 3, Scripps Estate site, La Jollan; No. 4, La Jolla Shores site, human fossils; No. 5, Texas Street site, interglacial; No. 6, Buchanan Canyon site, undated; No. 7, Border Road site, undated; No. 8, Yuha burial site, late Pleistocene; No. 9, Truckhaven burial site, undated.

River, they led him through forty years of time and hundreds of miles of seacoast valleys, brushy foothills and finally into the vast, brooding deserts of the Colorado and the Mojave. Here he found increasingly more ancient traces of these primitive hunters, artifacts so crude as to be scarcely recognizable and often sand-blasted and varnished so heavily as to have their flake scars practically obliterated on the exposed sides. These extremely early industries he first called "Malpais" (literally "badland" in Spanish). Later he concluded that they simply represented the earliest phase of the San Dieguito, so they became San Dieguito I. The two later phases II and III were based on evidences of increasing sophistication in lithic technology. In Rogers' view only San Dieguito II and III appeared in the San Diego region. The later aspects that he first considered following cultures and named "Amargosa" were also eventually merged into San Dieguito III.

Malcolm Rogers received his geological training at a time when accepted views of the past in terms of finite dates for major climate changes were extremely modest and conservative. The Pleistocene was thought to have lasted only about 500,000 years at the most, but in 1975 up to 3,000,000 years had been assigned to it. Man's antiquity in the New World had been arbitrarily fixed at not over 4,000 years by the most influential authority in the country, Alês Hrdlîcka, then a curator at the prestigious United States National Museum. Since the end of the Pleistocene had been correctly estimated at about 10,000 years ago, Rogers and other workers in the field had a paradox confronting them.

It was clear that humans were not likely to have inhabited the desert regions as Rogers knew them and as they are today. Lack of food and particularly water supplies made even the most marginal existence impossible. Also, there were obvious signs of prehistoric lake beds and streams; often artifacts were associated with these playas and elevated shorelines. So the people were there in a much more pluvial time when humid conditions promoted grass and game as well as water. But the last glacial pluvial had ended about 10,000 years before, and man could not possibly have been there that long ago, according to Hrdlîcka and others. There was only one answer: presume a Little Pluvial capable of producing the observed phenomena and sustaining the earliest hunters some 4,000 years ago.

These dating problems plagued Rogers throughout his career, and although he substantially revised backward his dates before his death, he was never able to accept and integrate into his own work properly the increasingly early data from radiocarbon testing around the country. Many other older scholars of American antiquity have suffered from the same handicap, hampering considerably the work of placing man in the proper time frame in the Western Hemisphere.

In addition to stone artifacts, Rogers found some intriguing features in the deserts, some of which were difficult to explain. There were in some areas long lines of carefully placed rocks, cairns and other arrangements which may have had some ceremonial significance. Stone hearths were also found and were obvious as to function. Ancient trails, some so faint as to be discernible only when the light was very low at sunrise or sunset led straight across the desert but to no recognizable modern destination, perhaps to a long-vanished spring or pond.

By far the most puzzling were the cleared spaces which could be found literally by the hundreds on the desert pavements. These were usually round areas in which all the stones except very small ones had been removed and placed outside the rim, sometimes as a border and sometimes just tossed out at random. Since desert pavement actually represented surfaces where the soils had been removed for many inches in depth by wind and rain erosion, concentrating all the rock material at the same level, it was probable that soil was also excavated from the spaces.

Rogers theorized that these spaces were cleared by the San Dieguito as "sleeping circles" and visualized the people lying in them close together "like sardines in a can"

A San Dieguito hunter making an offering at a cobble trail shrine in the desert.

to keep warm, perhaps piling brush around the edges to shelter themselves from the cold desert winds. It was true that historic Tierra del Fuegans were known to have curled up together to sleep in somewhat that same fashion. But here the sleeping circle theory was suspect, for the features came in a variety of sizes, some only a yard across and others up to twenty feet in diameter. Some were square rather than round, and some had borders of rocks piled up in two tiers.

Other explanations were offered, none entirely satisfactory. One of the most logical was that many were the floors of brush huts, although there were no door openings. They may have represented more than one use. Some may have been storage pits for mesquite beans or pinyon nuts, and may have been covered with brush or grass and then earth. One worker has suggested that some may have been excavated on surfaces that were subject to periodic flooding from now-vanished streams, and were fish traps. Desert shrubs have been known to scrape large circular patches bare of small rocks during windstorms, but this could not account for the piled borders.

The sleeping-circle theory and the brush wickiups would have been more likely if other evidence of human occupation were found with them, but hearths and artifacts were extremely scarce on the surrounding terrain. Hearths certainly might have been expectable where people who used fire lay down to sleep. Certainly lost or discarded stone artifacts or evidence of stone chipping should have been more plentiful in their vicinities.

George Carter has pointed out that identical cleared circles are found in Australia. They were made to pile up herbaceous seed-bearing plants. The plants dried, were threshed, the seeds scooped up and winnowed. There were various sized circles, and often groups of circles. Women gatherers used no stone tools, hence the usual lack of artifacts associated with stone circles. Australians also made ceremonial stone circles, sometimes with a stone or stone pile in the center. Their sleeping areas were crescent-shaped behind a low screen of brush.

Ceremonial objects were the descriptions offered for a typical kind of San Dieguito artifact, the crescentic stone. These were often found in later sites both in the desert and on the coast, and linked the many sites in vastly differing terrain to a common culture more securely than tool type similarities. They were carefully-executed small objects suggestive of pendants. They were frequently rather intricate variations on the crescent shape, usually two or three inches in greatest dimension, and might even have been mounted on a wand and carried as a political or religious symbol, as was done many millennia later in much grander form in the Valley of Mexico. Incidentally, this ceremonial designation is a traditional last resort with archaeologists who, upon being confronted with an unfamiliar man-made object for which they can think of no logical function, simply log it as a "ceremonial object."

In San Diego County the San Dieguito people appeared to have been somewhat nomadic as opposed to the sedentary La Jollans. Their sites were never as deep nor as well developed, and their artifacts were scattered over the county in such wide-spread and shallow distribution that one needed to visualize a people frequently on the move and without permanent camps. Far back in the late 1920's, when I knew them as the Scraper Makers, I recall crawling along the furrows of a recently plowed field in Mission Valley, along the north side where alluvium from the flanking terrace had enriched the soils, and finding the typical green felsite scrapers, dart points and knives. I also remember my younger sister's outrage when I suggested to her that the fine dart point she had found should be taken down to the museum and contributed to its collection.

No skeletal remains identifiable as San Dieguito have been found. It was presumed that they simply exposed their dead in the open, as many of the later Plains Indians did. Although such funeral practices could be highly ceremonial, the remains soon disappeared, destroyed by the scavengers, gnawed by rodents and dissolved by weather. Some skeletal remains of early hunting people had been recovered in New Mexico and Texas, and appeared to have been little different in physical appearance from historic Indians.

Most of the earlier or San Dieguito II sites that Rogers found west of the mountains were well back from the coast. Those foothill locations appeared to be unrelated to modern water sources and were always on high ground, flat promontories or ridge tops. The midden soils were shallow, usually only a few inches deep, and sometimes extended horizontally for a considerable distance. No hearths were found in connection with the earliest San Dieguito sites, only sparsely distributed bits of charcoal in the soils. Rogers thought that this indicated a preference for small temporary fires with which to scorch their meats. But this observation has some relevance to the situation at Texas Street, where charcoal was mostly scattered rather than confined to carefully-constructed hearths, and where critics suggested that only definitely-prepared hearths would indicate the presence of man and not natural fires.

Later San Dieguito sites were near and even on the coast, and some of them even had shell in them, leading Rogers to conclude that these same hunters had finally been able to overcome their repugnance for shellfish. It was impossible to judge what their relations with the La Jollans might have been; whether they attacked and drove away the apparently inoffensive little shell midden dwellers or merged and interbred with them. Unless the San Dieguito people were simply absorbed by the La Jollans, a seemingly unlikely possibility, they must have moved on following the game that their weapons and tools suggested was the basis of their economy. The distant descendants of the La Jollans, mixed and modified by later arrivals, may well have been the Diegueños.

The above views of the aboriginal prehistory of the San Diego area were widely and generally accepted in 1975 with only slight disagreement in minor details, and they had

This is a cleared space in the Yuha area of the Colorado Desert. The large rocks around the periphery of the cleared space apparently have been brought from elsewhere and arranged here. Neither the function nor the makers of these cleared spaces are precisely known, but the feature strongly suggests either the remains of some kind of brush dwelling or a ceremonial space. The weathering and alteration of the rock indicates a very long period of time. Many hundreds of these rock-lined spaces are found over the Colorado Desert, most often in the form of circles, occasionally in the form of rectangles. The late Malcolm Rogers, who first recorded their presence in detail, speculated that they might have been used as "sleeping circles" in which primitive people might have curled "like sardines in a can."

54

been held for over twenty years by most archaeologists familiar with the area. Only the suggestions of considerable antiquity for the La Jolla culture were relatively recent, and not widely known nor universally accepted.

It was not surprising that George Carter's announcement of a far older human occupation had been greeted with skepticism, for Malcolm Rogers' reputation for thorough and painstaking investigation was widely known, and it must have seemed strange that no traces of this more ancient settlement had called themselves to his attention. It was true that when he was active the evidence at Texas Street was deeply buried in interglacial silts, the crude tools scarcely recognizable as human artifacts. If he had seen the massive quartzite choppers of later discovery to be described in following chapters, I believe he would have been astonished, for they were far different from the artifacts of the La Jolla and the San Dieguito people he had come to believe were the earliest inhabitants of the San Diego region.

Discovery in Buchanan Canyon

The coarse gravels in the stream bed sparkled in the March sun, and their delicate grey colors were enriched to more vivid pinks, lavenders and golds where they lay still submerged in clear pools of water from the recent storm. The odors of drying sage and buckwheat were pungent in the canyon, and bees were again busily about their business. The liquid notes of a canyon wren sounded repeatedly from the hillside.

As I picked my way over the freshly exposed cobbles of the canyon floor, a strangely symmetrical piece of chipped quartzite caught my eye, as much for its color as its shape. It was a rich mahogony brown, quite different from the ground-down opaque tints of the cobbles among which it lay. About six inches long, it was shaped like a pumpkin seed and had long, regular grooves or flutings flowing down its sides and meeting in a rather blunt point. I could think of no natural explanation for such a form, and when I held it in my hand and examined it I felt beyond any doubt that this was the work of an incredibly ancient human inhabitant of the canyon.

Like so many of the deep canyons that gave the city of San Diego its unique and distinctive flavor, this one was a beautiful wild oasis surrounded by dense population and bustling urban activity. Traffic poured down Cabrillo Freeway at its foot and the sounds of sirens, amplified rock music and jet liners interrupted at times the drowsy drone of insects and the accents of bird song. But the over-all impression was one of peace and isolation, and the rabbits, skunks, coyotes and foxes that had come to reasonable terms with man lived in the chaparral and could be glimpsed at times from the rim.

Buchanan Canyon was the southeast-trending fork of a larger canyon, part of the natural drainage that dissected the San Diego mesa. It opened into Mission Valley only a little over a mile west of the Texas Street site; the branch took its name from a once-projected avenue shown on the city maps as running up the bottom but actually never constructed. It was about three-quarters of a mile long and the sides and bottom were completely undeveloped although most of the land was privately owned. The floor varied from thirty to eighty feet wide for most of its length and had a relatively gentle gradient; it dropped only about two hundred feet from a point just a little below its head to the juncture with the valley. The sides were quite steep, particularly the southwesterly-facing slopes which were weathered, chalky and sparsely vegetated. The opposite walls were heavily grown with tall native shrubbery and had thick layers of rich, organic topsoils.

The area of mesa top which this canyon drained was modest, being less than three hundred acres for the whole length, and of course far less than that for its upper reaches. Before the modern settlement the amounts of runoff collected by the canyon must have been fairly light even in the wettest, most pluvial climates, given the cover of vegetation that surely clothed the mesa. But by 1970 the entire natural watershed above the canyon had been covered with urban development. Paved streets, concrete sidewalks and roofs had replaced the grasses, chaparral and live oaks that once thirstily soaked up the rain. Large caverns and ravines had been placered out below the street drainpipes on the canyonsides, and cobble ramps below them broke the force of the alluvial discharges.

On the last day of February in 1970 a small local cloudburst suddenly poured nearly three inches of rain on University Heights, the district of the city surrounding Buchanan Canyon. I had reason to venture out during the downpour and found water cascading in rivers down the streets and overflowing the curbs and sidewalks. The heaviest shower was over in two hours, but enormous torrents were sent roaring and churning down the bottom of the canyon, perhaps in greater volumes because of the transformed watershed than ever before in its long history.

My house stood on a ridge overlooking the canyon, and I used to walk up the trail frequently, enjoying the wildness and solitude. On the morning after the deluge I had descended to the canyon floor and found an amazing metamorphosis. The flood had swept away tons of overburden from the bottom and cut a wide gulley ten feet deep in places. Exposed was an ancient stream bed of coarse sand and gravel. In places the cobbles had been removed to depths of over two feet, and scattered through this jumbled mass were bits of crockery, shattered glass, fragments of brick and broken plastic toys.

The discovery of what appeared to me to be a massive stone artifact was completely unexpected. Nothing had been further from my mind than any evidence of ancient human occupation in my quiet city canyon, but a lifetime of automatically examining the ground beneath my feet, checking cutbanks and old beach lines, and reading the records of small animal tracks in the trail dust, had made such careful scanning an unbreakable habit. I may have been the only person for miles around likely to recognize so crude an artifact as the product of human activity.

In the weeks that followed during that rainy spring I found many more such stones in the stream bed, lying in the lowest exposed levels among the cobbles. Their distinctive brown coloring made them easy to spot even at some distance, and they seemed to be limited to about half a mile along the wash. Since they were all mixed in with modern debris they had obviously been redeposited from some unknown source, and they were collected with careful notes made of the general area.

All of the pieces were of quartzite or felsitic porphyry, with the former very heavily favored. Most I could identify as massive choppers and chopping tools, heavy scrapers formed from thick plates of quartzite, pebble tools with much of the rind or cortex remaining, and the same strange bipolar cores that Carter had found at Texas Street twenty years before.

I took some of the quartzite specimens in great excitement to the San Diego Museum of Man and showed them to the curator of archaeology, who was of the opinion that they were not artifacts but had been flaked by stream action. Such massive pieces were completely unfamiliar to her and they lacked strong evidence of percussive flaking. This was a serious disappointment, and for the first time I began to understand and appreciate what Carter, Renaud, Lee and Simpson must have gone through.

Frustrated, I wrote to Carter describing the finds and enclosing a snapshot of the collection. He wrote back confirming that the stones appeared to be artifacts. But photos are seldom completely adequate and although we corresponded throughout the following year he was never able to appreciate the nature of the specimens, so in the fall of 1971 I bundled them all into cardboard cartons and drove to his home in Texas. It was pouring rain the evening I arrived but neither of us could wait and we carried the boxes, streaming water, into his kitchen and plopped them on the table. Carter took a look and said in utter amazement, "Good Lord! They're all Texas Street!"

The next day we took them to his office at the university and compared them piece for piece with what was left of the Texas Street collection. As we laid out pairs of almost identical cores, flakes and tools, one from each site, the correspondence in material, size, shape and technique from the two locations was amazing; they were indistinguishable. It was perfectly obvious to us that this was the same industry and culture, but there was one crucial and all-important difference in the two collections. The Buchanan Canyon assemblage also included specimens so symmetrical and carrying such clear evidence of purposeful percussive flaking and use wear as to seem to us indisputably man-made, and indeed their human authorship has seldom since been questioned.

From that time on we were convinced beyond any doubt that man had inhabited the San Diego area during an interglacial no less than 70,000 years ago, and probably far earlier. The Buchanan Canyon material appeared beyond question to be man-made and solidly supported the human origin of the specimens found at Texas Street. In effect the pieces from the two sites represented a single and unique cultural horizon, since reinforced by other sites in the region. The interglacial age of this culture level was demonstrated by the terrace formation at Texas Street in which the lithic evidence was solidly in place, a formation whose pre-Wisconsin origin seemed obvious to us.

Unfortunately we also knew with equal certainty that this evidence, convincing as it was to us, would still be considered as "inconclusive" by those who found it difficult to believe suggestions of great antiquity for man in the Western Hemisphere. We decided to seek Foundation support for an exhaustive and complete investigation of the San Diego sites. Since it was already too late to meet deadlines for the following spring and summer, we decided to plan for 1973. Carter would make application to various foundations while I organized the project in San Diego.

In the meantime a great deal was learned about the geology of Buchanan Canyon. Its original formation must have occurred very early in the Pleistocene, if not before, and its relatively modest size and stable condition could be attributed to a tough capping of clay and conglomerate called the Sweitzer Formation. This top layer, forty to fifty feet thick, had preserved the softer sandstones composing the so-called San Diego Block from being completely eroded away. I was insistently reminded how easily early man could have scraped away caves under this rock-hard conglomerate; indeed, generations of children have been doing exactly that in the vicinity.

It was originally hoped that living floors high on the canyonsides might have been

View of Buchanan Canyon, in San Diego, looking southeast. Located almost in the geographical center of the metropolitan area, this medium-sized canyon dissects the San Diego Mesa and empties into Mission Valley and the San Diego River.

preserved by collapsing sections of the capping, but if man actually did live there it was felt that the chance of locating such a habitation was quite remote.

The soils on the floor of the canyon presented several perplexing problems. It was difficult to judge without major excavation what lay between the sandstone basement and the surface. We could see exposed in the cutbanks recent slopewash to depths of three to eight feet, and below that the gravel in which the artifacts were distributed. We had no way of knowing whether the soils had been completely flushed out numerous times or whether this had ever happened. Were the artifacts originally deposited in the gravels and then simply redistributed or were they washed out of more ancient soils or down the slopes from living floors on the top or sides?

Both Carter and I felt there should be a lower stratum of fine silts representing the same arid interglacial climate as was demonstrated in the terrace at Texas Street, or at least some remnants of such soils out near the base of the walls. In the early winter of 1973 just such a stratum was exposed up near the head of the canyon and underlying the heavy gravels. In March a remnant of this ancient-appearing, highly plastic clay was uncovered by a freshet farther down the canyon, and solidly *in situ* in it I found an obviously man-made quartzite chopping tool. So now we knew that a dig under controlled conditions would have some hope of demonstrating that this was the soil of original deposition and the source of the surface finds, and offered the remote possibility of discovering a living floor or skeletal material.

With regard to the collected specimens, the first necessity was to examine thoroughly and eliminate if possible any lingering theory that all the pieces might be merely the products of some kind of natural or ınhuman process. Anthropology students were often told that one could walk down anȝ rocky dry stream bed and collect what appeared to be bona fide artifacts but were actually "nature-facts." Even in professional circles there was a rather persistent belief, perhaps in a few cases well-founded, that various natural processes could produce chipped stone objects closely resembling man-made artifacts. Stream beds were regarded with suspicion, since cobbles were undeniably rolled about, struck against each other and even occasionally fractured if the force of the current were sufficient.

The natural agencies capable of breaking rock in the vicinity of the wash in Buchanan Canyon were carefully reviewed. Cobbles could be broken by being tumbled down steep slopes or by being struck by other rocks crashing violently against them. They could be fractured and spalled by extreme temperature changes, particularly the heat of brush fires. They could be chipped or fractured by stream action, but only under extreme flood conditions or exceptionally high current velocities. Earth pressures and seismic activity could fracture rock under certain circumstances. Simple weathering and chemical decomposition broke down and exfoliated some rock, notably granites, leading to an appearance somewhat resembling flaking. All of these possibilities required examination.

In the case of gravity, we knew that the cobbles from which all the material derived were originally deposited in Tertiary times, the period preceding the Pleistocene, as gravel beds on the ocean beaches. This ancient marine formation, now uplifted to form the San Diego Block into which the canyons had been cut, showed bands of cobbles called lenses exposed by erosion on the sandstone walls. As the canyon slowly enlarged itself over some three million years all of this heavier material weathered out and was concentrated on the floor to be moved gradually downstream or deeply buried. The individual cobbles would either have been lowered gently by slow erosion, or in many cases tumbled violently down as the result of brush burn-off or heavy slope wash, and these had undoubtedly accounted for much of the broken rock seen in such washes and canyon bottoms. But these circumstances could only produce one such violent journey for each cobble, and it was difficult to conceive of a stone bouncing or being bombarded enough times in exactly the right contact positions to leave a set of rhythmic and symmetrical flake scars forming a functional cutting edge or shaped point. And then to have manufactured a whole series of pieces in precisely the same fashion along a limited section of the canyon floor? To us, the possibility was considered remote.

In several places along the walls there were what might be called cobble chutes, where large masses of rock had been catapulted down from the rim during construction or during periods of heavy runoff. These chutes were exhaustively examined, and although broken fragments were plentiful in them, no pieces resembling artifacts were ever found among the thousands of whole cobbles and jagged pieces in the drifts — negative evidence, perhaps, but tending to support the view that symmetrical flaking simply did not occur under those conditions.

Extreme temperature changes had also broken rock here over the millennia. Brush fires must have raged unchecked through the canyons uncounted times in the past. Extreme heat not only fractures rock but in the case of quartzite might spall off thin sheets and flakes very similar to what could be produced by percussion, and just as functional. It was quite probable that such heat-spalled flakes were utilized by humans. Frost could accomplish the same thing but of course neither left the telltale marks on the flake scars that were usually produced by deliberate percussive flaking. In addition, heat sufficient to break quartzite generally left an indelible red stain easy to recognize. While a few of the artifacts had received this heat-reddening, the heating could have occurred after their manufacture, since fire was a constant presence in man's habitations. And a great many of the pieces showed unmistakable signs of percussion flaking; small cavities at the striking edge called erailleure, small bulges or hollows called bulbs of percussion, and in some cases marks typical of bipolar flaking to be described later. Such evidence effectively ruled out temperature changes as the formative agent.

Of all natural agencies invoked by critics to explain lithic specimens offered as artifacts, but considered to be doubtful examples of human manufacture, stream and flood action was most often cited, especially of course when the specimens in question were actually taken from a stream bed or wash. The possibility that the Buchanan Canyon assemblage could actually have been formed by stream battering was very carefully studied for over two years, with the result that here at least such a theory had to be firmly rejected.

As has been mentioned earlier, Buchanan Canyon drained an extremely limited area of mesa top. Based on the modern topography, which might have changed considerably throughout the Quaternary without substantially affecting the drainage pattern, only runoff from about one hundred acres could have found its way into the upper reaches of the canyon. Thus the wash in the bottom could not be thought of as a formerly active stream bed, for even during the wettest pluvials the watershed would have been insufficient to maintain a running stream of any consequence. Spring-fed pools and an ephemeral stream were more likely, with occasional strong freshets. The sands and gravels were not formed by fluvial action here but were deposited from the lenses of the canyon walls as the canyon slowly enlarged itself throughout the Pleistocene. During freshets some additional stream work had been done on them; every time two cobbles knocked together a little powdering occurred at the point of contact and a tiny amount of cobble became sand. Pieces of glass and brick that could only have been in the wash a few winters were collected and served as excellent examples of stream action. The brick fragments were already smooth spheres like tennis balls, while the glass fragments were ground-down, opaque objects no longer resembling glass.

But only during heavy rains could there have been enough volume and current to move cobbles and boulders downstream and cause substantial contacts. In the canyon's natural state even in arid regimes there would have been enough vegetation on the mesa top and the slopes to retard excessive run-off except in exceptional circumstances.

This was not true by 1970. The watershed had become concrete, asphalt and rooftops, and considerable volumes poured down the canyon after every substantial rain. But many of the artifacts were found weathering out of gully cutbanks in soils that had clearly not been disturbed during the last century at least, so that their manufacture could not be attributed to modern hydraulic forces.

In respect to stream action on stones in an active stream bed, many observations were made that could easily be duplicated by anyone interested in the problem. In Buchanan Canyon the stream produced by heavy run-off was closely examined while the freshet was still at its maximum, in order to note the behavior of the cobbles. In the heaviest current, while the individual stones were sometimes carried along for some distance downstream, they rarely collided with sufficient force to fracture in this way, even under flood conditions quite probably more severe than ever could have occurred before modern settlement. They clacked together and minute batter-marks and powdering appeared, a few faulted ones broke and the din was ear-splitting, but general breakage and flaking simply did not occur. Rather than producing distinct edges the tendency was always to blur and smooth away irregularities in cobble surfaces by pecking and powdering. After the freshet had subsided, freshly fractured pieces could rarely be found even by diligent search.

It was quite possible that in some high mountain cataracts flaking might be produced under exceptional circumstances, but Abbé Henri Breuil, a European anthropologist and scholar of human antiquity, had this to say on the subject of stream breakage: "In normal times a stream or river does not break anything resting on its bed. Should a flood occur, however, all the stones on the bed are carried farther along, and are knocked together fairly gently. ... No current is able to fracture stones in any way comparable to human chipping, or to split slabs of flint, still less of quartzite."

It was admittedly possible for a rock to be struck at just the right angle and velocity, when wedged into a stream bottom, to have a flake removed and leaving a scar that would have been quite indistinguishable from human work. It was immaterial who held the hammer, man or the river. But as in the case of tumbling falls it was difficult to imagine precise bifacial flaking around a continuous edge from such random action, and particu-

Typical artifacts from San Diego's Buchanan Canyon. All examples shown here are of quartzite, although occasional pieces made of porphyritic felsite occur in the canyon. The top row shows a tool type called a skreblo *in Siberia, where it occurs commonly in paleolithic sites. It is also one of the most frequent of the readily distinguishable tool types in Buchanan Canyon, and has been found in many other sites in America, including the Texas Street site. The second row shows ovate bifaces, somewhat similar to skreblos but flaked all around the periphery rather than being backed as the latter are. These are also numerous in the Buchanan Canyon assemblage, and usually show considerable use wear, the kind expectable from contact with bone or wood and believed to be distinguishable from stream damage because concave edges are often the most heavily abraded. In the third row are smaller scraper-like tools which may be either unifacial or bifacial, while in the bottom row are pointed or generally elongate objects which may be picks. In addition to the tools illustrated here, many other types are present in lesser quantities. These include chopping tools with one side or end bifacially sharpened, unifacial plane-like scrapers, heavy mauls for bipolar flaking which are extremely battered on their wider or business ends (shown on page 80) and many other objects thought to have been used as tools but of such indiscriminate shapes that they are difficult to classify. The most obvious feature of the majority of tools from the canyon is their large, heavy, massive quality. Lack of secondary flaking also distinguishes them from other prehistoric stone industries in the vicinity.*

larly the production of numerous similar specimens in a limited area by such means.

Attribution of the flaked artifacts to earth pressures gave rise to the same objection as that for temperature changes. While rock could certainly be shattered this way, such a process would hardly leave percussion marks on the flake scars, nor could whole series of similarly pointed or edged specimens conceivably have been produced by this random shattering. It was possible to find pressure-broken fragments resembling intentionally-struck flakes, but such fragments never exhibited overlapping flake scars on their backs as many in the assemblage did. The latter could only have been struck from an already worked core; their overlapping scars representing several previous removals before they themselves were detached.

Physical abrasion due to wind or water-carried particles certainly modified the shape of quartzite but could hardly produce a flaked appearance. Many of the artifacts had been blurred and softened by these forces through the years, and eventually would have been reduced to cobble form again. Indeed, it was quite possible that many rather ir-regularly-shaped cobbles in stream beds were in fact artifacts that had now become un-recognizable because all their flake scars and edges had been erased by these wearing-down processes. Chemical weathering and decomposition weakened and crumbled some rock, especially granites, but not quartzite, the material from which most of the specimens were made; for it, like glass, was chemically inert.

Since it appeared that no formative agency other than purposeful human activity could convincingly be proposed to account for the specimens, what evidence of their human authorship could be cited? Three aspects could be mentioned. Perhaps the most compelling of these was based on common sense. Specimens which looked identical to tools collected from established prehistoric sites in the Old World, sites bearing skeletal material and other convincing evidence of human occupation, could not be dismissed merely because of preconceived notions of man's modest antiquity in this hemisphere. The heavy quartzite mauls and anvils found in the canyon functioned perfectly when wielded to produce cores and flakes resembling those collected from the site.

Many of the flake scars on the specimens bore the typical marks of human manufac-ture usually displayed on artifacts of finer-grained stone like flint or chert. These in-cluded erailleures, small cavities near the lip of the scar at the point of percussion; bulbs or small swollen areas just below the point that had received the blow, and occasional conchoidal fractures in which the flake scar somewhat resembled the surface of a cockle shell. Many of the cores believed to have been produced by bipolar flaking showed bat-ter marks on their ends where they had been repeatedly held against an anvil and struck violently enough to detach a flake. Flake patterns were symmetrical and consistent, and flake scars appeared to have identical degrees of weathering and abrasion, suggesting that all were struck away at the same time and not gradually accumulated.

And finally, wear patterns were found on many functional surfaces and edges and not on nonfunctional parts. If one picked up a tool and held it comfortably, the minute chipping and batter marks appeared just where they should have been if the tool was visualized in use chopping wood, turtle shell, armadillo armor, marrow bone or what-ever. Those specimens that were identified as scrapers and blades showed, when their edges were microscopically examined, that the points of all the minute peaks had been ground down to flat-topped mesas of the same height by back and forth abrasion impos-sible to visualize in Nature. Pieces thought to have been hammers or mauls used in stone-to-stone contact for flaking other tools displayed the kind of crushing and battering that was easy to recognize on quartzite, once one had experimented with such tools and ex-amined the resulting wear. It looked very much like thumbnail marks forced into damp clay. The possibility of stream battering, or some other unguessed-at agency, ever pro-ducing such distinctive markings seemed remote. Even if the piece were wedged into the bottom in a position to receive repeated blows, those blows would have had to be de-

64

livered by sharp-edged and jagged objects rather than smooth cobbles to produce such a pattern, and all the blows would have had to be delivered at maximum force. Lesser blows would tend to smooth away earlier disconformities.

Clearly then, the specimens found in the wash at Buchanan Canyon were artifacts and represented a human occupation at a very primitive culture level. The questions to be answered next were (1) Did the tools represent a culture already known in the area, and if not (2) Could the tools be related to any known culture level anywhere, and (3) How long ago were these people living in the canyon? The answers to these questions required a great deal of study and investigation, and the third one regarding the time factor may never be known precisely.

The Testimony of the Tools

To anyone familiar with the collections of Paleo-Indian artifacts from sites around the country, with their neatly flaked spearpoints and scrapers, the rows of crude, massive quartzite tools seemed incredibly primitive and strange. Had they been assembled from the fossil beds of Africa or the limestone caves of Choukoutien on the Mongolian Plateau they would have seemed perfectly appropriate. But to have been plucked out of a gravel wash in the center of a bustling city, associated not with the bones of mammoths or cave bears but with old tires, broken china and discarded tennis shoes gave them an air of incongruity difficult to overcome. Nevertheless, one needed only to handle them and visualize the brawny, dark-skinned hand of the maker with its chipped and broken nails and curling black hairs to feel the Alice-in-Wonderland setting recede into unimportance.

It had become increasingly apparent as their numbers mounted that the Buchanan Canyon artifacts were extremely similar in type, materials and method of manufacture to those found at the Texas Street site, that they were unquestionably of human origin, and that they were quite different from those of previously described prehistoric cultures in the San Diego area, with the exception of the Texas Street assemblage. Typological studies of several kinds were undertaken. The pieces were first classified on the bases of shape and probable function. They were then compared with those of the other recognized lithic industries in the vicinity, with assemblages from other sites in North America that were of possible great antiquity, and with artifacts from lower paleolithic culture levels in Asia in order to identify similarities, differences and possible relationships. Finally the technique of bipolar flaking was studied so that it might be recognized elsewhere with expectable variations.

In attempting to separate the collected artifacts into type classes a good deal of difficulty was encountered. There were some obvious types which occurred in substantial numbers, and others which had to be rather loosely defined in order to encompass pieces of considerable variety. Some were so crude as to suggest quarry discards; others could have been tossed into any one of several baskets. Clearly the canyon floor had been a quarry workshop, but the fact that large numbers of obviously finished and well-used tools were also recovered made it evident that the canyon had been inhabited over long periods of time.

The broad type classes into which the materials were eventually separated suggested function as well as form, although exactly how some were used remained a matter of conjecture. The largest class by far included what have usually been referred to as choppers and chopping tools. These were generally rather massive core tools, meaning that they had been made by striking away flakes from a cobble work piece in order to shape the tool, rather than modifying a flake for use as a tool. Most were bifacial; they had been shaped by removing flakes from alternate sides forming a rather sinuous cutting edge. Some had been struck directly from cobbles while others were more discoid and were made from split cobbles or thick plates perhaps struck from boulders.

Many of the chopping tools displayed wear patterns on their edges which could not be ascribed to contact with stone. Chopping such things as bone, hardwood, ivory, antler and shell leaves tiny chip marks easy to recognize. Certainly chopping wood not only for fuel but for the manufacture of wooden tools and weapons must have occupied a great deal of time. Many of the very ancient sites in the Old World where bone refuse has been preserved have suggested that splitting bones for marrow was a universal practice, since marrow is tasty, nutritious and sweet long after flesh has decomposed.

The collection and preparation of tough plant foods also required the use of chopping tools. Two of the foods which were heavily relied upon by Indians in Baja California when the Spaniards first marched up the peninsula may have been staples in San Diego during the warm third interglacial. These were pine nuts where available, and more importantly the hearts of the agave called mescal. The latter had tough, fibrous leaves which could be stripped away to leave the bulbous central portion, palatable and nourishing when roasted in a fire pit lined with rocks. Such plant materials would have left few traces of wear on a quartzite cutting edge other than general dulling.

The second largest group of tools were classified as scrapers. These varied considerably in size and shape and had in common only their apparent function; to remove excess material by exerting pressure with a sharp edge in a movement parallel to the surface of the work piece, as opposed to cutting, chopping, hammering or drilling. They ranged from large unifacial planes made from split cobbles to small side scrapers made from flakes. A series of backed side scrapers made from split cobbles or thick flakes and possibly used for skinning and butchering big game was considered diagnostic of this culture and will be discussed in more detail later.

Many specialized scrapers called spokeshaves were found. They had a depressed or concave area on the functional edge which was the right size and would have been highly appropriate for dressing down a wooden spear or lance shaft. The complete absence of any stone projectile points suggested that heat-hardened wooden spears were used, although if shafts were tipped with bone or antler, no trace would be likely to have been preserved. The massive size of many of the chopping tools and scrapers insistently suggested use on the bones and hides of very large animals.

Like the choppers, the pieces classified as scrapers frequently showed appreciable wear beyond the expectable all-over abrasion caused by stream transport. A few of the larger ones appeared to have been used as choppers or hammers perhaps after they became too dull to function properly. Many may also have been used as blades; since retouched edges were almost unknown in this industry, cutting and slicing must have been done with any edge sharp enough to serve the purpose.

A third well-represented class was designated picks, perhaps for digging in soil and sandstones. These were elongated objects from four to eight inches in length and shaped to a point at one end. Many of them showed the kind of abrasion on their pointed ends that would have been expected from digging. Ground-down wear was not exhibited elsewhere on the tools. Excavation in the canyon bottom for wells or in the soft sandstone walls for caves, as well as the harvesting of roots, tubers and agave hearts might well have made such pointed implements useful.

Cutting tools or blades were represented by simple flakes, often bearing dorsal flake scars showing that others had been struck from the same area of the core or work piece. Many were recovered that were either extremely long and narrow or appeared to be broken remnants of such blades. They were believed to be the products of bipolar industry first recognized by Carter at Texas Street, and accounted for the large numbers of long, exhausted cores at both sites. The flakes themselves were less plentiful than the cores, being light and fragile and thus more subject to breakage and stream transport.

The cores were found in abundance in Buchanan Canyon, and constituted a very important type class because of their diagnostic possibilities. They were from four to seven inches long, about two inches or less in diameter, and were trilateral, quadrilateral or polygonal in cross section. They often came to a point or wedge shape at the anvil end. The other end often displayed what appeared to be a striking platform, as though the end of the cobble work piece had been knocked off first. As at Texas Street, many smaller sections appeared to be snapped-off cores. While anvil-supported bipolar flaking seemed not to have been limited to these axial cores and flakes, but apparently was employed to produce many of the tools, the elongated cores were easily recognized and unique. Because they often lacked percussion marks on the flake scars they undoubtedly have been rejected by workers in the past as being the products of some natural process, although to what process one might attribute them would have been hard to specify.

Large stone pieces apparently shaped by flaking for use as anvils were part of the collection. Some were flat or slightly concave while others were shaped like little peaked-roofed houses with the peaks battered and indented. They were all of quartzite and weighed from ten to twenty pounds. Some of the larger non-portable boulders in the wash undoubtedly offered the same supporting function.

Finally the hammers and mauls by which all this stone work was produced had been collected in respectable numbers. These were of two kinds. There were small ovoid and battered hammerstones of two to three inches in diameter which would have been highly appropriate for hand-held trimming. They showed the pecking and abrasion expected of such pieces. The others were better described as mauls because of their massive size. They were quite heavy, some being over five pounds in weight, and were roughly triangular. The small ends had been shaped for convenient grasping, while the business ends were broad and extremely battered. Of all the wear patterns found on artifacts in

Buchanan Canyon these were the most obvious and the easiest to reproduce. There was little question that these were the tools used to produce the mysterious broken stones first found by Carter at Texas Street.

For purposes of comparison with the lithic assemblage from Buchanan Canyon, the better-known La Jolla and San Dieguito industries were extremely well represented in the San Diego Museum of Man collections, thoroughly described in professional literature and easy to recognize. While it was possible that a few pieces might be confused, particularly types that appear almost universally in all stone industries, such as unifacial scraper planes, when site collections were viewed in their entirety the typical characteristics became more obvious.

The artifacts collected from the La Jolla sites as they were generally recognized differed in many ways from the Buchanan Canyon pieces; in size, in tool types, in choice of lithic materials and in methods of production. They were similar in their relative crudity and in the intergrading and apparent multiple use of tool types. The La Jolla manos and metates, handstones and grinding slabs for the preparation of seed foods, were the most diagnostic implements of that industry, linking together coastal sites and those well away from the sea. No evidence of milling slabs was found at either Texas Street or Buchanan Canyon, but it must be pointed out that most La Jolla metates were made of sandstone and subject to more rapid disintegration than quartzites and volcanic rocks. An oval object somewhat resembling a mano was found in overburden at Buchanan Canyon in later operations.

The La Jolla tool kit consisted mainly of unifacial choppers, sharpened pebble tools, scrapers and scraper planes, hammerstones and many flakes and small blades presumably used as knives. Some of the later sites had crude stone projectile points. Lacking were several Buchanan Canyon types such as the massive bifacial chopping tools, ovate bifaces, the pointed digging tools or picks, the specialized large scrapers or cleavers believed to be big game butchering tools, and the heavy mauls, anvils and long cores associated with bipolar flaking.

Both industries utilized cobbles almost exclusively, and the same raw materials were available to both. The La Jolla stone knappers were content to use whatever cobbles came to hand and no particular preference was discernible. Their tools were made of rhyolite, andesite, metabasalt, felsite, porphyries of many kinds and only rarely of quartzite. In general smaller cobbles and pebbles were used, so that the over-all impression was one of medium-sized tools. The Buchanan Canyon people, perhaps because their needs were quite different, used much larger cobbles particularly for their massive choppers and mauls. They seem to have searched diligently for just the right kind of quartzite or felsitic porphyry for their tools, and almost all of them were made from one of these two materials with quartzite heavily favored. Neither kind of stone seemed to be especially common in the canyon bottom.

Although core tools were common in the La Jolla sites the vast majority were unifacial, with all the trimming blows struck from one side leaving an untouched flat face on the other side of the split cobble. Most Buchanan Canyon tools were bifacial although one side was often trimmed considerably more than the other. This was a somewhat puzzling situation since unifacial work was usually considered to be a more primitive expression and should expectably be older. Here the order was reversed because the extremely simple seed and shellfish economy of the La Jollans made little demand on technological skills, while the tool kit of Buchanan Canyon people suggested reliance on the killing and processing of large animals, which would have required the best tools and weapons of which they were capable.

The stone work of the other previously recognized very early culture in the San Diego area, the San Dieguito, was quite distinctive and abundantly present in the region. The artifacts attributed to these people were generally small, well-made and refined

69

when compared with the very coarse tools of both La Jolla and Buchanan industries. Edges were usually carefully retouched, pressure flaking was present in later phases and the preferred materials were volcanics, usually green felsite in this region, and black metabasalt to the south in Baja California.

Scrapers of many kinds were prominent in the San Dieguito sites, particularly domed scrapers and planes. Their small size, rarely more than three inches in diameter and more often less than two, suggested the working of fairly small hides like antelope, deer and jackrabbit. Stone projectile points were also common and frequently of good workmanship; they appeared to have been used on darts hurled by means of a throwing stick or atlatl. Carefully-made blades that might have been hafted knives were often found. Objects called crescentic stones of uncertain function were found in many sites and, as stated earlier, may have had some symbolical significance. Milling implements were not found in pure San Dieguito sites, but were occasionally seen in mixed sites where La Jollan was also present. The relationship between the two cultures remained unclear.

There was little possibility of mistaking the massive tools of Buchanan Canyon for San Dieguito as it was then understood, even though choppers did appear in the San Dieguito sites and were sometimes rather coarse. The earliest phase of the latter culture did produce cruder tools but quite different from Buchanan Canyon artifacts, and it had not been recognized west of the mountains.

Although a few of the smaller scrapers and choppers in the Buchanan Canyon collection might have caused no surprise if found in a La Jolla or San Dieguito site, particularly those made of felsitic porphyry, it was abundantly clear that the Buchanan Canyon assemblage represented a distinct and undoubtedly more ancient culture for the San Diego area. Those few specimens suggestive of La Jollan or San Dieguito were all collected from the surface or the disturbed overburden, and could well have been deposited far more recently than the more crude and massive quartzites. Although the canyon had evidently served as a quarry workshop for thousands of years, the vast majority of the specimens could not be attributed to the previously recognized cultures since on the bases of tool types, size of tools, quality of stone work and preferred materials they were decisively different. Furthermore, although the La Jollans occasionally split their cobbles on anvils, no evidence of their practicing the bipolar technique, recognized by Carter at Texas Street and demonstrated in profusion by exhausted cores at Buchanan Canyon, had ever been reported. That the Buchanan Canyon artifacts included finished tools and not merely quarry blanks and discards from a later culture was plainly evident from the wear patterns observable on many functional edges, indicating considerable and

Buchanan Canyon artifacts compared with specimens from the Texas Street site, San Diego. As can be seen, the tool types, quality of workmanship and preferred materials are extremely similar in the Buchanan Canyon pieces on the left and those from the interglacial terrace at Texas Street on the right, suggesting that the occupation in Buchanan Canyon and at the Texas Street location was contemporary and by the same people during an interglacial period. The two skreblos in the top row, one from each site, have identical small patches of heavy battering, as if their users had habitually used that part of the tools, thought to have been butchering implements, for splitting marrow bones or chopping through joints. The round chopping tool from Texas Street, second from the top on the right, is made of a purple porphyry common to that site but never seen utilized at Buchanan Canyon. All of the other tools shown are of quartzite, the commonest material in the vast majority of extremely ancient industries but seldom seen in sites of more modest antiquity. Shown on page 80 are cores, blades and implements of the bipolar flaking technique common to both sites but lacking in La Jollan and San Dieguito assemblages, and appearing to link Buchanan Canyon and Texas Street in a single bipolar complex.

repeated use.

Numerous undated sites in the Western Hemisphere, containing very primitive chopping tools, scrapers and crude blades similar to Old World materials described as lower paleolithic, had been dismissed as merely the workshops of relatively recent Paleo-Indians. The apparent crudity of the tools was attributed to the fact that such Indians were believed to have roughed out "blanks" which they intended to carry away and chip into more finished hand axes somewhere else, but for some reason discarded in large numbers on the sites. These were mostly surface sites like Black's Fork, Wyoming; sites on erosional surfaces that have been exposed for scores of millennia. Here excellent stone for chipping into tools and weapons has usually been accessible, in some cases throughout the Pleistocene. During periods when climates were favorable for human occupation they were also favorable for game and the growth of plant material, so that it was not surprising that quarry sites had been camped on repeatedly for long periods of time. It was also hardly surprising that artifacts collected from such sites could represent a temporal spread of many millennia and of several different culture horizons all apparently deposited or redeposited on the same surfaces. Well-developed stone projectile points on these ancient sites were sometimes cited as evidence of their recency, when in fact such finds were only evidence of their long duration and could hardly refute the antiquity of the older pieces.

The Buchanan Canyon and Texas Street sites were immune from such misrepresentation if the geological history proposed for them was accepted. At both the cultural evidence appeared to have been deeply buried throughout both the Holocene and the Wisconsin during most of the time since original deposit. At the Calico site also the specimens and features identified as evidence of human occupation had been covered and perhaps in part redeposited in the sediments at least throughout the last 70,000 years of the Holocene and Wisconsin, and possibly throughout the Sangamon interglacial as well, an additional 50,000 years. If so they represented a culture of long duration and great antiquity.

There were striking similarities between the assemblages from Calico and Buchanan Canyon. Flaked stones believed to be elongated polyhedral cores, mauls and anvils occurred at both, indicating a bipolar flaking industry which appeared to link the very old sites in the Western Hemisphere with Asia, since evidence of bipolar work had also been reported from lower paleolithic sites at Choukoutien, China, and on Kyushu, Japan. In addition, some of the pieces described as chopping tools from the lowest levels of Calico were compared with similar tools from Buchanan Canyon and found to have a remarkably close resemblance except for the lithic material, the former being of close-grained chert and the latter of quartzite. Since two more unlike stone textures could hardly be found, the chance of their having been formed by natural agencies in completely different environmental settings but presenting the same rather complex forms seemed rather remote, and tended not only to validate their human authorship at both sites but also to argue a close cultural relationship.

When compared with tools from Black's Fork, the Buchanan Canyon materials resembled most closely the specimens that to Renaud represented the Typical Culture, the artifacts from the middle terraces rather than the water-worn cleavers from the high and ancient gravels attributed to the Illinoian. Many of the former were similar in shape to those from Buchanan Canyon and were made of the same material, a light grey quartzite. The same heavy, massive and rough quality and large size characterized both assemblages, and in general the same tool types were present. The Black's Fork artifacts that the French-trained Renaud called "coups-de-poing" and Americans now called ovate and elongate bifaces, were present at both sites. The bifacially-trimmed pebble tools that reminded Renaud of the African lower paleolithic were collected in some numbers in the canyon. While Renaud was insistently reminded by his artifacts of the most ancient European tools, it was becoming increasingly apparent that they, as well as the Buchanan Canyon pieces, bore an even closer relationship to the Asian lower paleolithic, a relationship that was perfectly expectable.

Artifacts of quartz and quartzite believed to be up to 400,000 years old have been found in China. Judging by descriptions, illustrations and plaster casts, these tools are very similar to the Buchanan Canyon specimens. The earliest and best-known finds were at Choukoutien, the site of the discovery in 1929 of the fossil remains of *Homo erectus pekinensis*, or Peking Man. Among the similarities noted between assemblages from lower paleolithic Chinese sites and the Buchanan Canyon material were the presence in both industries of strong evidence of bipolar flaking, an emphasis on choppers and chopping tools of massive size, the absence of stone projectile points, and an almost complete lack of secondary flaking or retouching of edges. Another characteristic remarked on by archaeologists who studied the Choukoutien artifacts was a shading of one tool type into another, without definite and established patterns such as have been noted in the hand axes of lower paleolithic Europe. Chopping tools ranged from sharpened pebble tools to fairly symmetrical large bifaces; the same variations occurred at Buchanan Canyon, where fewer than half of the collected specimens could be decisively classified as to type or function.

In the Amur River Basin of Southern Siberia two sites have been reported that Soviet scientists estimated might date back into the late Middle Pleistocene, on the order of 250,000 years. The first of these, called Kumara I, was discovered in 1957 by an expedition under the direction of E.V. Shavkunov. Stone tools of a very primitive nature were found about six miles downstream from the village of Kumara on the Amur River. There were about twenty specimens of which eight were chopping tools and choppers and the rest were large pebble cores from which long, irregular flakes had been detached from one side, the opposite side having served as the striking platform. In 1968 the site was excavated and more choppers, artifacts with points or beaks, and pebbles with crude, flaked facets were found.

The other very early site, Filimoshki, was discovered on the Zeia River near a village of that name. It contained specimens that appeared to be even more primitive. The pieces were described as artifacts with "grooved notches" and large pebbles with flaked points or beaks formed by alternate blows at both faces. Such alternate flaking of bifacial tools is typical of Buchanan Canyon work, and has been seen in many other North American sites of possibly great antiquity.

In descriptions of other somewhat less ancient assemblages from Siberia, a tool long considered by the Soviet scientists a diagnostic trait of the Siberian paleolithic has

Next Page
Buchanan Canyon artifacts compared with typical La Jollan specimens of the San Diego region. The heavy, bulky nature of the former, shown on the right, contrasts with the usually more modest size of La Jollan tools. Although occasional large tools are found in La Jollan sites they are the exception rather than the rule. Both industries share the characteristic of rather crude, coarse workmanship, but tool types considered characteristic of Buchanan Canyon are not found in La Jollan sites; for example, the skreblos and ovate bifaces. La Jollan tools are generally unifacial and steeply flaked; such tools are rare in Buchanan Canyon and may well be later La Jollan intrusions. Although not shown here, milling tools are typical of later La Jollan sites but not found in Buchanan Canyon. Evidence of bipolar flaking is abundant in Buchanan Canyon; not seen in La Jollan sites. Finally, an outstanding characteristic of La Jollan assemblages is the variety of lithic materials employed. Shown here are La Jollan tools of quartzite, quartz, basalt, felsite and porphyry, while the Buchanan Canyon examples are all quartzite, as are ninety percent of the specimens recovered.

been repeatedly described and illustrated. It is called a "skreblo" in Russian, and the term has been adopted here for convenience. A skreblo might be described as a large backed side scraper or cleaver about five inches long. If a thick, oval-shaped plate of stone were bifacially flaked all the way around its perimeter and then snapped in two the long way, two skreblos would have been produced. But since sometimes the backing was mostly the rind or cortex of the original cobble, it was obvious that the half-moon shape was intentional. The tool looked extremely useful for skinning and butchering large animals; its sharp edge and wedge-shaped cross-section would have been ideal for separating hide from flesh and cutting through the connective tissue. The profile was duplicated in the skinning knife called the "ulu" and used for millennia by the Eskimos.

Over twenty specimens classified as skreblos were collected in Buchanan Canyon; some apparently almost identical to tools in collections from Siberian paleolithic sites. Illustrations of tools from the caves of Choukoutien showed very similar tools. Specimens of this distinctive shape were collected at Black's Fork, taken from the lowest

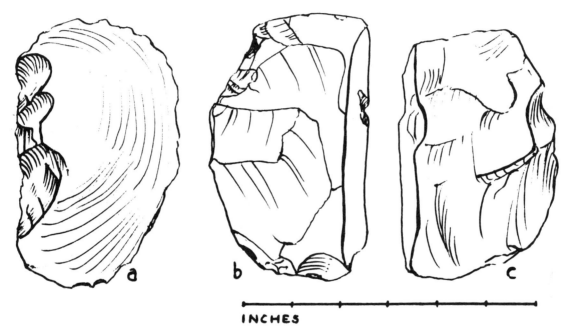

INCHES

Sketches of Lower Paleolithic cleaver-like tools. The "a" is from Choukoutien, China (after Bordes, 1968, no scale shown), and was excavated from Locality 15, one of the latest sites and generally attributed to the Third or Lushan glacial period (Illinoian in America) about 200,000 to 125,000 B.P. It is made of quartz and may represent a prototype for following industries in Siberia and North America. The "b" is from Diuktai Cave, east central Siberia. Soviet scientists call this tool type a "skreblo" and the term has been used by the author for similar to ls in the Western Hemisphere since it appears to be common to paleolithic sites in both northeastern Asia and western North America. The skreblo shown from Diuktai Cave has been tentatively dated as late fourth glacial (Wisconsin in America), perhaps 15,000 years old. Similar tools are illustrated elsewhere in this book from Black's Fork, Wyoming; the Calico site near Barstow, California; the Yuha Desert in Southern California; and the San Diego area. An enormous time-spread for the production of this tool type is suggested, probably 100,000 years in America, possibly much more. The "c" is an example from Buchanan Canyon, San Diego, also shown elsewhere in this book and presented here to show the rather extraordinary resemblance to the Siberian specimen.

75

Skreblos from four sites in the western United States. This cleaver-like tool type, typical of Siberian paleolithic sites, is also considered to be a diagnostic or typical implement of very early cultures in Western North America, and may be present throughout the Western Hemisphere as well as Northeast Asia. The specimen in upper left was exposed over twenty feet below the surface in Master Pit II at the Calico site near Barstow, California. It was in the general area of the cobble feature identified as a hearth by the late Louis S. B. Leakey and Ruth De Ette Simpson, the investigators. The tool in upper right is from the Yuha Desert near El Centro, California, and was collected by Morlin Childers of the Imperial Valley College Museum. It is an undated surface find and has been heavily abraded by blowing sand, but its resemblance to the Calico piece is striking. In lower left is a similar specimen from Buchanan Canyon, collected from the exposed gravels of the wash by the author. The example in lower right was also collected by the author, from the highest and therefore oldest terrace surface flanking the Black's Fork River in Wyoming. While the Calico assemblage has been controversial because of the obviously great antiquity of the deposits, the close similarity of the specimen shown here to others of the same type tends to support the contention of the human origin of the Calico lithic materials.

level of the pit at Calico, and found weathering out of the interglacial terrace at Texas Street. This was seemingly not a tool Nature could make, nor was it found in La Jolla or San Dieguito sites. Since it appeared to be a big game hunter's tool, it spoke not of antelopes and jackrabbits, the likely prey of San Dieguito people, but rather of longhorned bison, camels and giant ground sloths, creatures that wandered over our slopes and valleys far back in the distant past. Of all the tools found at Buchanan Canyon the skreblo was by far the most exciting to contemplate; even a modern hunter in handling it knew instantly what its purpose was.

Intriguing as the skreblos might have been, the bipolar cores were far more important diagnostically, for they proclaimed a technique of manufacture rather than merely a distinctively shaped tool. In order to understand thoroughly the resulting cores it was necessary to understand the process, so on a March afternoon in 1972 I descended to the canyon floor equipped with a collected anvil, a small hammerstone, heavy gloves and a clear plastic face shield. The following was taken from my notes:

"(1) The first unexpected aspect of the experiments was the great difficulty encountered in finding suitable whole, unbroken cobbles of the kind of quartzite that makes up ninety percent of the collected assemblage. Despite the tons of cobbles in the wash, this particular kind appears to be rare. Is this because of centuries of picking over for suitable materials in Buchanan Canyon, or is this kind of cobble scarce everywhere?

"(2) After numerous and persistent attempts to flake or split cobbles by striking them against the edge of the anvil without success, it was concluded that either some technique was employed that hasn't occurred to me, or direct striking was not employed. The only results were to batter and break down the edges of the anvil; yet there are such suggestive batter marks on the edges and ridges that some such process seems to have been employed.

"(3) Bipolar flaking was first attempted by placing a whole cobble vertically on the edge of the anvil and striking it sharply with a small, one-pound hammer shaped like a pear. The small end was used as the contact; the only results were to break down the

Next Page
Buchanan Canyon artifacts compared with typical San Dieguito pieces from the San Diego region. The marked contrast in size and quality of workmanship is very apparent here between the massive Buchanan Canyon quartzites on the left and the generally more delicate and sophisticated flaking of the tools classified San Dieguito by the San Diego Museum of Man and shown on the right. But the term "San Dieguito" has been applied to such a broad spectrum of prehistoric industries in the Far Southwest that a considerable variety of tool types can be found in assemblages so labeled. All of them appear to be decisively different from the Buchanan Canyon material. The large tool shown third from the left in the top row is from the Harris Ranch site on the San Dieguito River in San Diego County, but it is the least typical of those shown, being quite coarse and crudely executed. Directly below it is a beautifully flaked lanceolate knife from the same site, the type site for which Malcolm Rogers named what he considered to be a wide-spread but related complex. Although in 1975 it was becoming increasingly questionable whether such simplification was valid, the so-called San Dieguito industries all shared a preference for fine-grained volcanic stone like felsite, an emphasis on small scrapers, knives and projectile points and a tendency toward careful workmanship and fine flaking, although coarser work in quartzite was sometimes seen. A typical San Dieguito artifact of unknown function is the small crescentic piece just above the lower right, which may have been of ceremonial significance. Such careful and controlled work would appear to have been far beyond the capabilities of either Buchanan Canyon or La Jollan people.

edge of the anvil and powder the contact point on the cobble. Placing the cobble firmly on a solid, horizontal plane of the anvil and striking with the hammer was also ineffective; not nearly enough force could be delivered. This was tried with several cobbles and different hammer stones without success and the whole experiment was about to be abandoned when a remarkable coincidence occurred. In rooting around for cobbles a massive but apparently purposefully-shaped quartzite bludgeon was unearthed, similar to our Type 6 artifacts. In examining it, extremely deep batter marks were found not at the narrow end but at the wider back edge. It weighed five and one half pounds. Since several large twenty pound anvils have been collected in this vicinity, it seems very probable that this huge hammer was actually used with one of them. When it was held by its small end, this hammer could easily be wielded, and cobbles were both split and flaked against the flat surface of the anvil.

"This appears to be one answer to bipolar flaking. On re-examining our Type 6 pieces, I find heavy batter marks on the thick ends where I never thought to look, being so sure they were some kind of pick or digging implement. What I thought were small pointed anvils are probably massive hammers or mauls for bipolar flaking.

"(4) Our smaller Type 2 hammers work very well in normal hand-held percussion flaking once the cobble is broken down into blades or blanks. A small scraper plane was manufactured in minutes.

"(5) Although it seems most probable that bipolar flaking was accomplished here by the means just described, more experiments are needed and will be conducted. None of the long slender blades that run the length of the core have been produced yet.

"(6) Final observation: All those critics who insist that paleolithic quartzite artifacts are simply rocks broken by stream damage or rolling down hillsides should spend an afternoon trying to break quartzite cobbles by pounding them together. They are almost indestructible!"

From this and other experiments it became apparent that if the proper fairly coarse-grained quartzite was selected, the cobbles could be split and flaked using a very massive hammer shaped for the purpose, and an anvil solidly rooted in the ground. The flakes, cores and tools that were produced on the site with implements believed to have been actually used in antiquity showed the same weak structural evidence of human

Next Page
Bipolar striking mauls, cores and extracted blades from Buchanan Canyon, San Diego. The heavy mauls or hammers are always wider at the contact ends, which usually show the typical batter-marks of stone-to-stone contact, while other edges do not. Such selective placement of heavy abrasion on a whole series of similar specimens tends to eliminate the possibility that the battering is simply the result of random stream damage. The maul in the upper left was used by the author in experimental bipolar flaking at the Buchanan Canyon site, and had actually been found at the location where the experiments were conducted. Careful examination of wear on the contact edge before and after strenuous use showed only slight additional abrasion. The maul in upper right weighs almost eight pounds, but because of its shape can easily be wielded by a person of normal strength and no experience in stone knapping. Blows of low velocity and almost irresistible mass tend to produce cleavage in quartzite with little or no evidence of percussion on the removed flake or the core. The long slender blades show multiple flake scars, indicating that a series of blades had previously been removed before they were struck off. The cores also demonstrate the removal of successive flakes from the original cobble. Both cores and blades show only occasional bulbs of percussion and erailleure, the tell-tale marks of hand-held stone knapping still demanded by some authorities as proof of human manufacture.

A sketch of anvil-supported bipolar flaking. By striking the cobble with a heavy stone maul shaped smaller at one end for ease in grasping, long, slender blades running the length of the core can be removed. The end of the cobble has been knocked off first to provide a striking platform.

manufacture as cores found on the sites and questioned by critics for this apparent shortcoming. Blades were produced experimentally that were virtually lacking in visual evidence of the percussive blows. It was safe to assume that ancient man possessed far more manual strength than the average man today. His skill in stone knapping would have been developed from early childhood. An experimenter could achieve sufficiently impressive results to say with some confidence that this was the method employed by the ancients in bipolar flaking and these were the tools.

A skeptical critic of the Buchanan Canyon site remarked, "Those may be artifacts but they are meaningless out of context." The implication was that only if such pieces were found firmly fixed in an undisturbed geological stratum that was datable and also contained other material such as bone or charcoal to indicate a living floor and not chance deposit, could they be regarded as valid archaeological evidence. This was true, but only in a sense. The tools and implements did make a real contribution to our knowledge.

In form they closely resembled the worked stone specimens taken from Texas Street soils that were evidently deposited during an interglacial period. A logical conclusion was that they were over 70,000 years old. Since no natural agency could reasonably be proposed to account for their formation they stated convincingly their human manufacture. They were clearly different from all other known examples of human stone work in the region, except Texas Street of course, so they represented a separate and distinct culture. They bore an obvious typological relationship to artifacts from other sites in North America that appeared to be extremely old, and to industries of proven vast antiquity in

Asia. The specimens believed to have been used as mauls and anvils for bipolar flaking could be demonstrated to function perfectly for that purpose, leaving the same weak structural evidence seen on many of the collected specimens.

Malcolm Farmer, a former director of the San Diego Museum of Man, when asked what further proof critics might require to validate some archaeological evidence, is said to have replied, "A note in a bottle, I guess."

Discoveries in the Yuha Desert

Seventy miles due east from the cool, blue-shadowed walls of Buchanan Canyon, beyond the granite and timbered crests of the Peninsular Ranges the land dips down precipitously again to sea level and below. This is low desert; dry, hot and polished by blowing sand. Its vegetation is meager. The higher westerly reaches have ocotillo, slender clumps of waving wands tipped after the rare rainy spells with scarlet blooms, like bright feathers on clusters of Comanche lances. Along the sandy and usually dry washes that wind down out of the mountains there are green screwbean mesquite and the vague neutral greys of desert smoke tree. The tall stalks and golden candelabra of agaves stand like sentinels on the slopes, and cacti of many shapes and colors huddle among the boulders and spike the hillsides.

Farther downslope as the land levels out somewhat on a long incline the vegetation almost vanishes; only creosote bush and a few other tough, hardy and inconspicuous small shrubs survive. The tilted floors are paved with a rich mosaic of concentrated and varnished bits of stone on the rolling, eroded flanks of the mountains, and the washes and low-lying flats have drifts and hummocks of glittering sand pocked with the burrows of kangaroo rats. From these desert inclines on a clear day one can see far down in the distance the green of cultivated fields and the shimmering blue of the Salton Sea, a briny inland lake some thirty miles long and more than two hundred feet below sea level.

Here where Interstate 8 dips down from the mouth of the Inkopah Gorge on the long incline to El Centro, it cuts across the Yuha Desert, officially described as the Coyote Wells and Yuha Quadrangles, Imperial County, California. And here on these sunburnt and wind-polished surfaces, the bottoms and beaches of ancient Pleistocene lakes now eroded, dissected, tilted and thrust up toward the sky, the margins and banks of vanished streams that once flowed cool with snowmelt from the peaks, lie scattered among the gravels the stone artifacts made by generations of earlier people.

Many years ago Malcolm Rogers prowled over these high slopes and beaches, noting and collecting. Here and on other surfaces all along the eastern flanks of the mountains and in the canyons and desert valleys that indent the range for fifty miles, on the dry mesas of the Mojave now far removed from any water source, along the Colorado and the Gila Rivers and deep into Mexico, he found traces of the people he named San Dieguito: artifacts and cryptic symbols formed of stones in linear patterns, undecipherable and strange. The tools ranged from large, crudely chipped flakes barely recognizable as the work of human industry and so wind-scoured and varnished as to seem unbelievably old, to well-made and finely-flaked specimens which he identified as relatively recent.

Although they had been reported by early travelers and surely noted by prospectors, Rogers was probably the first archaeologist to see and puzzle over the cleared circles, cobble and boulder cairns and rock alignments that occurred by the thousands in the far Southwestern deserts. But as far as is known he never excavated any of those mysterious features beyond a little tentative probing; never wondered what lay under the piled rocks or how deeply the cleared spaces extended underground.

But Morlin Childers of El Centro wondered. Like Malcolm Rogers he had had no formal training in archaeology and related sciences; he had only an irresistible fascination with the distant human past in his particular corner of the world. For three decades he had been ranging over the Yuha desert in his spare time from private business, examining, noting and collecting. In the beginning he was the desert equivalent of a pothunter, a breed detested by serious archaeologists because such hobbyists remove or destroy evidence of potentially great scientific value simply to accumulate a collection which becomes meaningless out of context.

Slowly, despite his limited education, Childers began to understand the great geological events of the past, the effects of changing climates on the land, the physics and chemistry by which stone was shaped and modified by humans and by nature. He picked up archaeological and geological terms by ear, and read what he could find on those subjects. A broadly-built, husky man of gentle nature and great imagination, he lacked the professional patter and self-assurance that more formal schooling would have provided, but with dogged persistence in the field and the library, he acquired the kind of insights and methodical thought processes that mark a competent scholar, and later he became associated with the Imperial Valley College Museum as curator of paleoarchaeology.

In the years that Morlin Childers roamed over the Yuha Desert and adjacent areas and as he became increasingly sensitive to the implications of stone alteration by man and by the environment, he became convinced of a much greater antiquity for human occupation than Rogers and others had proposed. He saw extremely primitive stone artifacts firmly fixed in desert pavements on high mesas, eroded and dissected alluvial fans and ancient Pleistocene beaches now elevated more than six hundred feet above the lower desert floor of the Salton Sink. Some of the flaked specimens were so sand-blasted as to appear made of melted wax, yet they were often surrounded by stones far less polished. This suggested that the artifacts had been deposited and then abraded by centuries of blowing soils long before the desert pavements had been formed, a process itself requiring the passage of vast amounts of time and ultimately bringing to an end the wind abrasion. Such weathering suggested not only exposure throughout the recent period since the end of the Wisconsin about 10,000 years ago, but long periods of earlier exposure under very arid conditions during the interstadials of the last glacial period and

84

perhaps even during the Sangamon interglacial.

The alterations of stone surfaces that Childers saw often covered the flake scars of artifacts, and thus were attributable to the action of the environment during the time since they had been flaked by man. The surface modifications were of two kinds. In addition to the action of wind-carried sands and silts, which simply scoured away the outer layer of stone and softened and polished the contours, the surfaces were discolored by patinas and desert varnish.

Patina could be acquired in two ways, depending both on the mineral composition of the stone and the nature of the soil matrix in or upon which it rested. Exposure to oxygen in the air caused some mineral components to oxidize somewhat as iron rusts and copper turns green. The longer the exposure the deeper the color became, but of course the degree of oxidation produced on any specimen also depended on the amount of susceptible elements in that particular piece, and also on a great many other variables including amount of sunlight, air temperatures and humidity. The other form of patina, properly called soil-patina or soil stain, appeared on parts of the stone embedded in the soil and was also a chemical reaction; in this case a reaction to mineral elements in the soil absorbed into the porous surface of the rock which became increasingly porous and stained from this interaction with iron and manganese salts when present in the soil. Even in chemically inert materials like obsidian the stain could be absorbed by capillary action over a long period of deposition in a soil rich in iron oxides.

Desert varnish was less well understood. Unlike patina, it was a layer deposited on the surface of the stone rather than a modification of the stone itself, and produced in extreme cases a rich dark brown color as though heavy coats of varnish had been applied. It coated all stone surfaces equally, regardless of their mineral content, and when polished by blowing dust assumed a beautiful soft luster. The coating was thought to be composed of iron and manganese salts, but just how these were transmitted to the stone surfaces was not clear. In the low desert it was believed by some to result from the decomposition of a species of lichen and its spores, which contained iron and manganese salts and which upon decomposition became oxidized through long exposure to intense sunlight.

No one knew better than Childers the futility of trying to date lithic materials simply on the basis of their surface alteration. The length of time necessary to produce patina or desert varnish was unknown; it was probably many millennia and probably varied tremendously depending on specific conditions both of the particular stone and its matrix and climate environment. Specimens of the same age could present completely different aspects because of having been buried for long periods and then re-exposed, having had one or more coats of desert varnish or patina scoured off by blowing sand and then slowly re-acquired, receiving thicker layers of soil stain from concentrations of oxidizing elements in the soil matrix. Malcolm Rogers had broken artifacts and carefully measured the depths of chemical alteration for comparative studies, but such efforts were useless for the determination of finite dates in terms of years or centuries, and probably not reliable even for comparative dating.

Nevertheless, there was little doubt that materials from surface sites on which all the artifacts were of an extremely crude and unsophisticated nature, and in addition were strongly altered by weathering and the accumulation of thick layers of desert varnish, were far older than specimens from sites upon which all were fresh and unmodified. Pieces that lay loosely on the desert pavement were undoubtedly deposited much later than those that were solidly incorporated in it. Furthermore, concentrations of artifacts on surfaces that represented the beaches of lakes believed to have vanished no later than the end of the pluvial climate of the Wisconsin could surely be associated with the period of the lake's existence with some confidence. If such pieces also had even minimal patination and varnish it would have been specious to deny the probability of considerable antiquity for them.

That probability greatly increased after the advent of radiocarbon dating in 1944. In the 1950's it became apparent that lake tufa, a thin coating of micro-organisms laid down on stones and preserved indefinitely after the lakes had evaporated and vanished, could be dated and would offer an indication of when the lake had last been present. Since human occupation was presumably contemporary with the lake, a minimum age for the artifacts found on such beaches could be deduced.

Although ephemeral lakes had been present in the deserts in quite recent times, the higher beachlines dating back to the more pluvial Wisconsin over 10,000 years ago could be identified through radiocarbon analysis of tufa and fresh-water shell. It was noticed that artifacts on such beachlines, almost certainly as old as the period of the lake's existence, were never as heavily patinated and varnished as those fixed in desert pavements on the high mesas and alluvial fans, although they could be heavily wind-scoured and surf-abraded. Since patina-building would have increased in arid periods when the stones were exposed, and been retarded or even suspended during the humid periods of the Wisconsin, how long ago must the materials on the fans have been so greatly altered?

In 1970 Morlin Childers heard of the forthcoming Calico Conference arranged by Dr. Louis Leakey and Ruth D. Simpson. Although obviously not an invited participant, Childers boxed up some of the crude, heavily-weathered specimens from what he considered to be the oldest sites of the Yuha Desert, and headed for Bloomington and the San Bernardino County Museum where the conference was being held. Naively unaware of the resistance that any suggestion of Lower Paleolithic man in the Western Hemisphere produced in many American anthropologists, he felt that this would be an excellent opportunity to acquaint the scientific world with what was clearly new evidence of man's extreme antiquity.

Unfortunately and perhaps predictably, Childers and his collection of broken stones were largely ignored. Ruth Simpson was cordial and interested, as was Thomas Lee of Ottawa. Approached in his motel room, Louis Leakey was also receptive and examined the specimens with care. He agreed with Childers that the artifacts represented an extremely early culture, and intimated that when the Calico investigation was completed he would like to come down and examine the Yuha sites. But because of his many commitments and his failing health he was unable to do so before his death.

One other participant viewed the Yuha specimens with close attention and even considerable excitement. George Carter knew the terrain well and was already convinced of man's antiquity in the region because of his earlier work at San Diego. He was most encouraging but not in a position to undertake a personal investigation then. He filed the information on a mental spindle and went back to Texas. Childers returned to El Centro rather disappointed but still moderately hopeful that Leakey might follow through. But within a matter of months Childers was to discover what was then one of the oldest datable human skeletons in the Western Hemisphere.

Scattered over the Colorado Desert and the Mojave are rock cairns, features in which stones including good-sized boulders have obviously been collected by man and placed in a pile. In the Anza-Borrego Desert State Park on the western edge of the Imperial Valley, Robert Begole, a retired professional engineer turned archaeologist, has mapped hundreds of these cairns which have been placed in long lines across the land. Judging by coatings of desert varnish and soil patina, many of them are extremely old, having the same amount of alteration on their exposed surfaces as the surrounding rocks. Others are more recent, and the overriding impression is that, whatever their purpose, they represent an extremely long period of occupation by man.

The possibility that some of the cairns might represent grave markers had occurred to Childers and some of his friends at the Imperial Valley College. At one such cairn near Truckhaven, a tiny desert community near the Salton Sea, Childers had seen bits of fos-

At the left is typical desert pavement of the Colorado Desert. All fine sands and silts have been removed by weathering over many millennia to produce a concentration of rock material solidly wedged together at the surface. In the more humid climates of the Late Pleistocene these same rocks may have been distributed throughout a soil layer many feet thick. Examination of the desert varnish, patina and ground stain on individual pieces suggests that they have been undisturbed over very long periods of time since the pavement was formed. When artifacts are found solidly incorporated in such pavements and display the same degrees of surface alteration as the surrounding rocks, it can only be assumed that they were flaked by man at some time even earlier than the formation of the desert pavement. At the right are the remains of a rock cairn on a highly elevated beach of a vanished Pleistocene Lake in the Yuha Desert near Coyote Wells, California. The rocks have been scattered, probably by someone digging down in search of skeletal remains. The finding of a skeleton nearby in 1971 by Morlin Childers, following the dismantling of a similar cairn, had been well publicized. Such rock cairns are fairly common in the Colorado and Mojave Deserts. They occur in a variety of shapes and sizes, sometimes in carefully aligned series, and their presumably ceremonial functions can only be guessed. It is doubtful if all of them could have marked burials, although bone under certain conditions can be destroyed fairly rapidly by elements in the soil without a trace remaining. Most rock cairns appear to have been assembled all at one time from rocks in the vicinity. Somewhat similar rock features are the so-called trail shrines, composed of stones not found near the site and thought to have been built up gradually by ancient travelers depositing cobbles as offerings to propitiate the Spirits.

87

sil bone in a rodent burrow under the rocks, and the site had been excavated by an archaeological team from the college. It proved indeed to be a burial site but the skeletal remains were almost completely disintegrated. Radiocarbon dating was attempted without success by Dr. Rainer Berger of the University of California at Los Angeles. A second sample sent to Geochrone Laboratories in Massachusetts produced an age of around 5,000 years but was considered much too young in view of the geological context and the condition of the cairn rocks. The find did confirm that at least some of the cairns marked burials even though the bones had disintegrated almost entirely and been leached out of the soils or become contaminated for dating purposes.

In the spring of 1971 Childers saw a cairn about forty miles south of Truckhaven in the Yuha Desert that closely resembled the excavated one. In addition, the lower rocks in this cairn were heavily coated with caliche or calcium carbonate, a whitish, organic compound that sometimes forms from water deposited as seepage in a very arid climate, and capable of being dated by the radiocarbon method. If fossil bones were still present beneath the cairn and coated with caliche, the caliche could be tested and would provide at least a minimum age for the bones.

The site was excavated in the fall of 1971 by the Archaeology Department of the Imperial Valley College under the direction of Erlinda Burton. The cairn, which measured about nine feet by twelve and was about a foot high, was carefully dismantled and removed. The first bones, heavily cemented with caliche, were encountered a few inches below the surface. They proved to be parts of the skeleton of an adult *Homo sapiens* who had been laid on his back with the lower legs partially flexed, in a shallow depression. The corpse had been covered with rocks piled as a cairn or monument to mark the grave, or possibly just to discourage scavengers. A down-wash of finer materials had apparently infiltrated the cairn and covered the bones to the present level.

The spinal column below the neck, the pelvic region, both tibiae and all of the foot bones had been completely destroyed by elements in the soil, the skull was badly crushed and fragmented, but the remaining bones had apparently been protected from disintegration by a coating of the same caliche that cemented the surrounding matrix. Samples of the caliche were removed from the bones and the soils immediately over them for radiocarbon dating before any attempt was made to remove the skeletal remains.

The cairn was located at an altitude of about four hundred and fifty feet above sea level. Directly to the west a valley or depression about two miles wide, which showed evidence of having once been either a narrow lake or a broad drainage channel, separated the ridge on which the cairn stood from the slopes of the range. A few miles downslope to the east at an elevation of one hundred and fifty feet lay the terraced beachline of a much larger Pleistocene lake. Here radiocarbon dates from lake tufa, fresh-water snail shell and mussel shell have ranged from 37,000 to 50,000 years before the present.

Caliche scraped from the fossil skeletal remains beneath the cairn yielded a radiocarbon age of about 21,500 years, implying that the remains themselves were at least that old and could have been considerably older. The situation was remarkably similar to the Lake Mungo finds in Australia. There, too, a burial near an ancient Pleistocene lake in the desert yielded skeletal remains encased in caliche and associated with mussel shells. But there charcoal was also found, and it was significant that radiocarbon dates on the charcoal and on associated shell gave dates of over 30,000 years, while dating of soil carbonates (caliche) showed only about 20,000. The Australian scientists considered that the charcoal dates were the most accurate and actually dated the skeleton, hearth and shell.

In 1975 the Yuha skull was being carefully restored and reconstructed by Rose Tyson, curator of anthropology at the San Diego Museum of Man, but she was still unable to say with confidence what its distinguishing features would prove to be. Since two crude, unifacial tools had been exposed in the excavation of the cairn, these and the cir-

About 21,500 years ago, the adult Homo sapiens now known as the Yuha Man was interred by his companions in a shallow depression and covered with a rock cairn, in what today is a desert near El Centro, California. The burial and fossil remains were discovered by Morlin Childers and excavated in 1971.

cumstances of apparently deliberate burial and location near a probable source of shell-fish, were all suggestive of the La Jolla people whose skulls had been collected in some numbers along the San Diego coast. But warping of the Yuha skull cap might prevent sufficiently accurate restoration to permit valid comparative conclusions.

The two unifacial tools found associated with the skeletal remains were of a type designated "ridge-backs" by Childers and seemingly unique to this area. They were oblong cores four and one half and five inches long respectively, and had had long flakes or blades struck off around the perimeter from the flat underside. They could have been described as choppers, pulping planes or simply discarded cores; whether they had been intentionally interred with the remains could not be determined, but since several flakes were also found this seemed unlikely.

The ridge-backs of the Yuha Desert presented somewhat of an enigma. They were not considered to be the oldest lithic material, seldom being found strongly altered, and certainly representing an industry of some sophistication. They were found in great numbers and Childers had collected dozens of them through the years. The strangest thing about them was their great similarity in shape but extreme disparity in size. Some were only two inches long, others were huge objects a foot or more in length and weighing several pounds, and they came in all sizes in between. They were distinguished by always being unifacial, usually oblong and often pointed at one or both ends, and with the flake scars meeting along a ridge or at a point on the dorsal side. Sometimes the flakes had been struck at a surprisingly low, flat angle, producing a shallow cross-section.

But the two pieces from the burial were steep-sided.

The mystery lay in their purpose or function. If they were simply discarded cores from which useful flakes or blades had been struck, why did they need to be of such carefully controlled shapes? If they were tools, how were they used and how could such a variety of sizes have served the same need? Unifacial planes were common in many cultures but normally they had flat tops or cobble cortex between the flake scars from opposing sides, and the extremely low-angle edges on many ridge-backs were rare in other industries. Since they appeared in many different kinds of stone, some peculiarity of the preferred lithic material could not account for their unique aspect; they cut across all lithic classifications.

The discovery of the ridge-back cores in the Yuha burial was most useful in suggesting a time-frame for them, and the two examples presumed to be over 21,000 years old were apparently early forms since they were less well-developed than most, although clearly belonging to the same industry. But many elements of the puzzle remained undeciphered.

Early in 1973 Dr. George Carter came to San Diego, before the start of the Spring semester at his university, to make preliminary plans for archaeological excavations at Texas Street and Buchanan Canyon, scheduled for the following summer. He stopped off in El Centro to visit Morlin Childers and ended up spending several days with him. They walked over many of the Yuha Desert sites that Childers felt were significant. As Carter examined the eroded and sun-baked surfaces his earlier feeling that human occupations of far greater antiquity than had been suspected were represented here became a strong conviction.

In general two different kinds of surfaces with artifact material on them were examined. There were ancient beach lines of vanished lakes including a huge body of fresh water which had nearly filled the Imperial and Coachella Valleys at various times in the past and referred to variously as Lake Cahuilla, Lake Le Conte and Blake Sea; and a string of smaller lakes at a higher elevation along the eastern slope of the mountains. Traces of such lake shores were found over four hundred feet above sea level, but how much of the elevation was due to subsequent uplift of the landforms could not be determined. Above the beaches were fossil alluvial fans composed of materials eroded from the higher slopes as at the Calico site, surfaces now dissected and no longer actively building. These had solidly-formed desert pavements in which the closely-packed stones had accumulated moderate to heavy coatings of desert varnish and a few had been heavily wind-abraded, indicating that they had been deposited long before the formation of the pavement and when the surface was still subjected to blowing sand.

On these high mesas and fossil fans artifacts of quite different industries and ages were found. Recent Yuman stone projectile points and broken pottery occurred on some of them, often in locations camped on during journeys from the lower deserts to the coast. Older but still relatively fresh and unvarnished artifacts of types attributed by Rogers to San Dieguito II were also found lying on the desert pavement but not incorporated in it. But firmly embedded in these ancient stone mosaics were tools considered to be highly significant in terms of age.

These were mostly thick flakes, some quite large, which in many cases appeared to have been naturally formed and then modified by man by unifacial flaking at very steep, almost vertical angles along parts of their perimeters. Some had been chipped along one edge and then turned over and flaked along the opposite edge from the other side, an extremely primitive expression. A few were bifacially flaked with the scars alternating from one side to the other to produce the typical sinuous edge, almost a zigzag. They usually had the maximum amount of desert varnish on all exposed surfaces including the flake scars, and a rich soil stain or patina on their undersides. In some cases they were patinated on all sides, suggesting burial in the soil for a long period before being ex-

90

An elevated Pleistocene beach in the desert near Plaster City, California. The land is slowly rising here along the eastern flanks of the Peninsular Range, and subsiding just to the east in the wide trough of the Imperial Valley, but the movement is so slow as to be imperceptible from one year to the next — only a fraction of an inch in a year. Traces of water-laid deposits formed when the land was at or near sea level can be seen in the background as tilted sheets or plates of hardened silt. Evidence in the vicinity suggests that several distinct freshwater lakes or channels occupied the area at different times during the Pleistocene. Among the scattered, highly wind-abraded and polished stones lying on these surfaces are elongate polyhedral cores similar to those found at Texas Street and Buchanan Canyon on the coast, but here on the desert they have been reduced to a state resembling melted wax.

posed by pavement formation.

Such tools were first called "Malpais" by Rogers but later he included them in his classification of San Dieguito I. Many archaeologists still referred to them as Malpais. Robert Begole believed they could be distinguished from a later industry properly called San Dieguito I, and that the term "Malpais" should be retained. Regardless of name they were generally considered to be the oldest evidence of man in the region; the principal difference of opinion was in the age assigned to them.

Rogers never felt that even the oldest artifacts of the Colorado Desert could be attributed to periods earlier than late Wisconsin times, and even placing man into the Pleistocene near the end of his career had required painful revisions of thinking on his part. But he had few yardsticks then against which to measure their antiquity. The same type of steeply-chipped flakes and thin cobbles worked into crude cleavers were found by me on the highest gravel beds at Black's Fork, Wyoming, but here they showed strong evidence of having been rolled in streams that had vanished at least 125,000 years ago and possibly far earlier. Simply on the bases of their form and workmanship, both the latter specimens and the Malpais flakes on the fossil fans of the Yuha Desert argued a respectable antiquity.

George Carter was perfectly familiar with the Malpais specimens. He had worked with Rogers during the 1930's in many parts of the Colorado and Mojave Deserts. In 1951 he had published some extremely revolutionary ideas about the antiquity of man in the Western Hemisphere called "Man in America: A Criticism of Scientific Thought." As might be expected, he drew a storm of criticism on his own head.

In the article Carter pointed out that in his experience stone projectile points in the Mojave, even the crudest and presumably oldest dart points, showed little surface alteration nor did they occur fixed solidly in desert pavements. On the other hand he had observed that crude flake and core tools like the Malpais were as heavily varnished and patinated as any of the rocks around them and were an integral part of the pavements.

Carter cited his work on the coast, particularly the age relationships demonstrated by La Jollan artifacts and the revealing soil profiles beneath which they were embedded, and drew the following conclusions:

"From detailed study of such features as an alluvial fan at La Jolla we know that acid clay-pan soils formed two or more times during the Wisconsin period. That artifacts are found beneath the full series indicates that man was present during all of Wisconsin time. Rolled artifacts from the 60-foot valley-fills of the rivers of this area are evidences of still greater antiquity. They represent man in third interglacial time. This is perhaps the explanation of the discontinuity from traces only of desert varnish and desert pavements to the extreme development of these features that we mentioned in discussing the desert cultures; that is, the artifacts with extreme coloration associated with maximum desert pavement development may also be of third interglacial age. Actually, it seems more logical to think of them as of third glacial (Illinoian) age, for only during the increased humidity of glacial times would the deserts be so inviting and habitable as to allow primitive man to occupy the area where his house sites (cleared circles) are now found.

"The evidence from the coast and the desert leaves little ground for doubt concerning the priority of the lower Paleolithic level of culture. The upper Paleolithic hunting cultures equipped with the throwing spear (dart or atlatl) are of Wisconsin and Recent time just as they are in the Old World. The lower Paleolithic peoples equipped with extremely simple stonework were present in America during all of Wisconsin time, probably during third interglacial time, and possibly even earlier. ..."

These were powerful and even prophetic words, for in 1951 Carter was still puzzling over the strange cores at Texas Street. More than twenty years later in 1973, particularly after the discoveries in Buchanan Canyon, the bipolar flaking industry with its long poly-

Ridgeback artifacts from the Yuha Desert near El Centro, California. According to Morlin Childers of the Imperial Valley College Museum, specimens of this type are not considered to be the oldest artifacts in the area, but have been somewhat of a mystery as to their method of manufacture and function. Ridgebacks are unifacial, with one side flat and unworked. Trimming blows appear to have been struck from the flat side all around the periphery of the pieces, with the flake scars terminating in a point or along a ridge on the dorsal or worked side. Whether they represent cores from which useful small flakes have been struck, or were so shaped for use as tools, is unknown. The mystery of their manufacture concerns what seem to be the impossibly low angles at which some of the flakes have been removed. However, Childers has produced a similar result experimentally by flaking on a much larger work piece and then separating the finished specimen from its larger core with one blow, shearing it off to produce the flat base last as the final flake scar. The two dark metabasalt specimens in the left center and lower left were found near the skeleton of Yuha Man in the cairn-marked burial dated about 21,500 years before the present.

hedral cores, its age significance and its relationship to very early sites in both hemispheres was becoming better understood. And now in January of 1973 during his survey of the Yuha Desert Carter was shown the same bipolar industry with the same long axial cores on sites in the desert with implications of equal or perhaps even greater antiquity.

On the dry lakes and beaches at various levels were areas of distinctly different tool industries and ages. Artifacts closely resembling those of the coastal La Jollans, including manos and metates for seed-grinding and unifacial, steeply-flaked choppers and pulping planes, were found on shorelines now far above sea level and the desert floor. These stone specimens had acquired light coats of desert varnish, suggesting by reference to the condition of early stone projectile points ages of many thousands of years. But on elevations only about one hundred feet higher on another beachline were crude stone tools so sand-blasted as to be scarcely recognizable as artifacts, their flake scars almost completely obliterated by millennia of exposure to the slow abrasion of the weather.

On one beach that displayed features suggesting a lake basin that had been filled, dried up in a long arid period and then filled again much later to a lower level, the familiar bipolar cores were found. These were the same size and shape as the once-mysterious broken stones first seen at Texas Street, and then found to be abundant in the fossil stream bed at Buchanan Canyon. On this desert site they were mostly of black basalt, but some were of quartzites and porphyries as on the coast, cutting across all lithic boundaries and reinforcing the theory of their human origin as opposed to natural breakage of some kind.

Here on the prehistoric beach the bipolar cores were so abraded by wind-driven sand and possibly by lake-shore surf that they appeared wax-like and slightly melted. Had they been of less distinctive shape they would have been completely unrecognizable as the work of man. There seemed to be little doubt that they represented the same industry first seen at San Diego and attributed by Carter to an interglacial period by reason of their geological context there. But here an interglacial climate might have been too arid to sustain the lakes and support human occupation, so that either an early Wisconsin age of about 60,000 years or an Illinoian presence twice that long ago began to seem more likely. Except for the suggestion of great antiquity implied by their extremely worn and polished appearance, they were undatable. In such objects all traces of percussive blows had long since been obliterated, and even their human origin could not be proven nor even guessed by one unaware of similar artifacts in other places. It seemed significant that such distinctively-shaped specimens, easily spotted and unique in their surroundings, had been seen at only one other place in the region by Morlin Childers. That was on a site just north of the ancient lake bed described above, and closely related to it. Had these cores been the manifestation of some natural process and not the work of human stone knappers, they would expectably have been distributed generally over the countryside, and not confined to one extremely restricted area. Could their resemblance to the elongate cores of Texas Street, Buchanan Canyon, Sheguiandah and Calico be merely coincidental?

Stone specimens believed to be elongate bipolar cores and blades from the Yuha Desert near Plaster City, California, about one hundred miles east of San Diego. These are found on the surface of an ancient beach now elevated far above the floor of the Imperial Valley to the east. Although they are extremely polished by wind erosion and possibly have also been abraded by surf action, they are apparently products of the same bipolar industry as that at Texas Street and Buchanan Canyon. According to Morlin Childers, curator of paleo-archaeology at the Imperial Valley College Museum in El Centro, California, they have only been found in two limited areas of the Yuha Desert, about three miles apart, and although similar stone and similar beachlines are quite common in the area, the elongate cores apparently do not occur outside of the two sites, strongly reinforcing the judgment of their human manufacture. Although some of the cores and their extracted blades are made of quartzite as at San Diego, here they are also of felsite, porphyry and even metabasalt, seeming to refute the suggestion advanced by critics that the Texas Street cores originally found by George F. Carter were formed by some natural process inherent in the crystalline structure of quartzite.

94

The Yuha Desert and in fact the entire arid sweep of country that lies in the rain-shadow of the Sierra Nevada and the Peninsular Ranges must have been, in the more pluvial and humid climates of the Wisconsin and the earlier glacial cycles, a very different land. The grassy lowlands would have had scattered lakes and running streams. On the mesas and slopes the pavements of polished stones would have gradually been penetrated by juniper and piñon, slowly covered with new organic soils and ground cover, perhaps suspending for centuries the weathering of flaked tools and cores discarded centuries before. Creatures of many kinds including man could then have flourished.

As the great ice sheets far to the north retreated under the warmer suns of major climate fluctuations, and precipitation diminished all over the Northern Hemisphere, the lakes and rivers would have begun to shrink, the grass in the lower valleys would have vanished and the topsoils that had covered the slopes would have been scoured away by the wind in great brown clouds of dust. And gradually the desert pavements would have reappeared to resume the slow process of concentration and burnishing under the sun. A few species of mammals, camels perhaps and ground sloths, possibly pronghorns and mule deer and peccary, would have adapted over the centuries of slow change as long as a few springs or shrunken lakes existed or perennial streams ran down from the mountains. It is known that the Colorado River changed its course and filled the Salton Sink at times regardless of climate. Man, too, probably lived in the Yuha as long as permanent water sources were available, but in times of maximum aridity even those vanished and only the truly desert-adapted creatures could have survived.

Malcolm Rogers' San Dieguito people of the second phase must have abandoned the desert during such a period, probably sometime less than 10,000 years ago, and moved through the mountain passes into a greener land, perhaps only seasonally for many generations. Eventually they occupied the coastal valleys. But what of the earlier people whose artifacts in the desert suggested far greater antiquity, stone specimens which could only have received their rich patinas and varnish before the pluvials of the Wisconsin? Did they also gradually filter out of the lowlands beyond the mountains during the increasing droughts of the Sangamon interglacial and slowly work their way down to the coast, to leave their distinctive bipolar-flaked cores on the floor of Buchanan Canyon and under the cliffs of Mission Valley near Texas Street?

Excavation at the Primary Sites

More than a quarter of a century after his first glimpse of the broken stones and hearths at Texas Street, Dr. George Carter and I found ourselves scrambling up the steep, crumbling and eroded cliff in Mission Valley, pecking at the red-streaked earth and bits of broken rock with geology picks. The same tawny summer-dried wild oats and foxtails covered the benches, and on the slopes above stood the same grey and brittle remnants of April's surge of yellow mustard, but the valley had undergone a striking transformation. Instead of the peaceful sycamore-shaded river bottoms and the empty fields the scene below was a busy metropolis of concrete and steel, and the surf-beat roar of traffic on an eight-lane freeway never stopped. The city had overflowed the rim and poured over the land in a torrent of shopping centers, restaurants, office buildings and luxurious hotels. A magnificent new church now stood on the remnant of an ancient river terrace just to the east, while below where the gravel pit had been was a Scottish Rites Temple surrounded by acres of parking lot. From nearby a loudspeaker blared out frequent instructions to used car salesmen on their sprawling establishment down the valley.

Carter and I, along with James Moriarty of the University of San Diego, were about to launch a new investigation of the Texas Street site and a simultaneous excavation at Buchanan Canyon, in the hope of finding additional new evidence of a much earlier hu-

The upper bench at the Texas Street site, as it appeared in 1975. Winter rains had continued to erode the cutbanks behind the narrow benches, depositing stones, occasionally including artifacts, on the bench surfaces. Above the cuts heavy vegetation prevented noticeable erosion of the valley walls behind the terrace. Because of the considerable publicity given the investigation locally, the site was well known to San Diegans interested in archaeology, and they continued to collect from the benches and cutbanks an unknown number of lithic specimens during the rainy seasons, according to George F. Carter, who occasionally received letters to that effect.

98

man occupation than had previously been recognized. As we clung precariously to the exposed face of the terrace, poking into the weathered soils where traces of repeated fires were concentrated, I felt the same sense of unreality again that had gripped me in Buchanan Canyon when I first picked up a massive paleolithic chopping tool. How strange it was to handle the burnt earth and charcoal from campfires tended in antiquity by primitive, unknown human creatures while being bombarded by the complex modern world with all its noise and confusion!

The land here was now owned by the Scottish Rites Corporation, proprietors of the temple below. At the back or south end of their property rose the cliffs to which we clung while trying to select a suitable excavation site. The original terrace had extended well out from the valley wall but had been cut back by a gravel firm and engineered into three almost sheer faces of about twenty-five, thirty and twenty feet in height, counting from the bottom, and separated by horizontal steps or benches about sixteen feet wide, with gunnite drainage channels to prevent excessive erosion. The lower bench was thickly planted with large shrubbery, acacia and hibiscus mostly, while the upper bench had only weeds and wild oats on it. The cliff faces were furrowed and eroded despite the drainage channels, and had so little growth on them that the clearly separated strata or layers of soil and pebble conglomerates were well exposed to view.

The geological composition of the terrace and the processes that had caused its formation were well understood, thanks to Carter's previous research. Few very early archaeological sites in the Western Hemisphere could be placed so confidently into an interglacial period before the Wisconsin glacial cycle. Because of the great importance of this situation in dating very early man not only locally but throughout the hemisphere, these processes needed to be appreciated.

The San Diego River drained a large area of the foothills and mountains behind the coastal plain, which was an uplifted zone of ancient sea bottom. From a belt of hills about ten miles inland the river had deeply cut a wide valley to the coast. Other rivers to the north and south had done the same, leaving the now-divided sections of the upraised plain as flat-topped mesas. Mission Valley, through which the San Diego River flowed intermittently, separated LindaVista Mesa to the north from the central or San Diego Mesa. The valley's floor sloped gently down to the shallow bay at its foot, and was a little over a mile wide in its lower reaches.

During historic times, because of the arid climate, the river had seldom covered its flood plain. Nevertheless, as the present interglacial cycle advanced and before the modern development began with its upstream dams and water use, the valley was slowly filling with sand and silt and had been doing so for thousands of years since the end of the last glacial period, with its much wetter climate and lowered sea level. The sandstone floor of the lower valley was now covered with over two hundred feet of silts, the depth reflecting the low sea levels of glacial periods when vast amounts of the earth's water were locked up in ice on the land. During the periods of much heavier amounts of rainfall and a steeper slope of the valley floor down to the lowered sea level, the river excavated a broad channel through the silts of the previous interglacial flood plain. Such streams tended to cut downward in a relatively restricted bed rather than spreading across a broad flood plain or meandering in wide curves. Increased volumes from freshets tended to increase the velocity rather than the width of the channel, and deposition of excavated materials was at the delta rather than on the river banks. In such times the delta would have been far to seaward of the present Mission Bay, which would itself have been a tree-covered flood plain.

The periods of valley cutting during the glacial cycles or pluvials, as they are called in unglaciated areas of the Northern Hemisphere, alternated throughout the Pleistocene Epoch of the last three million years with long periods of valley filling as the warmer interglacial stages were reflected locally by more arid climates and sea levels rising far

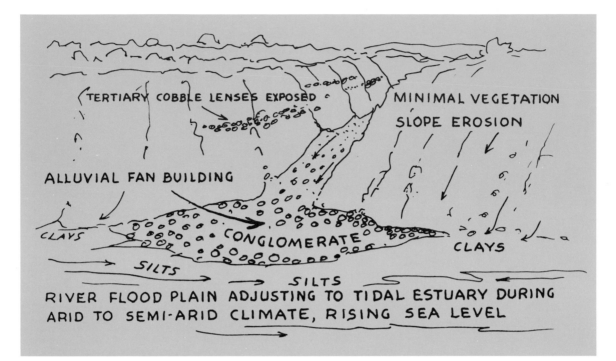

The Texas Street site during interglacial aspect, with its semi-arid climate and eustatic high sea level. Mission Valley is slowly being filled.

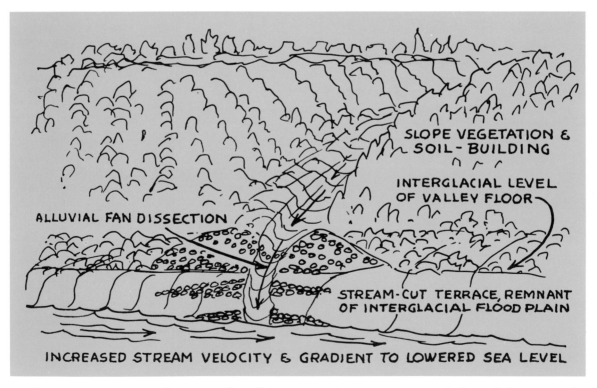

The Texas Street site during a glacial (Wisconsin) aspect, a time of pluvial climate and eustatic low sea level. Mission Valley is shown being excavated, leaving terraces along the walls.

100

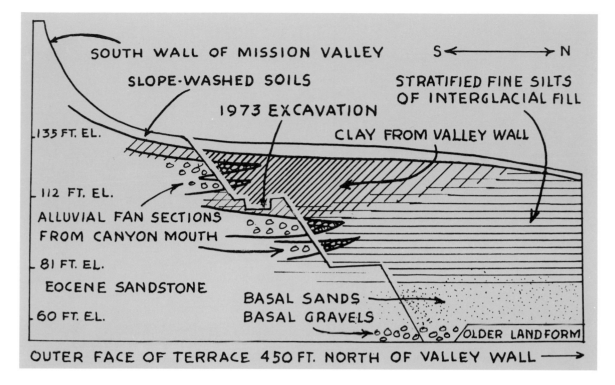

The Texas Street site in San Diego showing a section through the 1973 excavation. The soils north of the engineered faces were observed by George F. Carter prior to 1950 and their removal by sand and gravel borrow pit operations (no scale).

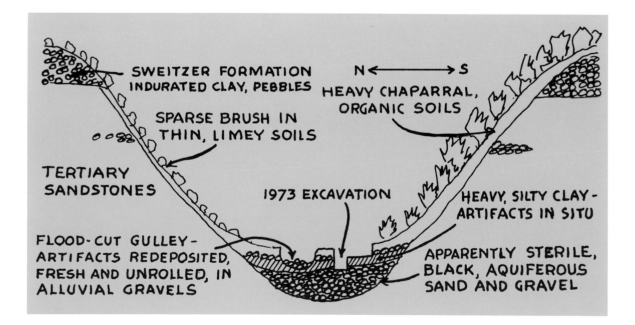

The Buchanan Canyon site showing a section cut through the 1973 excavation.

above the present bays and beaches, creeping up the valleys and into the lower canyons. The records of these dry valley-filling stages had been preserved as terraces along both flanks of the valleys; remnants of ancient flood plains and estuary sands. They stood at different levels along the valley walls where they had not been obscured by urban development, and their heights in general proclaimed their relative ages with the lowest ones the youngest and ages increasing with altitude above present sea level. Altitude was not, however, an infallible index of their ages since older terraces could be reshaped and even buried by later stream action.

Dr. Peter Birkeland, a geologist of the University of Colorado and the U.S. Geological Survey, had published in 1972 studies of the marine and stream-cut terraces in the vicinity of the Malibu Coast of Southern California, some one hundred miles to the north. On the basis of laboratory testing of shell from terraces thought to represent three different high sea levels during the Sangamon or third interglacial period, he assigned dates of approximately 80,000, 100,000 and 120,000 B.C. respectively. If these dates were correct the terrace at Texas Street probably dated to the second or 100,000 B.C. high sea level.

How far up Mission Valley tidewater came during that period was not known, but estuaries must have been near the site at Texas Street and would have provided an abundant and attractive food resource. During Carter's earlier work on the site, shell was taken from the vicinity of a hearth and was sufficiently intact to be identified as *Dosinia ponderosa*, a large clam now limited to warmer waters and not found north of San Quintin, Mexico, some two hundred miles to the south.

The valley was fringed with lateral canyons which had built alluvial fans of gravel at their mouths on the different flood plain levels of the river during the high sea levels of the interglacial period. Near the canyon mouths the terraces contained alternating layers of these cobbles and finer gravels separated by zones of silt deposited during floods by the main stream. As at Buchanan Canyon these smaller canyons had accumulated throughout their history loads of gravel from the sides and top as the soils were progressively eroded away and the rock in them exposed. Under flash flood conditions during the arid climates with only sparse vegetation, the gravels, including fair-sized boulders, were moved down the canyon floors for deposit on the fans. With the onset of the Wisconsin glacial cycle the down-cutting of the valley floor, plus the greatly increased cover of vegetation in the canyons, tending to minimize erosion, halted the fan-building. Canyon stream discharges cut and dissected the fan structures on the terraces, leaving remnants on both sides of the gullies running down to the lowered river level. Thus there had undoubtedly been no fan-building activity on the terraces since the onset of the Wisconsin, and one saw in effect hanging canyons connected by gullies and ravines to the valley floor.

A section of the remaining soils of the interglacial terrace at Texas Street which, unlike the bench where the excavation was conducted in 1973, is well out from the valley wall, about eighty yards from the engineered face and over a hundred yards from the canyon mouth. A clearly-defined unconformity can be seen as a horizontal division in the lower third of the photograph, separating two quite different kinds of deposit. The lower zone, composed of heavy clays and gravel, represents alluvial materials from the adjacent canyon and the valley walls, while the upper zone is clearly silts deposited by the San Diego River at flood stage during a period of very high sea level at least sixty feet above the present. The dark material at and just below the surface of the lower stratum is ash-stained earth containing bits of charcoal and red and broken rock; its isolation in this basin-like depression suggests a man-made fire.
A large church now stands on this remnant of ancient flood plain.

In more arid interglacial times the mouths of the canyons and their broad outwash fans would have provided cobbles and small boulders, good sources of stone for humans at a lower paleolithic stage of development and a resource which the sandy floor of the valley and perhaps the mesa tops might have lacked. It was not surprising to find evidences of human presence concentrated in such areas, and both Texas Street and Buchanan Canyon appeared to have been attractive to humans over vast periods of time.

When Dr. Carter first saw the site at Texas Street, the almost vertical cross section exposed by the commercial operation permitted detailed examination of the stratigraphy and composition of the landform. At the base of the terrace were coarse sands and gravels resting on remnant soils from an even earlier valley fill. The sands and gravels suggested a period of valley down-cutting since considerable stream velocity would have been required for their deposition. Above these coarse materials was a very thick stratum of fine sands and silts whose quality was quite similar to that of the present riverbed, but the top of this layer of silt was more than sixty feet above the modern flood plain. It was apparent that these deposits could only represent climate conditions somewhat comparable to the present, which was arid to semi-arid valley filling.

Near the valley wall the silty sands alternated with layers of clay loams which seemed to have been formed by deposits of soils from the walls, and in the vicinity of a lateral canyon which bisected the site successive layers of coarse gravel fan deposits were seen between thicker beds of silt and loamy clay. Chemical analyses of the soil surfaces showed them to be extremely acid and indicative of very long periods of weathering under decidedly humid conditions.

In the vicinity of the canyon mouth at the Texas Street site the successive gravel layers representing alluvial fan activity could still be seen in cross section on the cleanly cut walls of the former gravel pit, tapered spurs of coarse conglomerate marking periods of fan-building on each new level of the river's flood plain as the sea level slowly rose during the interglacial. It was difficult to see how any interpretation other than a period of valley filling during an arid climate and a much higher sea level than the present one could be offered to explain the structure of the landform in which the evidence of human occupation could be seen. And the sea had not been substantially higher than it was at present for well over 70,000 years, so the site must have been that old or older.

Late in June of 1973 we were at last ready to dig at Texas Street and Buchanan Canyon, although all of Carter's attempts to obtain foundation funding had been fruitless. The best we could do consisted of limited financial support from Texas A & M University and equally limited participation by the University of San Diego, a Catholic institution. The latter school would offer a summer class in field archaeological methods under Professor James R. Moriarty III, a man of considerable experience in archaeological excavation and also one of the most knowledgeable persons in the area on the La Jolla and San Dieguito cultures. Moriarty, since granted a doctorate in anthropology by U.S. International University, was strict in demanding site discipline. Originally highly skeptical of Carter's claims at Texas Street, the finds at Buchanan Canyon had convinced him of their human authorship and he was eager to establish their antiquity.

I had made all the arrangements necessary for excavating at the two sites. Since the operations at Buchanan Canyon were to be carried out at least partly on public property (mythical Buchanan Avenue) a city encroachment permit had to be obtained. Both sites were on locations covered by a land conservation ordinance which gave the Planning Commission control of all development on steep slopes in San Diego, so land conservation zone permits covering the sites were needed. The city utilities department had to bless the project since their sewer lines ran down Buchanan Canyon. Liability insurance, a performance bond and a portable toilet in the canyon were required. The terms of official permission demanded that both sites be securely fenced with chain link and locked, so a road had to be bulldozed up the floor of the canyon to truck in the toilet and

Excavation at Texas Street, San Diego, in 1973. Left to right: Brian Smith, a student at the University of San Diego and photographer for the project; Dr. George F. Carter manning a shovel in the rear, and the author waiting for an artifact to be photographed in situ *before removal. Smith had the distinction of finding the first artifact in the pits, almost where Carter is standing.*

the fencing materials. Maps had to be drawn and submitted showing exact areas of operation and access, and agreements had to be executed promising not only to backfill all pits and remove all structures by September 1, but also to provide and replant any shrubbery, including native growth, damaged or removed during the work. Finally private owners had to be contacted and their written consents obtained, since in the early stages of planning the precise location of the pits in the canyon had been in some doubt.

All of the private owners and city officials contacted were very much interested in the project, and were unfailingly cooperative. At the University of San Diego a large, handsome room with heavy wooden tables was placed at our disposal. Here the previously collected artifacts from the two sites being investigated could be displayed along with similar material from other sites for comparative studies and inspection by visiting scholars.

Before digging could commence the exact areas to be excavated had to be selected and marked off in order to fence the sites, and this presented difficult problems to be solved. Every chance of success hung on these decisions; we might spend all summer digging dry holes, so to speak. In Buchanan Canyon the final selection was strongly influenced by the discovery, mentioned earlier, of a quartzite chopping tool *in situ* in a clay stratum exposed during the spring at the base of the gully wall. This also happened to be one of the few places in the bottom where the canyon widened enough to provide an open and level stretch convenient for fencing. The pits were marked off here beside the gully, the hope being to penetrate the overburden and get down to this clay stratum closer to the canyon wall under conditions of good control in an undisturbed context.

At Texas Street, convenience and promising hints of culture-bearing soils determined our choice. If we sank our pits on the lower of the two benches we would have to remove and then restore a great deal of mature shrubbery, and the interglacial silts would give way to sterile gravel after only a few feet. Access to this bench by truck would be difficult if not impossible. The upper bench was clear of shrubbery, offered easy access for vehicles from the adjacent church parking lot, and showed streaks of burned earth and fire-reddened broken rock about thirty feet west of the intersecting canyon mouth. Digging on the surface of the bench here would mean penetrating potentially culture-bearing soils from the outset, since this surface was already twenty feet or more below the original surface of the interglacial terrace and was undisturbed. The fenced area was located at this spot abreast of where the burned material was weathering out of the cliff top.

On June 25, 1973, an orientation session was held at the university to acquaint the crew with the general situation, purposes of the investigation and proposed methods of operation. The size of the group at our disposal, including students and volunteers, was disappointing. Only about sixteen young men and women attended, and this number diminished alarmingly when it was realized that heavy, monotonous work under the hot summer sun was contemplated. But as usual the most energetic and enthusiastic people remained, and many of these had had experience on other field projects, so that for the six weeks of digging operations we usually had from four to six workers at each site. For

The upper photograph shows a quartzite artifact in situ *in Buchanan Canyon, San Diego. This specimen, an unretouched biface about four inches in diameter, was found near the head of Buchanan Canyon weathering out of the wall of a narrow gulley cut by heavy rain runoff. It was exposed in a stratum of heavy clay overlain by a bed of sorted pebbles, the latter suggesting a period of continuous stream flow. Below, George F. Carter points to what was identified as an excavated hearth at the Texas Street site, San Diego, during the investigation in the summer of 1973. The top of the interglacial terrace in which the excavation was made is nearly twenty feet above the pit where Carter crouches, and the soils must have been deposited at a time of very high sea level. In the rough, cobble-formed basin profiled by the wall of the pit can be seen soot-blackened and burnt earth and bits of charcoal. Artifacts and heat-reddened broken rock were distributed throughout the excavated area, as were definite zones of soot and charcoal. The soils had developed into an extremely plastic clay, rock-hard in the summer and impossible to screen. Charcoal from this terrace was tested during Carter's earlier investigation and found to be beyond the range of radiocarbon dating, then about 40,000 years.*

the most part they worked carefully despite the uncomfortable conditions and the seemingly snail-like progress.

All of us were eager to get down to culture-bearing levels and expose indisputable evidence of human occupation such as bones, shells, hearths and artifacts despite the difficult soils encountered, but careful controls had to be exercised if results were to be useful and accepted by others in the field.

Moriarty supervised the laying out of several six-foot squares to be excavated at both sites. These were staked and strung with cord to establish boundaries and reference points, so that vertical and horizontal positions anywhere in the pits could be described exactly. Azimuth orientation, or the relationship of reference lines to compass bearings, was established at both sites. Moriarty then directed the actual excavation at Buchanan Canyon while Carter took charge at Texas Street with Moriarty making occasional visits there to supervise his students.

Each site had been provided with a frame backed with quarter-inch mesh for screening removed soils, a rough wooden table, water cans, a wheelbarrow and picks and shovels. Smaller handtools and brushes were also available, although the workers were encouraged to provide their own. Students were required to keep careful notes, and a student photographer divided his time between the two sites and took routine photographs of progress as well as all specimens *in situ* and all significant features that were exposed.

At the Texas Street site we knew before we began to dig that we were in an area where fires had repeatedly burned, for the evidence was weathering out only a few feet from our marked-off squares. As I began to take off the loose soils on top, I found myself surprisingly excited and fearful of becoming too impatient. The old joke about pulling out the pick with a skull impaled on it came to mind, but only a few inches below the surface the texture changed to a tough, almost rock-hard clay speckled with charcoal. Some of the black fragments were as large as kidney beans. The first reaction was that this might be evidence of a recent brush fire, but as we proceeded something about the way the streaks were scattered through and embedded in the clay made this seem doubtful.

We quickly found that our screening gear would be useless here. Progress could only be made by laboriously prying out heavy clods with a geology pick or screwdriver. These clods we would then attempt to break up and sort through, but this was time-consuming and unprofitable. The second week was well advanced when we realized that at the rate we were digging with our small tools we would be lucky to be knee-deep by fall, so recalcitrant was the soil. We shifted our tactics of necessity and began to dig with picks and mattocks as carefully as we could.

Shortly after it had been unanimously decided to dig down as rapidly as possible to a level two feet below the datum point, Brian Smith, one of the students, exposed the first artifact in a matrix so tough and indurated as to be unquestionably undisturbed. This was not only promising but highly significant, for the tool was a quartzite skreblo, and shortly after its discovery, in the same square and at the same level, the unmistakable profile of a basin-shaped hearth began to be exposed on the wall nearest the outcrop previously seen. This feature contained dark grey material which was identified as soot-stained earth, bits of charcoal and distinct color variations between the soils in the basin and below it, suggesting intense and repeated heating. The cobbles were not placed as carefully and convincingly as at Calico, but they were reddened and had bits of red and broken rock scattered throughout the basin and between them.

A total of five specimens considered to have been shaped and used as tools were exposed in the pits, and these were accepted as artifacts by experts who examined them. Dr. Paul Ezell, then Chairman of the Department of Anthropology at San Diego State University and previously one of the most skeptical critics of Texas Street, later told me that he considered specimens from both Texas Street and Buchanan Canyon as clearly of human manufacture.

108

A quartzite artifact exposed in interglacial soils at the Texas Street site during excavation in 1973. All features and specimens of interest were routinely photographed as the work progressed, using the cardboard indicators shown here. The D2 refers to the grid section, the arrow points to the feature being recorded and is also carefully placed to indicate true north, the scale is marked off in inches. This particular artifact is a wedge-shaped slab which may have been produced by block-on-block splitting; that is, hurling a small quartzite boulder against another solidly-implanted one with great force. The resulting fragments would have had extremely sharp edges and many would have been usable without further refinement for cutting. Others like the slab pictured here were flaked along one edge to be used as chopping tools; the wear pattern on this specimen suggests such use.

The pits at Texas Street were excavated to a depth of thirty inches, not a very imposing accomplishment to be sure, but totally in culture-bearing strata. In addition to the basin-shaped hearth profile other more generalized concentrations of charcoal, soot-stained and burned earth, and red, broken rock were exposed. All of us had hoped to reveal some dramatic and overpowering evidence: human fossil material, split marrow bones or other food refuse. But if such remains had ever been deposited at this level, no trace remained in the well-leached and weathered soils.

Scholars of many disciplines visited the sites during the project, including anthropologists, geographers, pedologists, geologists and geophysicists. Some agreed completely with our interpretations of the evidence while others were politely noncommittal, as they had been in Carter's earlier experience. A few offered, as at Calico, ingenious explanations for the phenomena observed. One archaeologist suggested that the streaks of charcoal were actually "peat from a ponding situation," even though these strata clearly slanted down in conformity with the original slope of the terrain. Laboratory analysis later confirmed that the material was charcoal as expected.

At Buchanan Canyon the operations were completely different from those at Texas Street. Here the problem was to remove great quantities of overburden with picks and shovels in order to get down to the hoped-for clay stratum glimpsed at the bottom of the gully. The soils were loose, organic slopewash first, then a thick layer of sand and gravel. Both had clearly been disturbed and rearranged, probably by workmen servicing sewer lines in the canyon. Nevertheless, Moriarty's professionalism required that every object encountered be examined and every man-made artifact, whether of glass, china, rusted steel or of quartzite worked in the ancient past and redeposited, be carefully logged and saved.

This digging was hard physical work and was done by husky young students urged on by Dr. Moriarty shouting down from the pit rim. It seemed never-ending; the project had only days to go when the clay stratum was at last reached in one of the pit squares. There was only time remaining to excavate a small patch of clay about the size of a bathtub.

George Carter and I were fortunate enough to be present when the miracle occurred. We had decided to visit the Buchanan Canyon site only a few minutes before, and were standing on the rim with Moriarty when Richard Coyer, a USD student, exposed a small scraper plane of felsitic porphyry solidly in place twelve inches deep in the clay. It was indisputably of human manufacture, a common and easily recognized type of primitive tool, other examples of which are in the collection. The long shot had payed off! The only reasonable assumption must be that if one can pluck a tool out of so limited an exposure there must be hundreds more in the underlying clay stratum along the canyon floor.

However, as at Texas Street, no organic material capable of yielding a finite date was found in the pit at Buchanan Canyon. But charcoal taken from the terrace at Texas Street in the earlier investigation, when tested by the Carbon-14 method, proved to be beyond the range of 40,000 years, which was the maximum for this process. Thus even had such materials been exposed their usefulness would probably have been minor. The only suggestions of age seen in the excavation were based on the appearance and nature of the clay matrix. The fine silts from which the clay had been formed were suggestive of an extremely arid climate; while their present state, highly plastic and acid, could only be the result of long weathering in a humid climate.

About two feet below the surface of the silty clay its texture gradually merged into a sand and gravel layer, wet and highly plastic and of a uniform dark grey color. When I had the pit backfilled in September the back-hoe operator dug down with his mechanical shovel and at the limit of his equipment's reach encountered the sandstone basement or bedrock of the canyon floor twelve feet below the surface. He spread out each big shovelful on the ground for my inspection. It was all the same almost black, aquiferous sand and gravel and I could see nothing resembling an artifact nor even any broken rock. I suspect this stratum represents deposits of Illinoian age or earlier, but this is pure conjecture.

The extreme wetness of that lowest stratum is significant, for it suggests that even in midsummer in an arid interglacial period it might have offered early man a source of water, if wells were dug, in a land and climate of extremely limited water supplies. One is reminded of today's Australian aborigines who roam the barren, parched deserts of the Outback and seem to know instinctively where to dig in the dry sand to encounter water.

While the work of excavating occupied most of our time during the 1973 summer project, some supplementary studies were carried out. These included reconnaissance of other areas in the vicinity, review of hundreds of artifacts in the site drawers at the San Diego Museum of Man, and experiments with porphyry and quartzite. The search for other sites grew out of the realization that if man had been at Buchanan Canyon and Texas Street for the extremely extended periods suggested by the abundance of artifacts and the thickness of the Texas Street deposits, there must surely have been numerous other occupied locations in the vicinity. Dr. Carter had found during his earlier work the same exhausted cores and tools in a cutbank on the edge of the Sweetwater Valley some ten miles to the south, but there they were unaccompanied by the signs of fire. So now one afternoon he drove south to see if he could relocate that or a similar situation.

As he travelled it became increasingly obvious that the quest was nearly hopeless. Terrain attractive to ancient man has clearly been equally attractive to modern man, and he has covered it with houses, shopping centers and freeways. Everywhere the story was the same; even to stop and examine what few cutbanks were exposed along the freeways was to invite annihilation. At last he was as far south as he could go in the United States. The border loomed ahead and he turned west and drove down the Tijuana River Valley toward the sea.

Here at last were cultivated fields, cattle and drainage ditches, flocks of blackbirds and a peaceful rural atmosphere. The road, a modest two-lane blacktop, ran down the south side of the valley beside a low, brushy terrace sloping gently up to the bordering hills perhaps half a mile away. About two miles from the sea a dry arroyo came down from a cleft in the hills, crossed the flanking terrace and intersected the road where a culvert provided a drainage channel. As he drove by something in the sandy depression near the culvert caught Carter's eye, and he parked his car and walked back. The object proved to be exactly what he had been seeking, a massive bipolar flaked core. But the most exciting and significant aspect was that this artifact was not in the familiar quartzite

Next Page
A section of the gravel-strewn wash at the Border Road site near San Ysidro, California. This view looks north across the Tijuana River Valley toward the city of Imperial Beach; behind the viewer a quarter of a mile are the international border fence and Mexico. The situation here is similar to that at Buchanan Canyon; a heavily populated urban area in Mexico is sending huge volumes of runoff water down the draw after each rain, causing excavation of ancient soils and redistributing prehistoric artifacts into the surface gravels. Here they are mainly of green felsite rather than quartzite, but otherwise closely resemble specimens from Texas Street and Buchanan Canyon and are completely unlike artifacts from the more familiar and presumably later prehistoric industries in the region. The Border Road site was discovered by George Carter in 1973, and is on private property belonging to a family farming the rich bottomlands visible in the background.

111

or porphyry of the others, but was a beautiful green felsite. He walked on up the arroyo and found several more worked cores and flakes, all clearly belonging to the same industry as Texas Street.

The next day I went with Dr. Carter to Border Road where we collected several more specimens from the wash, including a well-executed unifacial scraper plane and a heavy chopper. All were in the close-grained green felsite. The source of all these artifacts could not be determined but appeared to be the canyon or cleft in the hills on the other side of the International Border. The pieces showed surprisingly little abrasion from stream transport but the rock materials were scattered and the arroyo is mostly sand, so that a minimum of tumbling wear might be expected even under flood conditions.

Perhaps the most important benefit derived from this discovery was the demonstration that the same bipolar industry had employed a completely different lithic material. We had often been confronted with critics who, upon examining the quartzite artifacts, chuckled indulgently and said "Well, yes, quartzite has a tendency to just break naturally this way," an infuriating pronouncement from our standpoint and difficult to refute. But now we had an instant and convincing rebuttal to any such suggestion, for nothing could be more different from quartzite in its structure and behavior under stress than felsite, a fine-grained volcanic as opposed to a coarse-grained metamorphic rock. We had only to produce one of the beautiful green cores to silence any such argument.

It might be interjected here that early in 1976 it was learned that an archaeological survey of a very early man site in the eastern Sierra Nevada by Clyde E. Kuhn of Claremont Graduate School, Claremont, California, had revealed elongate polyhedral cores identical in form to those at Texas Street, but in obsidian, a black volcanic glass. As with the Tijuana River felsites, it was impossible to conceive of such material exfoliating or "peeling" under any kind of natural conditions; only extremely skillful human workmanship could produce such objects in obsidian.

Near the summer's end another site was located. Mount Soledad is an isolated highland above the community of La Jolla, a few miles to the north and part of the city of San Diego. During the Sangamon it would have been a high penninsula as the sea ran far up the small valley called Rose Canyon to the east. The slopes may have had groves of the Torrey pines which still thrive on the uplands just to the north. On a high shoulder of Mount Soledad and on relatively bare ground Carter discovered more of the same polyhedral cores which first attracted his attention to Texas Street. Although they were few and scattered there was no mistaking their origin as the result of human activity here, for this was an erosion surface and could not ever have provided the circumstances claimed by critics as responsible for the natural formation of the broken stones; that is, stream breakage or falling down hillsides. This was the top of the hill and streams are rare on hilltops.

Unfortunately this discovery came almost at the end of the summer and most of our visitors had come and gone. In contrast to Carter's earlier difficulties, however, we had had few disbelievers once they had inspected our extremely impressive artifact display, for in addition to similar specimens from Buchanan Canyon, Texas Street, Imperial Valley and Border Road, we had some Old World artifacts borrowed from the Museum of Man whose resemblance to the local pieces was compelling.

For nearly forty years the Museum of Man at San Diego had been surveying, examining and collecting from archaeological sites in San Diego County as well as from adjacent regions. Originally the collection was stored in old bureau drawers that Malcolm Rogers had brought from his citrus ranch at Escondido. By 1934 the museum had begun the system of site drawers for artifacts, with overhead racks for pottery. When I worked there briefly in the 1930's this system was just being organized, and Carter spent a lot of his time putting artifacts into the proper drawers. During World War II the building was taken over by the Navy, and an enormously confused storage problem resulted. After the war the staff under Malcolm Farmer began to sort through the mass of material in order to make it more useful for study. Site assemblages and type collections were made available in the drawers, with site books keyed to them giving the pertinent information about the sites and materials.

In 1973 under General Lowell English, U.S.M.C., Ret., the administrative director, and Dr. Spencer Rogers, the scientific director, the institution was a useful and impressive resource for the study of early man in Southern and Baja California, as well as many other aspects of anthropology in collections, library files, public displays and special events. In addition the staff was carrying on valuable field and laboratory research and public education projects.

During our search for parallel sites we went to the Museum of Man and carefully sifted through the hundreds of items in the site drawers. It had occurred to us that since the more ancient culture was unknown and unrecognized during the time most of the collections were made, some of the sites might have had mixed horizons including the older culture, particularly on surface exposures. In other words, just as desert quarry workshops could accumulate materials from many prehistoric levels, so here in San Diego the same might have occurred and not been noticed, since workers were unaware of the existence of the bipolar flaking industry.

The result of this survey was indecisive. Only a few pieces were found that resembled the quartzite tools of the earliest period, and these came from San Dieguito sites in Mission Valley and on Linda Vista Mesa just to the north. In one way this negative result suggested how separate and unique an industry we were dealing with, for in handling hundreds of La Jollan and San Dieguito artifacts we were in no doubt whatever that they belonged to the designated industry and not the earlier one. The exercise failed to establish whether or not the older pieces were on the sites, for the bipolar cores, even had they been present, would probably not have been recognized and collected.

This pointed up an aspect of the search for early man throughout the hemisphere that should be noted. It had often been maintained that if man were really as early in America as we believed, his artifacts should have already been found scattered from Bering Strait to Tierra del Fuego. Since they had not been, the arguments suggested, man's antiquity could not be as great as claimed. The fallacy here could be that these crude quartzite artifacts would have been recognized and collected, whereas nothing could have been further from the truth. Even what we now clearly recognized as tool types

Arrangement of artifacts from the Border Road site near San Ysidro, California. Discovered by George F. Carter during the 1973 investigations, this site consists entirely of surface deposits on an alluvial fan and is therefore undatable. The source of the artifacts found among the gravels is still unknown and is almost certainly across the border in Mexico, but the recovered specimens appear to belong to the same bipolar flaking complex as the Texas Street and Buchanan Canyon assemblages. Of particular interest is the fact that almost all the specimens are made of green felsite rather than quartzite, which seems to be rare in the vicinity. Shown in upper left is a well-made felsite pick. In upper center is a felsite core showing marks of anvil rebound typical of bipolar work for the extraction of long blades. In upper right is a backed skreblo of porphyry which, although somewhat longer than similar tools at Buchanan Canyon, clearly belongs to the same tool family. In the lower row are a unifacial chopper, a well-used hammer of felsite, and a felsite chopping tool also showing strong use wear. While the use of felsite suggests the San Dieguito industries, which show a marked preference for that material in their stone artifacts, the forms of the Border Road pieces and their large size are completely different from San Dieguito work and strongly resemble Buchanan Canyon and Texas Street artifact patterns.

114

many times repeated were so unfamiliar to most workers in the field as to have been disregarded, perhaps not even noticed on a quarry site containing large amounts of broken rock as well as later, more familiar types of stone work. On other terrain not even considered an archaeological site the chance of their being recognized as human work was even more remote; indeed little better than it had been twenty years before.

The original resistance to acceptance of "Carterfacts" was matched by unwillingness to accept the reddened and broken rock as evidence of high heating in campfires. Some visitors proposed "natural oxidation" could account for the color changes in the streaks of pink, red and violet rock fragments and whole cobbles in the Texas Street exposure. But it was pointed out that it was possible to examine similar cliff exposures all up and down the valley and in the canyon walls without finding such effects. Surely, if quartzite, porphyry and rhyolite oxidized to such strong colors at Texas Street, they would have done so equally in all similar exposures.

Another apparently logical explanation that was offered was that the colors were indeed produced by heating, but from brush fires and not campfires. While somewhat the same response as that above applied, there having been no reason to suppose that here and here alone brush fires would have burned fiercely and often enough to produce the small, concentrated fire areas in the terrace from top to bottom, an observation was made that also countered this proposal. In the excavation at Texas Street the undersides of the rocks were consistently the most reddened, suggesting that they had rested in and on beds of hot embers. In contrast, cobbles weathering out of the hillside behind my house, a slope over which a hot brush fire had passed some fifteen years earlier, showed no reddening on their undersides but were strongly heat-stained on top.

At the Calico site the same phenomenon was observed. Although the features designated a hearth by the investigators showed no visible evidence of heating when exposed, when one of the large cobbles was removed to be tested for magnetism, it also was found to be heat-reddened on the underside, indicating that it had rested on a bed of hot coals but had not been overrun by a brush fire.

A number of experiments in heating rock were made by Carter during his work in 1954, primarily to learn if heat fracturing could have been responsible for the flaked effect he was seeing on the cores. The results convinced him that heat could possibly cause flaking somewhat similar to what was being seen, and his conclusions at that time were rather indefinite. Now much more was known about bipolar flaking and also about the properties of quartzite. It could be stated with considerable authority that breakage from heating alone rarely and perhaps never occurred without leaving discoloration. To test this point new experiments were carried out.

Pebbles of quartzite and porphyry, both whole and already broken, were placed in an hibachi and charcoal briquets were piled around them and lighted. The stones were carefully watched, and as soon as breakage began to occur they were removed from the fire. All of the pieces without exception showed reddening to a very noticeable degree, and in these tests no fractures were seen that remotely resembled human flaking; the breakage was completely random and usually into halves or quarters. The purpose of the tests was to duplicate if possible the effects seen in the deposits at Texas Street, and it cannot be claimed that special circumstances such as already faulted rock or sudden cooling of highly heated rock by rain showers could not produce breakage without staining, nor simulate human flaking more exactly. But to invoke convenient rain showers during heating for all the tons of broken rock in the terrace was stretching credulity.

Another experiment was carried out in an attempt to duplicate the minute chipping seen on the functional edges of artifacts taken to be chopping tools. This type of wear pattern is often seen on concave edges where casual battering or pressure from other rocks is highly unlikely. At the Texas Street site I selected a suitable cobble and from it manufactured a fresh, sharp chopping tool, taking pains to insure that the functional edge

116

was slightly concave. Then a large beef bone was purchased and I began to chop at it in an attempt to expose the marrow. This was more difficult than I had anticipated but after about twenty minutes of steady chopping I had the bone well opened and the marrow exposed. I had made a special effort to use the same part of the edge in order to put maximum wear on it. When the edge was carefully examined the tiny flake scars duplicated the wear patterns displayed by many of the chopping tools in the assemblages.

Such wear is quite different from that resulting from stone to stone contact. When stone is the battering agent, crushing and powdering occur. Despite repeated attempts to produce the more delicate and minute flaking observed from the bone-chopping experiment by tapping the tool gently against stone, the same effects were never obtained. Only powdering occurred until sufficient force was applied to yield massive batter-marks.

Although the summer's excavations produced no very spectacular discoveries, important information was gained from them and particularly from concomitant activities. At Buchanan Canyon the finding of a convincing artifact solidly *in situ* in the underlying stratum supported our conviction that most of the recovered artifacts had originally been deposited in soils of obvious antiquity below the gravels in which they were appearing. While the age of that yellowish and highly compacted clay could not be ascertained except in the broadest terms, one could say with certainty that it was very old and seemed to have been deposited during a very arid period followed by a humid one of long duration.

At Texas Street the artifacts and charcoal supported Carter's earlier findings. The artifacts recovered were particularly valuable because they seemed convincingly man-made and, if so, would clearly establish man in a time frame that could only be attributed to an interglacial. Combined with the hearths and charcoal, and the earlier findings of burnt bone and shell at lower levels, the evidence seemed overwhelming. Man must have lived here more than 70,000 years ago.

Late in 1975, Dr. Edward J. Zeller, director of the Radiation Physics Laboratory of the University of Kansas Space Technology Center, offered to undertake the dating of burned hearth stones from the Texas Street site, using a process called "thermoluminescence." This method relies on the fact that the decay of radioactive materials in rocks releases electrons, some of which are trapped in the crystals of the rock structure. Substantial heating releases these trapped electrons, and this energy can be measured in the form of luminescence. Since it is accumulated at a constant rate, the elapsed time since previous heating can be estimated in the laboratory.

A rough estimate is a relatively simple procedure; that is, distinguishing between a period since previous heating of 10,000 years, for example, and one of 100,000 years or more. Direct, definitive dating in terms of years is considerably more complicated, and requires more elaborate equipment and much more time.

Burned rock specimens from the fireplace exposed during the 1973 excavation at Texas Street were sent to Zeller, and the results of his first runs, expressed in graphic form as "glow-curves," strongly indicated an age on the order of at least 100,000 years, and possibly much more. Further testing was in progress and was expected to yield more precise time frames, but even on the basis of the preliminary runs the interglacial age of the fireplace and its associated human artifacts seemed to be substantially supported.

The recognition of bipolar-flaked cores in the Yuha Desert, with suggestions of their vast antiquity, the discovery of the Border Road felsites which clearly represented the Texas Street industry in a completely different lithic material, re-examination of other sites like Black's Fork and Calico, all were important contributions to our growing insights into the human past. Studies of the artifact assemblages and hearths, plus the suggestions of bone and shell refuse found previously at Texas Street, have yielded a few clues to the cultural attainments and habits of the ancient humans who wandered into the San Diego region so long ago, but conclusions are rather speculative.

117

The massive Buchanan Canyon choppers suggest that big game was killed and butchered and the large bones split for marrow. Scrapers are of a size appropriate for working very large hides. Objects taken to be digging tools, common at Buchanan Canyon, might have been used for digging wells; or pits for roasting agave hearts, still practiced by Indians in Baja California; or harvesting edible roots and tubers; or perhaps hollowing out caves under the canyon rims in the soft sandstone. The shell remnants in the lower levels associated with hearths suggest that shellfish were a part of the diet.

The lack of milling implements and stone projectile points indicates that these cultural refinements were still unknown. Fire-hardened wooden spears and lances could have been highly effective against large slow game such as giant ground sloths, giant armadillos and elephant seals, and probably against more active game driven over cliffs or into estuary sloughs and bogs. The abundance of spokeshave-like tools would support the theory that wooden shafts were an important though now vanished part of the equipment of these early people.

Carter's reinvolvement in the problems of very early man in the San Diego region also led indirectly to an even more exciting and significant outcome: the dating by a newly-developed process of human skeletal remains collected from sites along the San Diego coast nearly fifty years earlier by Malcolm Rogers.

New Evidence from Old Bones

In 1926, almost a half century before the archaeological investigations at Texas Street and Buchanan Canyon and ten miles to the north, a steam shovel working at La Jolla Shores had turned up some interesting material. A low, hummocky area around a brackish pond and just behind the beach was being prepared for real estate development, and the workmen using the equipment were unusually astute. They noticed what appeared to be fragments of human bone coming up in the shovel.

The Museum of Man was notified, and its director at that time, Edgar Lee Hewett, ignored the information. But Malcolm Rogers, then an orange grower in Escondido, California, heard about the discovery and hurried out to examine the site. The material was indeed human bone; he collected several pieces from different levels, and made careful notes and sketches of the stratigraphy. The remains were in a low ridge or large hummock running parallel to and just behind the beach, and three distinct strata were noted although they merged into each other. The capping was a midden of shell; below it was a layer of red sand apparently washed down from the highlands behind the site. This stratum of red sand contained the remains of several burials which Rogers identified as La Jolla II, a mid-point in the La Jolla cultural development as he then understood it.

Below the red sands was a zone of white sand which Rogers attributed to the breakup of a landform to the north by the tides as the sea rose to a higher level. In this stratum were several bits of human bone that appeared to have been redeposited during the destruction of an older midden and burials. These included a frontal bone which had

119

formed part of the dome of a human skull, a rib bone with an olivella shell bead cemented to it, and various unidentifiable fragments. Since there was then no way the fossils could have been dated, they were simply collected and stored away in a bureau drawer at home with suitable identification.

Three years later in 1929 Rogers found an even more intriguing fossil. A human skull, mandible or lower jaw, and ribs were discovered weathering out of a terrace remnant above the beach, just where the San Dieguito River's estuary runs into the ocean at Del Mar, sixteen miles north of San Diego. The rest of the skeleton had apparently fallen into the sea. Although no artifacts were found with the remains, the bones were located about four feet below a thin layer of shell which Rogers believed had been the base of a La Jolla I midden, with the upper zones eroded away. A well-developed La Jolla II midden was on a slightly higher terrace to the north. The skull appeared to be somewhat more primitive than other La Jolla examples but was clearly within the range of modern humans. As in the case of the fossils at La Jolla Shores, Rogers made careful notes, took photographs of the site and stored the skeletal materials in the museum. During succeeding decades the skull was included in comparative studies of La Jollan fossils; its measurements were listed with others, but any special temporal significance was disregarded since its age could only be inferred by geological interpretation and this was highly speculative.

After the late 1940's when radiocarbon dating became available, fossil bone was occasionally tested by that method, but it required the destruction of such large amounts of the material being dated that, in the case of bone, one ended up with a date, if the sample proved suitable, but no specimen. It had occurred to no one to attempt radiocarbon dating of the finds described above, and the bones were simply forgotten and waited out the years in the dark recesses of the museum, as did thousands of other fossils stored in dusty boxes and drawers in basements throughout the world.

Skeletal remains of prehistoric humans had been found in many places throughout the Western Hemisphere during the last century. These finds were frequently, almost invariably, the subjects of heated controversies as to their antiquity, just as were the non-fossil-bearing archaeological sites with typological, geological and other implications of great age. It was impossible to know how many unpublicized finds like the Del Mar and La Jolla Shores fossils simply disappeared into museum storages and were virtually forgotten. The long-accepted but now discarded view that all humans before about 40,000 B.C. had so-called Neanderthaloid features, that is, heavy brow ridges, sloping foreheads and prognathous jaws, led in a great many cases to serious underestimation of the ages of fossil skulls. In addition, the same general resistance to any suggestion of great antiquity for the lower paleolithic chopping tool industries operated to hamper valid conclusions regarding the human fossil remains.

Many of the known human fossil finds were made by untrained people; workmen digging roadcuts or cesspools. Too often potentially valuable evidence was lost by improper removal and failure to note and record important data like the exact position of the bones, the surrounding matrix and significant associated materials such as artifacts, shell, charcoal and burnt earth. Even when the bones were exposed by competent scientists the geological interpretation of the deposits in which they lay was the subject of endless argument and difference of opinion. Unfortunately most fossil bone was unsuitable for radiocarbon dating because of mineral replacement of collagen, the material containing the carbons. Also, as mentioned earlier, anthropologists were reluctant to sacrifice valuable fossil specimens in exchange for a date.

One of the traditional methods of dating human remains both skeletal and artifactual has been a judgment based on their association with animals believed to have become extinct at certain periods in the past. Thus human remains found in the same level of deposition with mammoth or extinct bison bones were clearly contemporary with those now-extinct creatures, supposed to have vanished about 10,000 years ago, and could at least be attributed to the Pleistocene. But the disturbing question was: did the so-called Pleistocene megafauna actually become extinct then or did the changed climate eliminate the ideal conditions for preservation of their fossil remains? Negative evidence, or not finding something that is rare and fragile under the best of circumstances, is shaky evidence indeed, yet much of the chronological frame work of both archaeology and paleontology, the study of fossil bone, has been based on just such questionable presumption. Elephants and camels and ground sloths may have lived far into the Recent period in North America; man may have been present far back in the Pleistocene. These propositions could not be refuted simply by lack of evidence.

Clearly, if some method could be found to date fossil bone directly, without reference to its geological context or associated materials and without destroying the specimen itself, an enormous advance toward understanding the past would have been made. In 1972 Dr. Jeffrey Bada of Scripps Institution of Oceanography at La Jolla, a branch of the University of California, announced that just such a method had been developed and appeared to be feasible, at least under certain conditions of bone preservation. It was based on a phenomenon called "racemization" and known for more than a century. This is the gradual transformation of one form of amino acid into another after the death of living organic tissue. The molecular units of amino acids, called "isomers," occur in two forms in Nature, "L" isomers which are left-handed and "D" isomers which are right-handed. The "L" and "D" stand for the prefixes levo- and dextro-, left and right in scientific usage.

Living organisms utilize only the "L" isomers of amino acids, which have been called the "building blocks of Nature" and are essential in the growth of living cells. Since the enzymes will only react to "L" isomers, only these molecular forms are used by living systems.

When any organism dies all enzymatic activity ceases and the racemization process commences, a gradual conversion from a preponderance of "L" isomers to an eventual equilibrium where the ratio of "D" isomers to "L" isomers is 1.0. The period of time during which racemization is completed is, with certain exceptions, consistent and predictable, and it varies with the different amino acids, of which there are some twenty forms. Isoleucine, for example, reaches equilibrium in about ten million years, while aspartic acid is completely racemized in three to four million years, depending upon the temperatures to which it has been exposed. Theoretically then, if one could determine the rate of racemization and the ratio of "L" to "D" isomers of an amino acid in formerly living tissue, and an estimate of the temperature history of the fossil were available, one could then deduce how long ago the organism ceased to live.

In the early 1950's Philip H. Abelson, a scientist at the Carnegie Institute, Washington, D.C., discovered that there were amino acids present in fossil shells and that these were not decomposed when the animal died, as had previously been thought. His published findings led a young graduate student at California Institute of Technology, P. Edgar Hare, to undertake further research on amino acids in shells as the basis for a doctoral thesis and eventually, in 1963, after having obtained his doctorate in geology, to obtain a position at Carnegie Institute where he was able to continue research with Abelson. Among their areas of research were studies of the decomposition and alteration reactions of amino acids on the geological time scale. They used clam shells as the test material.

Abelson and Hare, with graduate student associates, continued their experiments through the next few years. In 1969, when they attempted to apply their developing dating technique to fossil bone, their findings suggested that bone presented unexpected complications and the dates were unreliable. They felt that their questionable results were caused by amino acids of more recent origin having contaminated the bone samples, perhaps transmitted by ground water percolating down through the soils in which the samples had been buried. The experiments with bone were discontinued, although research with shell went on.

Meanwhile Bada had been doing independent and parallel research but from a different viewpoint. His doctoral dissertation in chemistry at the University of California at San Diego in 1968 had concerned itself with the kinetics and mechanisms of the decomposition of aspartic acid and its geochemical implications. During this research he became interested in the racemization of amino acids, and began extensive laboratory studies of the kinetics and mechanism of this reaction in aqueous solutions. The results of these experiments suggested to Bada that if the same reaction occurred in Nature, it might be possible to use it as a dating method.

In 1969, Bada moved to Harvard University and there he began investigating the extent of racemization in deep ocean cores. These cores contained minute crustaceans that had died far back in the past. The tiny shells from the ocean floor were ideal for the purpose, since the deeply-buried material had been at a nearly constant temperature after its deposition and was not subject to contamination by fresher amino acid absorption His results seemed highly consistent; the deeper the fossils were in the core, the greater the extent of racemization of the amino acid isoleucine.

But Bada, like Abelson and Hare, was skeptical about the possibility of dating land fossils by the process since bones buried over long periods in soils would have been subjected to considerable variations in temperature over the millennia. Pleistocene climates in many parts of the world fluctuated drastically, and heat tended to speed up chemical processes, while extreme cold would retard them. As mentioned earlier, racemization was no exception, and since the exact temperatures to which fossils had been subjected would be difficult to calculate accurately, the resulting data would be unreliable.

In the spring of 1970, about the same time that Buchanan Canyon was first revealing its hidden store of ancient stone choppers, Bada was attending a seminar at Yale University. Here he met Karl Turekian, a professor of geochemistry who was aware of Bada's work on amino acid racemization, and who urged him to attempt the dating of fossil bone by the method. He convinced the younger man that there was a tremendous need for such a technique, and that while some fossils undoubtedly would prove unsuitable for such procedures because of having been subjected to severe heating or contamination, the locations of many others would have made them relatively immune to interference by outside factors. He suggested that fossils from deep subterranean caves would be ideally suited to experiment since such caves, like the deep ocean sediments, would have remained at constant temperatures throughout the periods involved.

Turekian suggested Muleta Cave on the island of Mallorca in the Mediterranean. Here in abundance were the fossil remains of an extinct species of goat which had inhabited the island during the Pleistocene. In early 1971 Bada and Turekian went to Mallorca and gathered a generous supply of fossil goat bones from the Muleta Cave's deep recesses, material which should be perfect for the purpose, and upon his return Bada began experiments on them. His results by the racemization technique he had developed produced ages for the bones of between 25,000 and 30,000 years.

While such ages seemed reasonable enough there was no way to judge their accuracy. But when samples of the same bones were sent to Rainer Berger, a geophysicist at the University of California at Los Angeles, independent radiocarbon dating produced ages of between 28,000 and 29,000 years. This was a remarkable correspondence by completely different dating methods, and solidly supported the new method at least in cases where contamination was minor or nonexistent.

In 1972 Bada published the results of the racemization experiments on the Muleta Cave fossils and other bones including a shark's vertebra from the ocean floor. The article came to the attention of George Carter who, because of the developments at Buchanan

Canyon, was again becoming actively involved in the search for early man at San Diego. The timing could hardly have been more fortuitous. Carter was surely the only person alive who remembered in detail the circumstances of Malcolm Rogers' fossil finds at La Jolla Shores and Del Mar, and even more importantly, had sufficient grasp of the geological contexts in which they were discovered to appreciate their potential great antiquity. He wrote to Bada suggesting that the human fossils might be extremely old, older than the dates usually assigned to man's first appearance in the Western Hemisphere, and urging Bada to try his racemization technique on dating them.

But Bada was reluctant to attempt the project. He was still uncertain that the process would be reliable under circumstances less controlled than the constant temperatures of Muleta Cave, but he realized the importance, the almost incalculable boon to anthropology, that such a dating tool would represent.

In the summer of 1973, while the investigations of the Texas Street and Buchanan Canyon sites were proceeding, Bada travelled to Olduvai Gorge in Tanzania, East Africa, where he collected a supply of late Pleistocene fossil animal bones to which, because of the unique stratigraphic sequence of the deposits, relative ages could be assigned. One bone was dated by the radiocarbon laboratory at UCLA at 17,550 years. Back in his laboratory in La Jolla he tested them by the racemization technique, in this case using aspartic acid. A very close correspondence was obtained with the stratigraphic evidence, and this time on material that had been subjected to varying temperatures in a completely different environment from the deep cave deposits.

Extensive testing was then begun to check the agreement between racemization and radiocarbon ages deduced on the same bone. Material from sites all over the world was tested. The two independent dating methods were repeatedly applied on nearly two dozen different samples, producing close agreement in every case. Bada and Roy A. Schroeder, a graduate student also working on the project, were cautiously optimistic now, and agreed to attempt the dating of the San Diego human fossils.

In the meantime the human bone had been retrieved from storage at the Museum of Man, and small samples were extracted by Mrs. Rose Tyson, curator of physical anthropology. In contrast to the large amounts needed for radiocarbon dating, only tiny samples of less than an ounce were sufficient for racemization testing, one of the advantages of the method. Rogers' notes and photographs bearing on the sites were carefully studied, and copies were provided to Bada and Schroeder. But one more critical ingredient was needed.

In order to deduce the amount of time that had elapsed since the commencement of the racemization process, Bada needed to know the rate of racemization in the Southern California area. Average temperatures varied widely in different parts of the world, and temperature appeared to play an important role in determining the rate in a given locality.

The solution was to obtain fossil bone from the same region and with the same climate history, which had been dated by radiocarbon methods. By noting the degree of racemization that had occurred in specimens of known age, the rate at which this had been occurring could be deduced, in addition to providing a valuable cross-check on the accuracy of the new technique. Fossil bone samples from the Southern California coastal area were obtained from UCLA and the Los Angeles County Museum of Natural History. Included were human fossil specimens: a piece of skull found in 1936 called "Los Angeles Man" and dated at greater than 23,600 B.C. by Carbon 14, and a sample of the Laguna Beach skull discovered in 1933 and dated at about 17,150 B.C. Analysis of aspartic acid isomers in these samples produced dates that closely corresponded with the radiocarbon dates, and provided racemization rates that could be applied with confidence to the San Diego fossil findings.

In May of 1974 Bada, Schroeder and Carter published in *SCIENCE* magazine the announcement that an age of 48,000 years had been deduced for the Del Mar skull, and

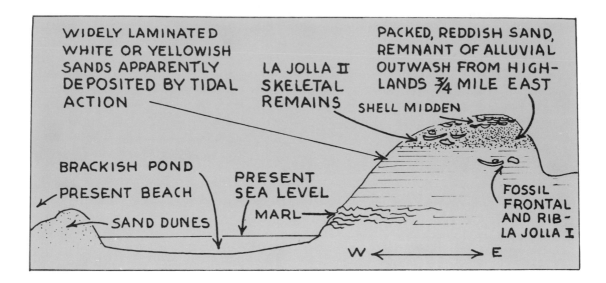

The La Jolla Shores site at San Diego, showing a section through the sand ridge where La Jolla I and La Jolla II fossils were collected in 1929 by the late Malcolm Rogers.

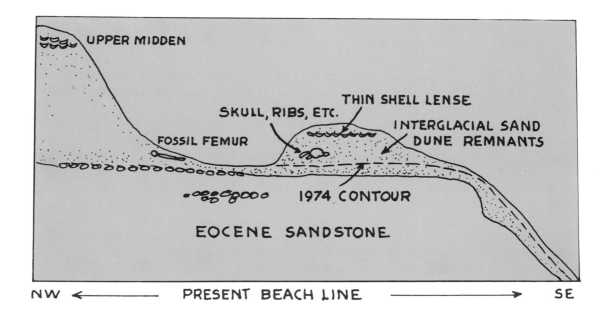

The site at Del Mar, California, showing the 1929 profile of a dune hummock where a fossil skull attributed to La Jolla I was collected.

ages of 44,000 and 28,000 years for the fossil frontal and rib bone from La Jolla Shores. The circumstances of discovery were reviewed briefly, and various cross-checks with radiocarbon dates were reported, as were the processes by which the data were obtained.

This brief three-page announcement meant that the widely accepted date of 20,000 years for the earliest human occupation of the Western Hemisphere had suddenly been revised backward almost thirty thousand years, more than doubling the age of man in America. The implications of the dates were much more far-reaching, for even in San Diego the fossils clearly did not represent the oldest inhabitants, the pre-Wisconsin people of Texas Street. Bada summed up his findings with the observation that to be in San Diego 48,000 years ago man must have crossed the land bridge of Beringia at least 70,000 years ago or earlier. However, in view of the apparent arrivals in Australia by boat at around 40,000 B.P., such a conclusion may not have been warranted.

The reactions of other scientists to the report were varied. P. Edgar Hare, who had attempted to develop the technique and then discarded it, felt that Bada had simply disregarded the importance of the contamination problem, and that his results were questionable. Keith A. Kvenvolden, a scientist with the National Aeronautics and Space Administration's Ames Research Center near Palo Alto, also had some reservations since he and his associates had made an unsuccessful attempt to date fossil bone from the La Brea Tar Pits in Los Angeles by the same method. Apparently the hydrocarbons in which the sabertooth bone had been preserved had also retarded the racemization process and had produced a date considered impossibly recent.

Bada had proceeded, however, with extraordinary caution, had been acutely aware of the heat and free-acid possibilities for contamination, and was well prepared to defend his procedures. Temperature factors had been carefully taken into consideration when his racemization rates were calibrated with fossils of known age from the same climate environment. He had found that extreme heat from localized causes such as brush fires or cooking in hearths completely destroyed certain of the amino acids in a sample, making such heat effects easy to recognize during chemical analysis. As for free acid contamination being absorbed from the environment to produce a false reading, such effects might influence the results in specimens several million years old, but in fossils less than 100,000 years old from normal soil matrices, such traces of washed-in acids would be negligible and have no influence on dating estimates. Moreover, contamination would produce a lower D/L ratio and thus the announced ages were at least minimal ages for the skeletons tested.

Archaeologists whose theories of man's recency in the New World would have been invalidated by the evidence from San Diego remained silent, feeling that the newly-announced dating technique was completely untested and needed careful scrutiny by the scientific community before it could be accepted as a reliable tool. Many were frankly skeptical. But in addition to the painstaking cross-checks with radiocarbon dating conducted by Bada and Schroeder, the circumstances of the fossils' recovery supported extreme antiquity for them. They were taken from soil formations that could only have been deposited far back in the Wisconsin glacial cycle, a fact not generally known and one which was not reported in the announcement in *SCIENCE* magazine.

The geological stratum in which the human frontal bone and the rib were found at La Jolla Shores was particularly convincing. The yellowish-white sands in which the fragments lay were described by Rogers as "laminated," indicating that they were water-deposited and not wind-blown dunes. The bones themselves appeared to be water-worn as though they had been transported from elsewhere, and they were described as "scattered." They were five to six feet below the surface of the ground and seventeen feet above sea level. The white sands merged at the top with a stratum of reddish sands which seemed to represent alluvium washed down from the red sandstone highlands behind the site and nearly a mile away. The hummock or low ridge was all that remained of that outwash plain after a long period of erosion, if indeed the red sands did represent alluvium. George Carter felt that, rather than alluvial material, the red sand was simply the extremely weathered top layer of the sand ridge. The undisturbed La Jollan burials in the red sand stratum had obviously been interred by the builders of the capping shell midden; these bones were determined to be 6,000 years old.

How could all this be interpreted chronologically? To begin with, the redeposited lower fossil fragments were clearly older than the formation from which they were recovered. The laminated white or yellowish sands containing them would have required a sea level as high or higher than the current one in order to have washed out the older burials during periods perhaps of exceptionally high storm-driven tides, and to have redeposited the sands and bone in thin layers behind the low beach dunes. The last previ-

Top
The skull of Del Mar Man, on display in the San Diego Museum of Man. Discovered and collected by Malcolm Rogers of the museum staff in 1929, the fossil remains had been seen weathering out of the side of a cliff above the beach at the mouth of the San Dieguito River in Del Mar, California. Much of the skeleton had presumably already fallen into the sea. Preserved along with appropriate notes and photographs in the Museum of Man, the fossil material was submitted to Dr. Jeffrey Bada of the Scripps Institution of Oceanography for dating at the suggestion of George F. Carter, whose studies of the beach terraces along the coast led him to believe that the fossil might have considerable antiquity. In May of 1974 Bada and Roy Schroeder, his graduate student assistant, along with Carter, announced that the age of the skull had been deduced to be approximately 48,000 years old, based on aspartic acid racemization analysis. This made it the oldest dated human fossil in the Western Hemisphere at that time. The skull is that of a young male Homo sapiens, and is similar to other fossils found in the San Diego area and attributed to the earliest La Jollan people. It is unlike most historic Indian skulls, and somewhat resembles those of prehistoric people found on Kyushu, Japan.

Bottom
The skull of Yuha Man in situ before removal from the matrix. This burial was discovered beneath a rock cairn in the Yuha Desert by Morlin Childers of the Imperial Valley College Museum and excavated by students under the direction of Erlinda Burton in the fall of 1971. Interment was on the back with the lower legs partially flexed. The spinal column below the neck, the pelvic region, both tibiae, and all of the foot bones had been destroyed by elements in the soil, but the remaining bones had been preserved by caliche (calcium carbonate) which partly coated the bone and cemented the surrounding matrix. Radiocarbon dating of the caliche scraped from the bone showed an age of approximately 21,500 years, with the obvious possibility that the bones were even older than the caliche deposited on them. Two unifacial artifacts and some flakes were also recovered during the excavation, but they gave no indication of cultural placement of the remains beyond suggesting, because of the steep unifacial flaking, the La Jollan industries on the coast. The location of the cairn on a low ridge between two lake basins might also be taken to imply some reliance on a shellfish diet as in the La Jollan culture, but shell middens as such are not seen in the area today. In 1976 the Yuha skull was being studied and carefully reassembled by Rose Tyson of the San Diego Museum of Man, a major undertaking since, although it appears to be fairly intact in the photograph, it is actually composed of many separate fragments, some of them seriously warped and deformed.

ous period when the sea level reached that of the present was during the mid-Wisconsin or Alton interstadial, thought to have occurred between 40,000 and 25,000 B.P. Those dates were perfectly consistent with Bada's findings of 44,000 for the frontal bone and 28,000 for the rib.

The sands which encased the Del Mar skull at San Dieguito Creek were less useful for geological interpretation of age, since they were undoubtedly wind-deposited dune sands built up during the high sea levels of the Sangamon interglacial, when a deep estuary or embayment ran far up the valley behind the coast. Dunes tend to shift unpredictably; sometimes they march slowly and inexorably inland almost like glaciers, and depth below a transitory surface is meaningless as an indicator of age.

The landform from which the skull was removed in 1929 was a hummock or remnant of dune sand resting upon a Tertiary sandstone peninsula jutting out perhaps fifty feet to the south from the higher land that framed the valley opening just behind the sea beach. This dune remnant was about ten feet high and twenty feet long; between it and the higher slope was an open space or notch some twenty feet wide. The fossils were seen weathering out of the hummock five or six feet from the top, which had a thin capping of shell. A piece of human femur was recovered from the area of the notch. The skeletal remains in the hummock that included the skull and mandible appeared to have been undisturbed, although much of the material had been lost below the ribs.

Rogers described the soil as "estuary sands" but made no effort to interpret the geological context in terms of age, simply remarking that massive erosion made it impossible to estimate the original depth and circumstances of the burial. The skull itself was in several pieces, but restoration was accomplished with competence, according to Dr. Spencer Rogers, the scientific director of the museum when the dating of the fossil was announced.

Naturally there was considerable interest in re-examining the site after the announcement. Unfortunately the entire hummock had since been bulldozed off of the point of land at Del Mar, almost down to the Tertiary sandstone. Nevertheless an effort was made in the summer of 1974 by the San Diego Museum of Man and the University of San Diego to excavate the remaining soils in the hope that some additional evidence might be exposed.

Under Dr. James R. Moriarty the archaeological crew carefully trenched the most promising area slightly to the south of where the hummock had stood. They recovered some charcoal, crude artifacts and shell, but these were all somewhat suggestive of a much more recent occupation and may have had no connection with the fossil deposit. Whether the latter was in fact an intentional burial or simply some kind of accidental or fortuitous interment could not be determined.

The sea, 48,000 years ago, stood far to the west of the site and far below it. The climate would have been considerably colder and wetter; this was during the first or Iowan advance of the Wisconsin glacial cycle and even the San Diego area would have been uncomfortably chilly in the winters. It requires little imagination to visualize humans burrowing into the lee side of an old interglacial sand dune to escape the bitter wind and drizzle. Even in modern times one reads occasionally of children being buried and suffocated by a suddenly-collapsing sand cave which had seemed to be a safe and secure retreat. If the dune was high and indurated in its upper levels the remains might well have had almost ideal protection from destructive elements, far more than a relatively shallow midden burial would provide.

The skull was in good condition, considering its age. It was that of a mature adult male between twenty and forty years of age. The teeth were extremely worn down, apparently from abrasive material in the diet, considerably more so than other La Jollan skulls in the museum collection dating from the Recent period. Even though sea food appeared to have been the mainstay of diet for coastal La Jollans in all periods, it should be pointed out that in more recent periods of high sea level mostly rock species were eaten: mussels, rock oysters, abalone and scallops. During the lowered sea levels of the glacial periods primarily surf and slough species of clams would have been relied upon, shellfish which had generous supplies of sand in their shells and which would have had a marked effect on dentition if eaten constantly for many years.

The cranial index, or ratio of width to length in the skull was low, 70.7, lower than any other male La Jollan in the collection, meaning that it was the narrowest for its length, usually considered an archaic trait. The cranial capacity was high, estimated to be 1,672 cubic centimeters, but La Jollans generally were large-headed and other skulls were known with even larger brain cavities. In general, nothing about the measurements of the Del Mar skull could be cited as evidence of great antiquity or decisively distinguish it from skulls believed to be 40,000 years younger. While this might lead to suspicion in regard to the validity of the claimed age, it also suggested that many undated fossil human skulls in America might in fact be far older than had been suspected.

Actually there have been discoveries of far more primitive-appearing skulls in North America. A case in point was the Utah Lake skull discovered in 1932 by some boys and thus without geological dating. It had weathered or eroded out of a bank during a period of lowered lake level and was studied by George H. Hansen, an anthropologist at the University of Denver, who reported, "the Utah Lake skull approaches the upper limit of Neanderthal possibilities." It was an archaic long-headed, low-vaulted and quite primitive skull type which would have fallen somewhere between the typical Neanderthals of Europe and modern *Homo sapiens sapiens*, but much closer to Neanderthal.

The Pericu Indians of Baja California, now extinct but many of whose skulls have been measured, also were clearly of a far more archaic mold than the Del Mar Man. Their skulls were extremely long and narrow, suggesting that they belonged to a more primitive race, at least morphologically, than did the La Jollan people. Whether they were indeed from different stock could not be known, but there was some reason to suspect that the earliest peopling of the hemisphere could have come from at least two quite different kinds of people from different sources and following quite different routes and customs.

In 1975 it was obvious that Bada's racemization dating technique was in its infancy but held tremendous promise for the future. In the San Diego region there had been minimal temperature fluctuations, and fossil bone samples of many ages were available for calibration of racemization rates and for cross-checking with radiocarbon dates. In other regions these conditions might be less ideal or entirely lacking, but it seemed likely that some formulae for dealing with more severe temperature ranges might be developed. As for acid contamination from the environment, the problems were still difficult to assess.

There were archaeological sites in many localities of the Western Hemisphere where non-human fossil bone was found associated with undisputed artifacts and other evidence of man. These fossil specimens would of course provide as reliable a date for human occupation as the skeleton of man himself. Even dates of something less than complete accuracy would in many cases be most helpful in assessing the antiquity of early sites. The situation at Valsequillo Reservoir near Puebla in Mexico was an excellent example.

In a paper presented to the American Society of Geologists at Dallas, Texas, in 1973, Harold Malde and Virginia Steen-McIntyre of the United States Geological Survey and the late Roald Fryxell of Washington State University reported some extraordinarily ancient evidences of man. The materials at the Hueyatlaco site were at the base of about thirty-four feet of deposits which were part of the Valsequillo gravels dissected by the Rio Atoyac more than one hundred and twenty feet below. Here were found well-made bifacial flaked tools associated with the bones of extinct animals. One such fossil, the lower jaw of a mastodon, actually had a flaked stone artifact solidly embedded in it. Above the tool-bearing stratum were several volcanic layers.

Three completely independent dating methods were employed. Open series uranium testing, a radiometric method somewhat similar to radiocarbon dating, produced from camel pelvis associated with bifacial tools dates of 245,000 and 180,000 years before the present. A purely geological test called "obsidian hydration," in which is measured the amount of moisture accumulated in closed vesicles of glass shards during weathering of volcanic deposits, produced from layers above the artifacts a date of 250,000 years before the present. A method called "fission-tracking" provided a similar age.

These dates were so astounding that they were widely disbelieved, and even suspected by the principal archaeological investigator at the site, Cynthia Erwin-Williams. But how such completely different methods of dating could be off so far, and yet agree so closely, could not be explained. Both Fryxell and Erwin-Williams had previously been known for their conservatism regarding man in the Western Hemisphere, so that it was ironic that their dates were considered far too early even by proponents of extreme antiquity. A major part of the difficulty in accepting the dates had been the nature of the flaked tools, which according to description seemed too well-made to be consistent with so great an age. Here obviously was a situation where amino acid racemization tests of fossil bone from the culture-bearing level might provide convincing support, if the method could be employed. But the suggestion of heating by volcanic layers might rule out the process.

Regardless of the outcome of the Valsequillo investigation, it seemed clear that the newest dating tool would find reliable employment in a great many archaeological situations around the world, adding immeasurably to knowledge of the human past. The title of "Oldest Human in the Western Hemisphere" was not expected to be held for any very extended period of time by the Del Mar skeleton from the San Dieguito River. His place of honor on display in the San Diego Museum of Man might even be yielded in time to an older claimant from the same region, for it had become increasingly apparent that far earlier human inhabitants had wandered over the pleasant mesas, valleys and ocean beaches of San Diego during the Pleistocene.

San Diego in the Ice Age

The Glacial Epoch or Ice Age, as the Pleistocene has sometimes been called, was an age of widely fluctuating climates with the shifts many thousands of years apart, in San Diego as well as in the northern latitudes actually covered by glacial ice; cool and humid in the glacial cycles or pluvials, and warm and semi-arid during the interglacials.

These shifts of climate can perhaps best be visualized by thinking of modern climate environments along the California and Baja California coasts. Conditions now found within a range of two hundred and fifty miles north and an equal distance to the south of the San Diego area would probably encompass the local climate variations of the Late Pleistocene. Thus during the Wisconsin pluvials of from about 70,000 to 10,000 years ago, the San Diego climate would have been somewhat like that of the present San Luis Obispo, while the driest and warmest periods of the preceding Sangamon interglacial approached the modern conditions at San Quintin Bay to the south in Mexico. But despite these variations the San Diego region must have offered, at least throughout the last 125,000 years, a physical environment extremely favorable for human occupation at the most primitive level.

Deep in the Sangamon interglacial, 100,000 years ago, a salt marsh and estuary ran far up Mission Valley. At flood tide a sparkling blue lagoon appeared, nearly a mile wide at its seaward limit behind the sheltering dunes. Like a miniature mountain range flung across the marsh's margin, these dunes were sculptured into rounded peaks and valleys. Only at the southern end were the ramparts pierced where a narrow, jade-green channel followed close beside the cobbled cliffs of the mesa. As the waters of the lagoon drained out this passage to the ocean on an ebbing tide, the booming of breakers on the beaches beyond the dunes subsided, and acres of eel grass and rich mud flats became exposed. In fall and winter and well into the spring thousands of birds took wing at each change of tide, some to feed on the flats with probing bills and twinkling small feet; others to find open water in the twisting, silvery channels or the quiet ponds up Mission Valley beyond the reach of the tide.

Over the marsh flew wavering lines of pintail ducks and widgeon. Geese of many kinds, Canadas, white-fronted geese and snows filled the air with their music. Whistling swans thrashed across the shallows to take the air finally in slow, majestic grace. Small compact flocks of green-winged teal burst suddenly like shrapnel from the flats and went rocketing off across the wind. As the tide rose again to flood stage flocks of black brant in broad, curving ranks headed low over the dunes and out to sea to rest on the thick copper-and-bronze kelp beds where herds of sea otters lay basking in the warm sun.

The salt marsh was like a living thing, throbbing with vitality. Its channels ran like arteries to every part, branching from the deep, swift currents of the entrance; to more slender ribbons winding through the eel grass pastures and the exposed mud flats; to the tiny trickles and rills draining and replenishing the bars and upstream reaches. Its slow, rhythmic heartbeats were the tides, rising and falling, flushing out and renewing the salt lifeblood in measured cadence through the years.

Multitudes of living creatures dwelt in the marsh or were attracted seasonally to it. In its rich mud were clams of many kinds. Rock oysters covered the rocks along the entrance channel and even clung to scattered blocks and boulders along its beaches. Massive and ancient sea turtles hauled out on the bars and cruised the deeper channels. Spotted harbor seals lay on the shingle beside the entrance and along the cliffy shore sunning themselves and scratching. Crabs swarmed over the flats at low tide; holes and burrows pocked the mud everywhere marking the havens of tiny creatures.

Beyond the marsh and the dunes to seaward were wide sand beaches curving around to the north and west, with smaller estuaries interrupting the strand and running up Tecolote Canyon and the larger Rose Canyon system. The thrusting finger of Crown Point and the higher Soledad landmass with its rocky cliffs pushing out into the ocean produced a shallow embayment behind the La Jolla peninsula. Just south of Mission Valley and its dunes and channel rose the rocky headland which 100,000 years later would provide the site for the first Spanish settlement and mission in California.

Beyond Presidio Hill the coast, rocky and steep, trended away to the southeast, to be interrupted again by another wide lagoon and salt marsh that ran far up the valley of the Sweetwater. These estuaries with their sand dune barricades fringed the coastline for hundreds of miles in both directions as the high sea levels of the Sangamon interglacial crept up the broad valleys of the rivers; streams that had cut their way down to a lower ocean through the upraised coastal plain in more pluvial times.

Between the valleys the ocean battered away at the seaward edge of the mesas, cutting back the cliffs and piling great chunks and blocks of sandstone on the wave-cut benches and terraces along the beach, strewing cobbles from far more ancient sea bottoms back on the shingle again. Here colonies of sea lions wintered, and the air was filled continuously in season with their raucous barking and the acrid smell of their excretions. The rocks were splashed and mottled with guano from millions of gulls, terns and puffins that nested on the cliffs and the mesa above, that added their din to the uproar and wheeled constantly overhead.

Along the rocky shores at low tide shoals of blue-black mussels were exposed, and abalones clung to the sides of the sandstone blocks and ledges. Spiny lobsters lurked in the pools and crevices, octopi felt their way daintily along the bottom and iridescent, gleaming crabs scuttled in all directions. Purple sea urchins abounded in the clear tide pools where careless sculpin and small rockfish were occasionally trapped on a falling tide.

About two miles offshore the long, blunt-nosed island that would become Point Loma lay parallel to the shore, wearing a fringe of Torrey pines along its humped spine. On its

132

windward side above the sea cliffs a few wind-twisted cypress trees still survived from a cooler and rainier time, while the canyons and draws to leeward had a few scattered sycamores and live oaks. Its only land mammals were rodents, rabbits, perhaps shrews and moles, and grey foxes in stable, balanced populations, but all along the seaward shore of the island elephant seals had established their rookeries. During the mating encounters of the huge herd bulls their roaring could be heard miles away on the mainland as they battered and flailed away at the bleeding, swollen necks of their rivals.

On the sand beaches and dunes animal life was less evident. The surf surged in endlessly, booming and boisterous at flood tide and in storms, then subsiding to long murmuring rollers of foam. Huge surf clams lay just under the surface of sand in the shallows; silvery shoals of grunion ran far up the beaches by moonlight to spawn, and gulls kept the margins under careful surveillance, poking and probing with inquisitive orange bills at the stranded flotsam cast up by the sea. Occasional visitors sometimes came to the beaches. Foxes, coyotes and dire wolves trotted along below the dunes on the lookout for small game or carrion. Trains of stately Columbian mammoths plodded ponderously along through the shallows, whisking bundles of wiry black rockweed into their mouths to savor the sharp tang of salt; huge looming shapes in the fog that drifted often over the headlands and beaches. Small bands of horses left their round hoofprints and droppings in the sand.

The dunes rose behind the beach in a broad band a mile long, two hundred yards wide and up to sixty feet high. They constituted a separate, self-sufficient world inhabited by small hunters and hunted who played out their destinies by night and disappeared in the daytime. A land of scaled-down white mountain slopes, narrow ridges and valleys constantly shifting; of gleaming sand embellished with brilliant purple and crimson mesembryanthemum and sometimes yellow daisies; of surfaces etched by wind into rhythmic herringbone patterns; its trails and burrows and small frantic footprints revealed endless games of desperate hide-and-seek. Lizards, mice, kangaroo rats, jackrabbits, grey foxes and rattlesnakes were the regular inhabitants, augmented by visiting hawks, shrikes and owls. On sunny days gulls and brown pelicans sometimes stationed themselves on the hummocks, staring at each other morosely with pale yellow eyes.

Up Mission Valley beyond the salt marsh, strings of freshwater ponds stretched along the course of the San Diego River, which sank below the sands in the summer and only ran briskly after the widely-spaced winter storms. The ponds were surrounded by tules and willows and were shaded by large spreading trees, mostly cottonwoods and sycamores. In places tangles of wild grape and blackberry vines festooned themselves over the thick underbrush in the shade of the trees and provided a cool contrast to the chaparral, sagebrush and grasses that covered the open country. Here in the heavy cover were tunnels and runways made by tapirs and peccaries, a labyrinth of passages leading in many directions and sometimes prowled by coyotes and sabertooth cats in search of a meal.

The ponds were inhabited by small turtles, frogs, crawfish, salamanders, sunfish and water snakes. Mallards rested on the quiet water and tipped up their white bottoms. Roseate spoonbills made their sprawling, untidy nests in the tops of drowned cottonwood trees. Troops of mammoths regularly went down to the ponds and stood in the shallows trumpeting and sending glittering cascades of water over their dusty bronze backs and flanks, the great sweeping curves of ivory tusk gleaming in the sun. Their exuberant offspring went squealing and splashing around and between the forests of massive legs rising like tree trunks out of the water. These and other large mammals dropped huge piles and windrows of steaming dung in concentrated amounts here where they gathered to water, so that the soils were well fertilized and fruitful and even during the semi-arid Sangamon interglacial produced lush vegetation in the watered bottom lands of the valleys.

The deep canyons that fringed the mesas had grass on the slopes: scanty and sparse on the south-facing walls where the chalky white sandstones of ancient sea bottoms were exposed and decomposing. On the shadier north slopes was more luxuriant cover: elderberry, hackberry and toyon. Yuccas and other agaves dotted the sunny slopes, and in the larger canyons there were sycamores. Small spring-fed streams wandered over the floor in all seasons, though almost vanishing in late summer during unusually dry years.

Many of the canyons and draws had cacti of several varieties including the viciously-spined chollas and the beavertail type, called *nopal* in Mexico, which bears the large

Mission Valley in San Diego during the Sangamon or Third Interglacial period about 100,000 years ago. The sea level was considerably higher than the present but the climate and plant environments are thought to have been quite similar to those the first Spanish explorers found in the area, or perhaps slightly warmer with somewhat more extensive grasslands. Pleistocene animals now extinct are shown gathered at a fresh-water pond. Three species of grazing mammals, the Columbian mammoth, western horse and giant long-horned bison, come in to water, while a teratorn vulture, a scavenger larger than modern condors, perches overhead. Since such creatures are known only through fossilized skeletal parts, features like hair length, color, shape and size of ears and other soft parts, feather patterns, etc., can only be guessed by reference to somewhat similar modern forms. Since the horses' feet and skull shapes were rather zebra-like they have been given short roached manes and striping. Although the very long hair of cold-adapted woolly mammoths is known from complete specimens preserved in glacial ice and the cave paintings of Europe, the mammoth species of the warm south may have been more like modern elephants.

juicy red tunas or prickly pears. These latter showed the scallop-shaped, gaping wounds in their fleshy green leaves where camels had been feeding on them, crushing the spines with their hard bony palates and with their deceptively tough velvety lips well apart and out of harm's way.

Up on top of the mesas the land went rolling off into purple distances; grasslands mainly but with islands of sage and scattered small groves of live oak and Bishop's pine. In late winter and spring the grasses were thick and green, rippling in the fresh breeze from the sea. By early summer they were tawny and golden, and by fall they were a lifeless brown, cropped short by the thousands of grazing animals that roamed over the coastal plain and renewed with their droppings the soil's fertility. At longer intervals the grasslands were additionally invigorated and freed of encroaching chaparral by wild fires set by lightning during the dry summer season; they swept unchecked across the land burning off brush and scorching the trees, causing hundreds of animals to stampede in panicky flight before them.

The most numerous grazing mammals were the horses, which ranged widely over the grasslands of North America during the Pleistocene. During the Sangamon at San Diego these were of the species called the western horse, *Equus occidentalis*. They were about the size of modern Arabians but more stockily built except for their hoofs, which were quite small. In this and other features they somewhat resembled modern asses and zebras, and they may have had faint stripes on their withers and flanks. Their manes also may have been zebra-like, short and stiff rather than flowing, and they averaged about fourteen and one-half hands high at the withers.

Extremely fleet of foot, the horses, when they were in their prime, could easily outdistance predators and although they lacked horns and antlers they could deal a devastating blow with their heels when cornered. The tiny newborn foals were able to run beside the mares in a matter of hours after their birth, but of course would soon falter from exhaustion so that many became prey to the dire wolves that lurked always in the vicinity during the foaling season. In the fall the high-pitched squealing of stallions and the thudding of hoofs against horseflesh marked the breeding ritual, when young bachelor stallions attempted to steal a few mares from the harems.

Almost as numerous as horses were the bison, belonging to two extinct species similar in structure but far larger than the modern animals. *Bison latifrons* was the most common variety during the Sangamon; bulls stood well over seven feet high at the top of the hump and had horns more than two feet long. *Bison antiquus* was present in limited numbers but was destined to replace *B. latifrons* during the more pluvial Wisconsin; it was slightly smaller but still much larger than the modern *Bison bison*. These huge animals ranged in very large herds and were extremely formidable with their long sharp horns and irascible tempers; few predators cared to face them until they were infirm from old age or injury, but their habit of wallowing in mudholes during the rare rainy periods caused the downfall of many. Often they were unable to find solid footing in the treacherous silts of the river bottom, floundering and bellowing with white-eyed panic as their hoofs churned the mud and they sank even deeper. The ever-present dire wolves moved closer, waiting with lolling tongues and eager, hungry eyes fastened on the massive brown hulk of a doomed bison. Overhead the huge teratorn vultures of the Pleistocene, with wingspreads of twelve feet, circled patiently, waiting their opportunity to move in.

The camels also were represented by two different species occupying separate ecological niches. The larger of the two, *Camelops hesternus*, was similar in structure and size to the Bactrian camels of Asia, towering more than eight feet from the toes to the top of the head. Whether these lofty creatures had a hump or humps is unknown, but with plenty of forage and water available this seems doubtful. They were browsers rather than grass-eaters, living on leafy shrubs, tree foliage and cactus, and since they were solitary rather than herd animals, they tended not to be numerous. The other camelid mammal, the stilt-legged *Hemiauchenia*, was more slender and llama-like, a grass-eater able to compete with other grazers only by reason of greater agility in reaching steep slopes and canyon bottoms. Compared with the bison and horse both species of camel were relatively rare in the region.

A very small antelope similar to the modern pronghorn, but only about twenty inches high at the shoulder, browsed on sage and other low shrubs on the mesas and the slopes of the canyons. This tiny animal relied on camouflage for concealment and then great speed if detected. Like the camels it was solitary and seldom occurred in groups of more than a few individuals.

The Columbian mammoths, enormous Pleistocene elephants of the south and southwestern United States, were well represented in the Southern California region during the Sangamon. Often twelve feet tall, they had tremendous curving tusks ten feet and more in length and weighing over a quarter of a ton apiece. Their massive bodies were supported on legs like tree trunks, and the whole animal probably weighed as much as eight tons. They had the same weakness as bison for water and mudholes, and because of their enormous weight were also occasionally inextricably mired, a mountain of meat for the predators and scavengers able to penetrate the thick, leathery hide.

These mammoths were primarily grass-eaters, able to gather and pluck enormous amounts of vegetation with their delicate and sensitive trunks. Because of their fondness for water and ponds they inhabited the valleys and lowlands rather than the tops of the mesas. They had nothing to fear from even the most powerful of predators unless they became disabled; nevertheless, like modern elephants they had highly developed senses of smell and hearing, and were constantly on the alert, fanning their ears into the wind and raising inquisitive trunks often to test the scents around them.

Present but relatively rare in the San Diego region during the Sangamon were the American mastodons, elephant-like creatures which browsed on trees rather than grazing. They looked rather like dumpy, heavy, thick-bodied elephants, standing less than seven feet at the shoulder; and their tusks, although very large, were smaller than the mammoths'. Unlike the Columbian mammoth they were broadly distributed over most of North America where woody shrubs were available.

Almost as massively built as the elephants were the giant ground sloths, *Glossotherium harlani*, which were also grass-eating grazers. Although only about four feet high in their normal grazing position, they were twelve feet from the heavy, blunt muzzle to the tip of the thick, massive tail. Their bodies and legs were equally massive and bulky, and although they were slow-moving and inoffensive, their long, powerful claws, primarily for digging up roots and tubers, were useful in self-defense. Embedded deep in the skin of their backs and shoulders were thousands of small, bony objects known as dermal ossicles which made their hides difficult to penetrate, so that only the most powerful predators could attack them with any hope of success.

Fearsome predators roamed the mesas and valleys, as might be expected where large game herds grazed. A huge member of the cat family called *Panthera leo atrox* and variously described as a giant lion or giant jaguar was nearly a quarter larger than modern Siberian tigers, the largest of the living cats. But in order to prey on the huge bison or camel great size and strength would have been required. There appears to have been considerable difference in size between the sexes of the species, females having been not much larger than the present-day jaguars of the Western Hemisphere.

Possibly more numerous were the saber-toothed cats, *Smilodon californicus*. These were about the size of African lions but built to different proportions, having extremely heavy and powerful forequarters and claws for grasping prey, a bobbed tail like a lynx and a rather small brain considering the bulk of the animal. Its jaws were remarkable; armed with enormous, dagger-like upper canine teeth and capable of gaping very wide, permitting the lower jaw to drop down and away like that of a striking rattlesnake and

No one knows exactly the physical appearances of the large extinct Pleistocene mammals like these giant ground sloths; details such as hair, color, markings and ears can only be guessed from fossil bones and teeth, although hair from a somewhat similar sloth has been preserved in caves in the arid Southwest.

bringing into play the huge, terrible, curving upper teeth. The structure suggests that the sabertooth leaped on the back of its prey and held it in a powerful grip while stabbing repeatedly deep into its vitals with the awesome daggers.

Two non-extinct cats, the cougar and the bay lynx or bobcat, were also present in the region during this period, but both probably preferred the more wooded country well back from the coast. Three species of bear also inhabited Southern California but would have been relatively rare on the grasslands. These were the grizzly, the black bear and an enormous extinct species called the short-faced bear, *Tremarctotherium simum*, the largest carniverous land mammal in the hemisphere. Until they became extinct late in the Wisconsin these huge creatures actually far outnumbered the smaller grizzlies and black bears, but little is known of their habits. Because their teeth were more like those of typical meat-eaters such as the dogs, they are thought to have been more carniverous than modern bears. If they stood erect as most bears do at times, they would have towered ten feet above the ground.

In addition to the coyote and grey fox the dog family was represented by the dire wolf, *Canis dirus*. About the size of the largest timber wolves, the dire wolf had a heavy, blunt muzzle with extremely powerful jaws. By far the commonest predators during the Pleistocene throughout the hemisphere, dire wolves also served as scavengers able to break and devour good-sized bones. They were somewhat similar to the Old World hyenas in their habits, and performed the same function of culling the game herds of weaklings and the infirm. There is little doubt that the shortage of human fossil bone can be attributed in large measure to the efficiency of these creatures, who patrolled diligently in the vicinity of human camps and habitations.

And what of man himself? Fossil skeletal remains of all the other Pleistocene creatures described above had been found in a number of sites in Southern California, particularly the Sangamon assemblage from Costeau Pit near San Juan Capistrano and the tremendously rich and varied assemblages from the famous tar pits of Rancho La Brea generally attributed to the late Wisconsin of about 40,000 years to the present. But only the broken stones and the hearth areas in the interglacial terrace at Texas Street, and possibly the quartzite tools from the clays and gravels of Buchanan Canyon, proclaimed man's presence here, and not only his presence but long occupation during centuries and perhaps millennia was suggested by the great thickness of the culture-bearing deposits found by George Carter and still available for inspection.

Possessed of fire, sharp stone tools, heat-hardened or antler-tipped spears and intelligence that towered over that of all other creatures in his world, man could have lived and prospered in the San Diego region with little hardship or discomfort. Food was everywhere for the hunter and gatherer during the Sangamon interglacial; all of the resources of the estuaries at his disposal; the beaches and rocky shores with their shellfish, nesting birds and eggs; plant foods like pine nuts, cactus and agaves, pond weeds, berries and wild grapes, edible roots and tubers. And game was everywhere, from rabbits, squirrels, quail and a species of wild turkey to large slow game like the sloths, seals and sea turtles. Scavenging in a world of large game herds would have been easy for a band of shouting, boulder-hurling humans who could also have carried flaming torches to bluff the most fearsome of carnivores.

The climate is believed to have varied during the Sangamon from arid to semi-arid, with annual rainfall averaging from a few inches to about ten inches, much as it does today. Tempered by its proximity to the sea, the temperatures would have been ideal for human occupation, requiring little or no clothing at any season and no need for complicated shelters. The soft sandstones of the canyon walls would have made the digging of caves easy with the simplest of stone tools, and stone in the form of quartzite and porphyry cobbles was always conveniently at hand in the gravel lenses weathering out of hillsides if not on the canyon floors. Since the streams in the region were flowing year round when the Spaniards first arrived, despite the modest rainfall, presumably water was available throughout the Sangamon.

Although destructive storms are now, and probably have always been, extremely rare in San Diego, they have been known to occur even in historic times. At widely spaced intervals, perhaps a century or more apart, the violent tropical storms approaching hurricane force that are called *chubascos* in Mexico wandered far north of their usual track and came ashore across the coastline here. Even more rarely huge winter storm fronts of unusual intensity and duration struck the region with torrential rains over periods of several days or even weeks. When these monster storms occurred the results in the lower valleys were devastating.

As the waters rose in every creek and stream, sluicing mud-laden runoff into the principal rivers, the floors of the valleys became raging brown floods. Great gullies and ravines were opened on the thinly-clad, south-facing walls of the canyons, and huge loads of silt were washed down onto the bottoms. The peaceful ponds in MissionValley with their spreading sycamore trees were gutted and swept away; the normally placid channel south of the dunes became a tossing, churning maelstrom through which were whirled out to sea tree trunks, matted rafts of vegetation torn from its moorings, and the corpses of animals caught in the flood and drowned.

Even the shellfish and other sea life along the shore were diminished, for the huge volume of silt-laden fresh water clogged the gills of fishes and the siphons of clams, and deposited layers of mud on the sensitive membranes of creatures accustomed to the crystal-clear sea water of the fresh ocean tides. But the scene in the valley after the storm had passed and the flood waters subsided was one of tragedy and complete desolation.

All along the landward margin of the dunes the wreckage of trees and shrubbery was piled in a giant tangle of branches and trunks interlaced at every conceivable angle. The peaceful marsh that had throbbed with life and vitality was a vast brown plain, a sea of mud several feet thick from which protruded other broken and smashed trees. The mud covered the flood plain far up the valley. Dotting this dismal expanse were the carcasses of bison and horses, swollen and bloated now in the returning sun, many of them already being torn and devoured by the huge teratorn vultures. A few of the larger trees still stood, and on these the vultures sat digesting their meals of carrion, too full to fly farther. The deep soft mud would yet prove a death trap for many more large animals as they came down their accustomed trails from the mesa to water, and the stench of carrion would linger in the air for weeks in this unhappy land.

Slowly over the years the marsh and the ponds would restore themselves. The creatures would gradually filter back in from other regions nearby, new seeds would germinate and new trees would grow and mature. The marsh, enormously revitalized and enriched by the flood, would reappear again with a completely new pattern of channels, and all the complex ecological niches would be almost miraculously refilled. The music of goose and swan would be heard in the valley again. A little band of humans would drift in from a few miles to the north and settle down again on the edge of the valley floor beside the marsh at Texas Street. They and their descendants might live there and up and down the valley for another century, maybe two, until the next devastation.

· · · · · ·

During the first or Iowan advance of the Wisconsin glacial period, 50,000 years ago, the ice lay nearly two miles thick across the Barren Lands of the Canadian Northwest Territories; closed all the passes of the Cordillera, and on the West Coast, we have been told, spilled into the Pacific and barred the passage of men and animals. Billions of tons of the earth's water remained for millennia locked in ice upon the land, not only in North America but in Eurasia as well. Global sea levels were lowered by this loss between three and four hundred feet; coastlines shifted out over the continental shelves for many miles in places, islands joined the mainland and became hills and mountains, and rivers cut far down into the coastal valleys to meet the lowered tidewater in a smooth transition. The same cooling trend and increased precipitation in the Northern Hemisphere that produced the glacier-building conditions in heavy snow country caused pluvials, or periods of increased rainfall and cooler climates elsewhere.

In the San Diego region the average temperature decreased by several degrees, producing frosty nights in the winter and occasional light dustings of snow along the coast, but the maritime air circulation prevented blizzards and lengthy hard freezes. Rainfall amounts more than doubled in the area, probably becoming from sixteen to twenty-four inches annually, with as much as thirty inches in exceptional years. The look of the land changed completely.

Now there were in effect two flat coastal plains at quite different levels. The ancient, uplifted sea bottoms that formed the San Diego mesas, and upon which much of the city now stands, became highlands more than six hundred feet above sea level. The sea cliffs of the Sangamon became eroded and softened slopes covered with oak and pine; between them and the distant ocean lay a fertile plain from three to ten miles wide and rising in a gentle incline from the sandy beaches and low dunes that now bordered the sea to west-

140

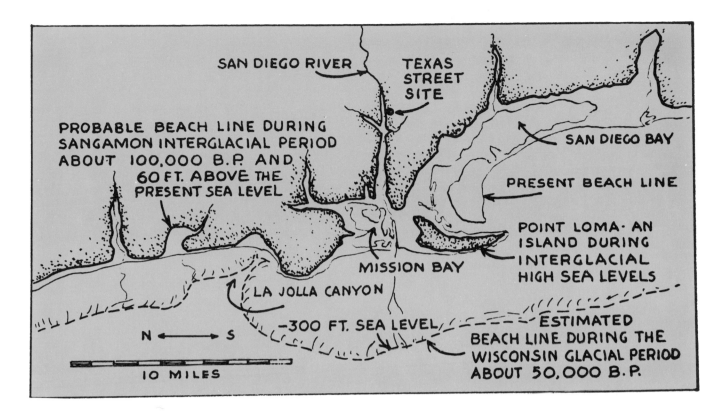

This sketch of the coastline in the vicinity of San Diego shows the late Pleistocene beach lines, including those of the Sangamon interglacial and Wisconsin glacial aspects. The location sixty feet plus above present sea level of the interglacial tideline is attributed to a combination of regional uplift and eustatic high sea level. The Wisconsin aspect is attributed entirely to eustatic lowering of the sea level, and is a minimal estimate.

ward. A few isolated buttes and chains of low hills stood on the grass-covered lowlands; the Coronado Islands were part of the mainland to the south, and the gently-rising slopes of Point Loma were rooted to the plain.

Although they were not glaciated, the higher mountains of the Coast Range behind San Diego received heavy snows in the winter. Generous amounts of meltwater drained off to the east into what are now desert basins, forming large permanent lakes beyond the mountains, where increased rainfall also watered the land and transformed it from the dry, arid wasteland of the Sangamon into a fertile green lowland of lakes, streams and grazing game. To westward the rivers ran down to the sea in all seasons; in the San Dieguito, Sweetwater and Mission Valleys they cut and excavated their channels deep into the silts of the Sangamon, leaving terrace remnants against the walls of the valleys and spreading out into broad, marshy deltas far out on the coastal plain.

Only in the vicinity of La Jolla and to the north along the Torrey Pines upland did the sea remain fairly close to the Sangamon shore. Just north of Point La Jolla a deep arm of the sea swung in close to the highland, and along the coast here instead of the broad sandy beaches, rocky ledges and steep, cobbled shores bordered the ocean. Here mussels and abalone still grew in profusion, tidepools were exposed at low tide and sea birds nested on the cliffs in great numbers.

The vast rolling grasslands of the Sangamon had long since disappeared. The more humid climate retarded the periodic cleansing action of fires, and little by little the land had been reclaimed by shrubbery and trees, although the coastal lowlands had vast stretches of grassland. But the tops of the mesas were now more like parkland, with mixed groves of pine and deciduous oak and spacious meadows in grass. Manzanita thickets and sage flats alternated with the trees, and in the canyons and hollows ferns grew in the shade, with perennial springs, streams and ponds common. Sycamore and live oak grew on the canyon bottoms, and the rims of the mesas facing the sea had thick stands of cypress. Oaks and pines occupied the well-drained, sloping hillsides and the flats in the foothills east of the mesas, and grew in limited numbers almost down to sea level. Along the highlands close to the sea the Torrey pines flourished, as remnants still do today.

Down on the coastal lowlands reclaimed from the sea the grass grew thick and tall in rich soils washed down throughout millennia from the tops of the mesas. A few clumps of live oaks dotted the landscape, and willows grew in profusion along the watercourses of the deltas and the edges of their swamps and marshes. In spring and summer the low-lying grasslands were vivid with wildflowers, and their sweet scents filled the night air that was clamorous with the piping of frogs and cicadas.

Wildlife flowed over the land in a richness and variety not equaled anywhere on earth today and only approached in the African savannahs of the Nineteenth Century. Their numbers can only be guessed at, but the catalogue of different species is well known from fossil recoveries at Rancho La Brea. There, however, the proportions would have been distorted, for creatures fond of entering water and mudholes and predators attracted by their distress would have been the principal victims of the pools with their deadly, entrapping tars.

Most of the Sangamon creatures survived far into the Wisconsin in Southern California and presumably at San Diego but in altered populations reflecting the reduced grasslands and increased cover of shrubs and trees. New species appeared in the region, browsers primarily or those requiring heavy cover, acorns or other specialized diets.

Late in the Wisconsin and early in the following Recent or Holocene period a great many species including the largest mammals, called *megafauna*, would become extinct from causes that are not known and have been the subject of wide speculation. Hunting by man employing such wasteful over-kill methods as stampeding entire herds over cliffs has been suggested; so has a variety of viral epidemics affecting either the victims directly or their plant foods. Man has been accused of setting vast fires which changed the plant environment with fatal results for some species. No one really knows, and perhaps never will.

Reflecting the increased shrub cover was an increase in the mastodons during the Wisconsin, and a different and primarily shrub-browsing ground sloth appeared in the region. This was *Northrotherium shastense*, a smaller animal than his giant grass-eating predecessor. Fossils and droppings from these animals have been recovered from caves in many parts of the presently arid Southwest, and they may have survived well into the Recent period. The remains of one from Gypsum Cave in Nevada still had bits of the hide and hair preserved, a tribute to the dry desert air.

Antelopes similar to the modern pronghorn appeared but not in great abundance. The same could be said for the Pleistocene deer, similar to the mule deer of California. Both of these species occurred in modest numbers perhaps no greater than at the opening of historic times in the region. Peccaries in large herds inhabited the mesas feeding on acorn mast and cacti as well as tubers rooted out of the ground. The small llama-like camel disappeared from the region.

Displaced also was the very large *Bison latifrons*, which may have become extinct at about this time. The smaller but still massive *B. antiquus* increased accordingly and grazed over the broad coastal plains behind the dunes all along the Southern California coast and in the inland valleys, becoming more numerous now than the horses, although the latter continued to thrive.

Most of the birds that are present today in Southern California, both permanent inhabitants and migratory species, were already in the region during the Late Pleistocene. In addition some very large birds lived in the vicinity of San Diego that are now extinct. The California condor competed with an extinct La Brean condor as well as the huge teratorn vulture which was one of the largest known birds of flight. Several smaller vulturine species are also extinct in the area.

A large species of stork, a pigmy goose and a large turkey similar to the living ocellated turkey of Yucatan were also common during the Wisconsin, the turkeys having been found in great numbers in the tar pits, suggesting that it was the prey species for a great number of smaller predators.

Undoubtedly the most numerous birds in San Diego in most seasons were migratory. Enormous flocks of band-tailed pigeons would surely have been attracted to the mesas to feed on the acorn crop during the fall and winter. Waterfowl also must have crowded every small lake and pond, to rise in clouds over the marshy river deltas. Plovers, curlews and shorebirds of many other varieties would have swarmed over the tide flats and the beaches, but in the absence of sea cliffs the pelicans, cormorants, gulls and puffins could no longer have nested widely along the coast, building their rookeries instead on the steeper Channel Islands offshore and in small enclaves like La Jolla.

The seals and sea lions would also have abandoned the area for the same reason, preferring the rocky offshore islands to the long sandy beaches of the Wisconsin in San Diego. A few sea lions hauled out at La Jolla, perhaps, but the limited extent of rock ledges there would have made them too subject to attention from predators to be suitable nurseries, while the island locations would have been largely immune from such dangers.

It seems certain now that humans occupied the area. Even before Bada, Schroeder and Carter announced in 1974 the aspartic acid racemization dates for man at San Diego, his presence during the earliest stage of the Wisconsin had been suggested by Carter but not generally recognized. Artifacts deep in the bay bar sediments at Crown Point, and artifacts and hearths beneath full Wisconsin alluvial covers at La Jolla, had been reported nearly twenty years earlier in *Pleistocene Man at San Diego*. Some of the human fossil bone found by Rogers had also pointed to early Wisconsin occupation because of stratigraphic and geological location, particularly in the case of the frontal bone from La Jolla Shores, but few archaeologists were aware of those finds or their significance.

The artifacts and evidence of concentrated fires at the Texas Street site belonged to the earlier Sangamon interglacial, and the Buchanan Canyon industry, although undated, seemed to be contemporary with Texas Street because of the close typological resemblance. The same was true of the Border Road site in the Tijuana River Valley. These sites were probably occupied because of their convenience to the tidal estuaries that formed in the coastal valleys during the high sea levels of the Sangamon. As the environment and the sea levels changed over the centuries the sites would no doubt have been abandoned, for Texas Street in the early Wisconsin was nearly ten miles from the sea.

What happened to the people? Could humans ever have intentionally abandoned so ideal a region, a land so well endowed with game and plant foods and shellfish, a climate so benign? Or did they continue to live in the area, slowly adapting to new conditions of life, never increasing very substantially but in perfect balance and harmony with their environment as were the other more successful creatures? And perhaps the most intriguing question of all: when and how did they first reach North America and ultimately the San Diego region?

The Arrival of Man in America

From the top of Potato Mountain on the Seward Peninsula of Alaska, on one of the rare July days without fog, one can look across fifty miles of blue water and see the Asian mainland; the low-lying, soft lavender cloud that is the Chukotka Peninsula of Siberia. Halfway across Bering Strait and more crisply visible are the Diomede Islands, wallowing like stranded whales; a mother and her calf. Often in wintertime, instead of a ruffled blue sea, the view is of glittering white pack ice in a strange sunless twilight except briefly at midday, and the presence of the Asian highlands is felt rather than seen.

It has been almost universally conceded that somewhere in this vicinity, although perhaps well south of the strait itself, the first humans entered the continent of North America. But the questions of when and how and even why they crossed and what sort of people they were have been shrouded in mystery.

In considering the problems of prehistoric man in the Ice Age, it is difficult to appreciate the tremendous spans of time involved in any given glacial cycle, used so freely here. The Illinoian and the Wisconsin glacial periods probably each lasted for 50,000 years, with interstadials or milder periods within them. The Sangamon interglacial, although also not uniformly warm throughout its length, is thought to have had a duration of over 50,000 years, while the second or Yarmouth interglacial that preceded the Illinoian has been assigned well over 150,000 years. Even the so-called Recent period or Holocene in which we dwell stretches back into the past nearly twice the length of all recorded history.

In the early 1970's the most widely-held view was that bands of well-equipped Paleo-Indian hunters and gatherers, physically quite similar to the people of historic Indian tribes, crossed Bering Strait when it was exposed as a land bridge by the lowering of sea level during the second major stage of the Wisconsin glacial period. These early hunters crossed no more than about 30,000 years ago and were the first human inhabitants of the Western Hemisphere. As the glaciers melted during a following, relatively brief interstadial of warmer climates, they were able to make their way into the interior of the continent south of the later reglaciated regions of Canada, and they gradually dispersed over the vast landmasses of North and South America, eventually reaching the extreme southern tip of Tierra del Fuego. As their numbers expanded they slowly developed the different physical characteristics, languages and customs of historic times. Some of the most pronounced differences might be attributed to the fact that after the first arrivals there were other waves in later times of peoples from different regions of Asia, crossing the strait and even wider ocean passages in watercraft or on pack ice in the Arctic after the land bridge had been submerged by rising sea levels.

Much of that view was perfectly sound; archaeological evidence from both Central Alaska and its North Slope demonstrated the presence and passage of such people. There was little doubt that such dispersals did indeed occur and that they accounted for some of the peopling of the Americas. But what of Bada's racemization dates of nearly 50,000 years on human skeletal remains, dates which placed man at San Diego far south of the Canadian glacial ice, a barrier that had sealed off passage from Alaska for the preceding 20,000 years? What of the broken stones and charcoal in the interglacial terrace at Texas Street, the massive choppers of Buchanan Canyon, the weathered bifaces on the fossil fans of the Yuha Desert, the deeply-buried hearth and stones identified as artifacts at Calico, the apparently stream-rolled quartzite cleavers far above the Wisconsin terraces at Black's Fork, the battered tools below the glacial till at Sheguiandah? What of the many other crude chopper sites throughout the hemisphere, some in circumstances that argued great antiquity — human occupation long before the onset of the Wisconsin ice at least 70,000 years before the present?

Since there appeared to be no evidence whatever of hominid evolution in the New World, the possibility of a much earlier human penetration of the Western Hemisphere needed to be re-examined. The general consensus that Asia and North America had been essentially one continuous landmass over scores of millennia during the Middle Pleistocene suggested that new conclusions might be reached regarding man's earliest arrival.

Humans might have spread from North China and Southern Siberia over the wide, later-submerged lowlands of Beringia as early as the second or Kansan glacial period, or perhaps during the early part of the third or Illinoian, when Beringia was again exposed. They could have been in the Yukon Valley of Alaska during the second or Yarmouth interglacial around 300,000 years ago, with northwest Canada ice-free and the way clear for dispersal far to the east and south into the heart of the continent. This would agree with the dates at Valsequillo Reservoir in Mexico of 250,000 years. If they first drifted across Beringia during the Illinoian, the same opportunity for further expansion existed again during the Ohe interstadial around 150,000 years ago, when the Laurentide or continental ice sheet melted and would have permitted ice-free passage south for several millennia at least.

Beringia, also called the Bering Land Bridge, has been studied at length by scien-

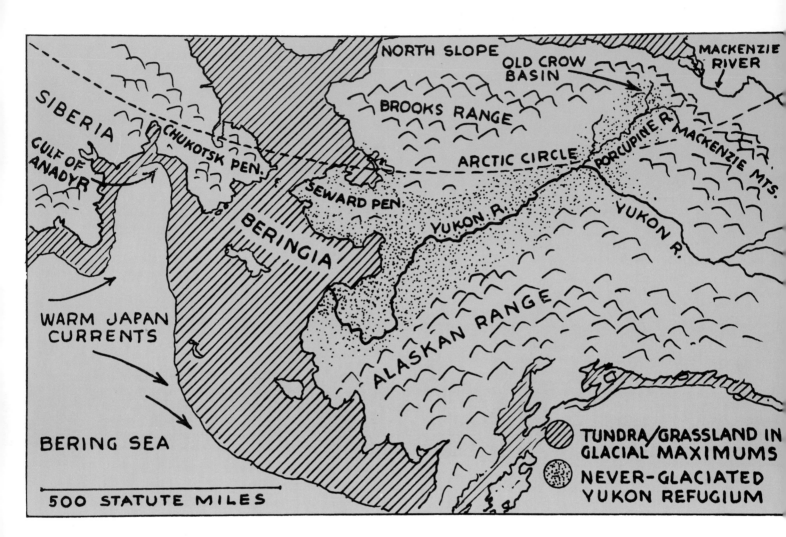

This is a map of Beringia, a vast area of rolling lowlands connecting Asia and North America that was exposed periodically for thousands of years and ice-free even during periods of maximum glaciation. Its eastward extension was the Yukon basin of central Alaska, which was an ice-free refugium during the glacial cycles.

tists of many disciplines and nationalities. In 1965 a symposium on the region was held by the International Quaternary Association at Boulder, Colorado. It was attended by American, Russian, Icelandic, German, English and Canadian specialists in geology, plant geography, oceanography, paleontology and anthropology. Most of the papers that were presented were collected in a book edited by David M. Hopkins, a research geologist with the United States Geological Survey. Entitled *The Bering Land Bridge*, it offered many views on the above subjects, some of them conflicting. Anthropologists presumed a first human appearance during the late Wisconsin years, the widely accepted view. On the whole there was broad general agreement on the history and past environments of this strange, appearing and disappearing landmass throughout the Middle and Late Pleistocene.

The land was thought to have been continuously exposed, merging the two continents, whenever, because of glacial accumulation of the earth's water in the northern latitudes in the form of ice on the land, the sea level was lowered by the process called

146

A pit hut woven of stunted willow and daubed with clay would have looked like a giant beaver lodge on the tundra. An opening in the top to let smoke out and a hide draped over the entrance could have produced a den capable of sheltering very early humans during the winters in the Arctic.

eustasis more than about one hundred and fifty feet below the present level. Since it fell more than three hundred feet during the Wisconsin and Illinoian and probably the Kansan glacial cycles, the Beringian landmass was well above sea level for very long periods of time, but little specific information was available for periods earlier than the Illinoian glaciation. The exposed continental shelves were one vast region of low, gently-rolling plains covering thousands of square miles, from the eastern Aleutian Islands in the south to latitudes well up in the Arctic Ocean.

From studies of fossil pollens trapped in sea bottom sediments of various ages it was deduced that during the Kansan glacial cycle over 350,000 years ago climates were more temperate and vegetation more varied and extensive, with grasslands and scattered groves of trees. My own view that humans might then have crossed was seemingly shared by none of the contributors. The Illinoian and Wisconsin glacial periods were thought to have been much colder, with permafrost and tundra vegetation on the Beringian plains. On the Siberian side during the Illinoian, perhaps 175,000 years ago, thick glaciers formed on the highlands bordering the sea in the deep Gulf of Anadyr just south of Bering Strait, and one Russian scholar has suggested that valley glaciers here discharged directly into the sea, barring the passage over the land bridge to mammals including man except in latitudes far north of the Arctic Circle.

Most anthropologists have assumed, in view of the supposed severity of the climate during the Illinoian and Wisconsin, that human occupation of Beringia would have had to await the achievement of rather sophisticated cultural adaptations in order for man to survive in so rugged an environment, although it was one in which modern Eskimos are perfectly at home. But that assumption was based on a premise that seems increasingly difficult to defend: that human dispersal in the region could not have occurred earlier than the Illinoian maximum glaciation.

Even if one postulated a first dispersal across the colder land bridge during the early Illinoian, before the formation of the valley glaciers at the Gulf of Anadyr, if they ever actually existed, humans at the most primitive cultural level might easily have survived and prospered. It was impossible to know how early in his cultural evolution man first utilized sewn clothing of cured hides, when he became capable of erecting temporary but snug shelters of mud-daubed willow branches, or began using animal fat or dung for fuel, or hunting with hurled spears tipped with horn or bone. Also one could not know, or have any prospect of ever knowing, what kind of physical adaptations to bitterly cold climates might have been acquired by very early humans, traits subsequently lost when no longer needed. Much more luxuriant body and facial hair may have been developed. It has been suggested that the network of small blood vessels just under the skin, particularly on the face and extremities, may have been far more extensive than in modern man, and that this combined with a high metabolic rate maintained by consuming large amounts of animal fat and protein, may have been a sustaining factor.

Many fossil mammal remains of Illinoian age and earlier have been collected in Central Alaska, which can be thought of as an unsubmerged part of Beringia. These have shown that both mammoths and mastodons ranged over the land, as did horses, bison, moose, caribou and musk oxen. Several of these, the bison, elk and musk-ox, represented species much larger than modern forms and now extinct. Also present were foxes, wolves, hunting dogs and large members of the cat family also extinct today. There were mountain sheep on the Alaskan and Siberian highlands but probably not on the Beringian plains. Giant beavers and muskrats inhabited the lakes and streams and would have been easy prey for primitive hunters. Two Asiatic mammals that reached Alaska never penetrated the continent beyond it; they were the yak and the saiga or steppe antelope. Other mammals were undoubtedly present in the highlands, the short-faced bear, for example.

If humans were living on the Beringian tundra 160,000 years ago during the Illinoian glacial maximum they could only have survived as meat-eaters, meat of course including fish, fowl, eggs and crustaceans. Such high-energy foods would have been essential in order to withstand the cold. Large animals could certainly have been killed at times by the most primitive of hunters, for like all predators humans would have preyed on the very young, the old and the wounded or sick members of the herds. Freezing winter temperatures would have preserved indefinitely any surplus of killed game or carrion on hand during that most difficult season, as would covered pits dug into the permafrost in summer.

In addition to the meat of animals killed with spears, hurled rocks and cudgels or scavenged from other predators, many other food resources would have been available on the bleak plains to very early hunters and gatherers. The tundra then as now was certainly the breeding and nesting ground for millions of migratory waterfowl and shore birds. In the late spring and summer their eggs and young would have been available in profusion. The adult birds themselves, swans, ducks and geese, went through their annual moult and were temporarily flightless as they dropped their big primary quills from the wingtips. Aleuts and Eskimos still run them down on foot at this season as they have been doing for many millennia.

Various other foods could have been gathered and consumed. The fresh tips of willow buds, bush cranberries and blueberries in the summer and fall, edible roots and bulbs dredged up from shallow ponds, and particularly the rich offerings along the southern beaches. It has often been said that when the tide goes out the table is set, and this is true in all latitudes free of ice. The most likely regions of Beringia for very early human habitation would seem to be the southern coastal zones, for here the climate would have been most ameliorated by the tempering effects of ocean currents swinging up from the warmer south. Here also must have been available shellfish of many kinds as well as

Running down molting and temporarily flightless geese on the Arctic tundra.

seals and walrus, and the mussels, clams and oysters would have been harvestable in all seasons, a very important aspect of this resource when one considers how bleak and rigorous must have been the winters.

It would have been the long, dark winters that most threatened human survival in all northern latitudes. The grazing game like caribou and musk ox would still have been available, and precipitation is believed to have been relatively light on the Beringian plains, but the very cold weather punctuated by freezing storms and the long hours of darkness would have made life difficult indeed for humans living at a minimum culture level. The same harsh conditions, however, would have culled the game herds of weaklings and made scavenging more profitable.

Human foragers would have prepared themselves for the approaching winter. Salmon surely swam up the streams of Beringia to spawn, as they have continued to do all around the northern Pacific Basin, and like the great Alaskan brown bears of modern times, human adults and their young could easily have gorged themselves during the spawning runs and laid on huge layers of fat, adding perhaps half again as much weight as they carried in leaner seasons. They would have faced the winter plump and rolypoly, only to welcome April's climbing sun as gaunt and surly as bears emerging from their winter sleep.

Salmon also ran far up to the headwaters of the Alaskan rivers, offering the same bountiful but seasonal resource. The valley of the Yukon in Central Alaska is an easterly extension of Beringia; it penetrates deep into the continent for nearly a thousand miles, gradually rising in elevation to meet the western Cordillera, the long chain of high ranges forming the rugged spine of North America. Some eight hundred miles inland the Yukon River is joined by the Porcupine, which rises two hundred miles farther east in the mountains just west of the Continental Divide. From the Old Crow Basin, a large intermontane depression drained by a tributary of the Porcupine, it is less than a hundred miles over the passes and down to the vast plains that spread over the interior of the continent and

149

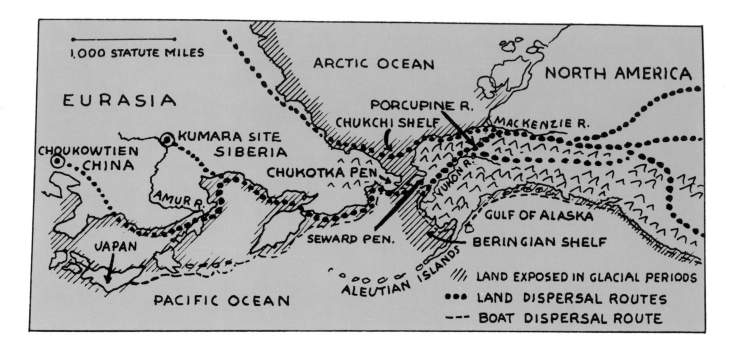

The dotted lines indicate the possible routes of human dispersal from Eurasia into North America during the Pleistocene epoch. In view of the primitive nature of the watercraft that might have been available, boat dispersals probably would have been limited to interglacial and interstadial periods, as would movements by land beyond and south of the Yukon basin.

run, broken only by scattered minor ranges, from the Beaufort Sea in the Arctic clear to the Gulf of Mexico.

Significant finds in the Old Crow Basin were reported in 1973 by W. N. Irving and C. R. Harington of Ontario, Canada. The basin was judged never to have been glaciated, and in effect could be thought of as part of Beringia despite its great distance from Bering Strait. Deep sediments in the basin indicated that it had contained an enormous Pleistocene lake, and river cutbanks yielded a great many fossils of mammals, layers of peat and preserved wood, and three bone artifacts indisputably of human manufacture. The latter, as well as the fossil remains, were dated by radiocarbon measure at about 30,000 years before the present, much later of course than is here being suggested for the earliest human presence. But the findings were of great importance for two reasons. The dates were deep in a glacial cycle and supported by extinct mammal remains, showing that occupation by humans was perfectly feasible here, and presumably would have been equally so during earlier glacial periods. A frequent argument against very early human occupation of the Yukon *refugium*, or place of refuge during the glacial periods, had been that human presence would have been revealed by his discarded stone artifacts, which certainly would have been found by now if they ever existed. But the more intriguing aspect of the Old Crow Basin site was that although no stone artifacts were found, man's presence there was clearly demonstrated by the bone artifacts and they had obviously been carved with stone tools.

Fossil bone recovered in the Old Crow Basin showed that mammals adapted to even warmer climates than the present had lived there, probably having spread northward during the Sangamon interglacial or an interstadial of the Wisconsin. These included camels, mastodons and giant beavers, all American rather than Eurasian species. Obviously if such creatures could disperse from southern North America into the Yukon region, man's capability of moving south, even at the most primitive stage of his development, would seem equally possible.

In considering the problem of human spread or dispersal from Asia to localities in North America south of the maximum advance of glacial ice, two factors were of paramount interest. They concerned the time element during which this first movement had occurred, and the route or routes by which it was accomplished. Dozens of other fascinating and more detailed questions offered grounds for speculation: the physical attributes of these first humans in the New World, their cultural attainments, means of communication, methods of curing hides and kindling fires, and many more.

The question of timing was intimately connected with what has been called the glacial-interglacial timetable. Man could only have crossed from Asia by land during a glacial period. He could only have spread south and east of the Yukon refugium during an interglacial period or a major interstadial, when the Laurentide ice melted enough to permit passage and provide an adequate environment for survival, if, as is generally believed, he went south up the valley of the MacKenzie River through the Northwest Territories. But it was apparent that he could have lived for many millennia in the Yukon Basin, unthreatened by rising sea levels or glacial ice, until conditions in the high passes of the Richardson Range beyond the Porcupine and those in the Upper MacKenzie permitted human occupation and the first bands slowly filtered south. And that would have had to happen no later than the Ohe interstadial between the two major stages of the Illinoian, around 150,000 years ago, to explain the suggestions of Illinoian or earlier occupation at Black's Fork and Calico.

Several alternate routes have been proposed in addition to the one suggested above. If very early man were sufficiently adapted to cold tundra environments he could possibly have crossed well north of Bering Strait over what is now the Chukchi Sea but was exposed as cold tundra during glacial periods. He could then have drifted along the Alaskan North Slope and into the MacKenzie Delta. None of these regions were glaciated during the Pleistocene, nor was precipitation heavy on them. As the Laurentide ice melted he could have slowly spread down over the Canadian Barrens and high prairies. There are two attractive aspects to this theory. The far northern route would have avoided the possible glacial barrier at the Gulf of Anadyr in Siberia, passing well to the north of it. Perhaps more importantly, throughout the entire distance of such a route, and perhaps from much farther west along the north Eurasian landmass, the environment would have been substantially the same, whereas by the Yukon route several very different environmental zones would have had to be passed through, requiring very long periods of adaptation and inhibiting further dispersal.

Another possibility was down what has been called the Rocky Mountain Trench, a series of connected river valleys leading south from the Yukon Basin but within the mountain systems of the Cordillera and the Rockies. This could have been open and available during periods of minimum glaciation, and human hunters might have filtered out of the Yukon region by way of the headwaters of the Yukon and the intermountain route to the south as the climate warmed and the valley glaciers disappeared.

The possibility of a completely coastal route from Asia to the tip of South America has long intrigued scholars of American antiquity, primarily because of its simplicity. Many perplexing questions would have been solved if such a route were found to be feasible. Little environmental adaptations would have been necessary since sea food and possibly marine mammals could have been the primary and unchanging diet. Very crude and primitive cultural baggage would have sufficed, and even in glacial periods the moderating effect of the sea on winter temperatures would have made life far less rigorous than in continental climates. The extremely primitive culture of the La Jollans and their shellfish economy, increasing evidence of great antiquity for them, similarities noted between La Jolla skulls and some early Japanese skeletal remains, and even their habit and necessity of moving on when shellfish supplies became depleted, all have lent credence to this theory.

But one serious and perhaps overriding obstacle has been raised, and that is a geographical one. Between the eastern Aleutians and the coast of Washington, a distance of some 1,500 miles, the coast is mountainous and deeply indented with fjords and channels. Sea cliffs plunge steeply down into deep water from high on the mountainsides. The continental shelf here is minimal or entirely lacking. Islands are in effect the tops of deeply submerged mountains, battered by frequent gales and crashing seas. During glacial advances the geological evidence insists that these rugged ranges were heavily glaciated, and that valley glaciers discharged directly into the sea in numerous places, blocking passage by land.

Two possibilities have been proposed to overcome these geographical blockades. One was the suggestion that during a period of heavy glaciation on the continent, with its enormous weights and pressures, the sea bottom in the Gulf of Alaska and along the North Pacific littoral might have been raised as the continental crust subsided under the load of ice, a process called *isostasis*. These could have provided wide beaches over which primitive shellfish eaters might have gradually drifted south, and would have required no glacial-interglacial timetable since the entire dispersal could have taken place within a glacial period. If such a shelf exposure was present, and there has been no reported geological evidence of it, the strip of habitable land would have had to be quite narrow and lacking substantial vegetation, for otherwise a great deal more mixing of Asiatic and American fauna and flora would be expectable than has been noted.

The other proposal has been the use of boats. It is impossible to say when humans first conceived the idea of water transportation. First reactions to the suggestion of very ancient use of boats are usually negative. It is difficult to conceive of people only a little past the *Homo erectus* stage being able to construct so sophisticated an object, although from floating tree trunks to dugout canoes is a relatively uncomplicated advance.

Some have suggested that all primates have an instinctive fear of water because, unlike most mammals, they sink in it. But a race of monkeys in Japan has overcome this fear, if it ever existed, and individuals of all ages enter the water willingly and often. Jacques-Yves Cousteau, the French oceanographer who invented the aqualung, visited the Indians of Lake Titicaca high in the Andes and found them spending their entire lives on the water, living on floating platforms and in canoes and yet completely unable to swim and believing that to immerse themselves in the water meant instant death.

Boats of many kinds were in use all over the world long before the beginning of recorded history. The first Europeans to reach California found the Chumash Indians of the Channel Islands and adjacent mainland using extremely intricate plank boats caulked with asphalt. In these whole families traveled between the islands and the mainland. These were people with a highly developed culture, but even the Alacaluf of Southern Chile, people with an absolutely minimal culture and economy based on shellfish and hunting, had also developed plank boats so advanced that they could actually be taken apart, moved overland to another channel, and reassembled.

Another argument for the early use of boats concerns the pygmy mammoths of Santa Rosa Island off the coast of Southern California. Fossil bones of these creatures, a dwarfed race only about six feet high, have been found broken and disarticulated as though they had been butchered, and burned and charred in pits in which at least one chipped artifact has been exposed. Samples of the burnt bone have yielded radiocarbon dates around 30,000 B.P., far back in the Wisconsin. But Santa Rosa Island is one of a group connected during the Wisconsin and now almost thirty miles off the coast. The maximum depth of water between them and the mainland today is over seven hundred feet; even at the height of the glacial advances and the consequent lowest falls of mean sea level it appears that there would have been an open water channel of at least two miles in width to cross. However, the evidence for humans on the island 30,000 years ago is well supported, and it seems certain that either there has been a subsequent lowering of sea bottom in the channel or boats were already in use by then.

Recent work in Australia has made it evident that man has been there more than 30,000 years. There seems to be no possibility that there could have been a land connection to the Asian mainland at any time during the Pleistocene. A land route from Java through the Lesser Sundas and Timor would still have left a gap of well over twenty miles of open sea to cross, even during the most minimum of sea levels. The same is true of a route through Taiwan, the Philippines and the Celebes to New Guinea, which was connected to Australia at times. That such land routes did not exist is plainly demonstrated by Australia's absolutely unique mammals, clearly isolated from the rest of the world for millions of years. Since man obviously did not originate and evolve in Australia he must have been using watercraft capable of substantial ocean passages 40,000 years ago, with a long time before that for development and dispersal.

I have been a seaman almost all my life, in freighters, war vessels and small craft. I vividly recall a winter voyage across the Pacific from Hokaido, Japan, to Seattle. The track arched far to the north on a great circle course, and the ship plunged and wallowed through a continuous succession of icy gales and endless, mountainous seas. That was normal for the season and we are probably in an interglacial period today. Knowing the destructive fury of the sea in those northern latitudes, even in supposedly inland passages, I have had great difficulty in believing the theory of a gradual, slow dispersal through those waters by very primitive humans in boats, human bands that would have included women and children of all ages. People who think of the northwest coast of North America solely in terms of the glassy-smooth fjords and channels pictured in travel posters are misinformed, and the waters can actually be more dangerous than those in the Arctic Ocean plied by Eskimo umiaks, the large open boats of walrus hide. Nevertheless, in view of the insistent evidence of man's early arrival in Australia, human dispersal down the coast of North America by boat, and even the crossing of Bering Strait at the same time ranges must now be regarded as a distinct possibility.

Possibly the first American scientist to suggest that man may have penetrated North America during the third interglacial was Dr. Raymond M. Gilmore, now a research associate at the San Diego Natural History Museum. As early as 1942, in a study of the transmigration between continents of Arctic voles in the region of Bering Strait, he mentioned the possibility of an "Amerasia" where man as well as many other mammals might have survived during the glacial cycles, and moved into North America or Asia during interglacial periods.

At the date of writing no generally accepted evidence of pre-Wisconsin man had been reported on any of the routes suggested above, although thick, heavy core tools, greatly weathered but undatable, had been found at Cape Krusenstern on the Alaskan side of Bering Strait. Yet the evidence from many parts of the hemisphere insisted that one or more of these routes was followed. Archaeologists have searched for traces of very early occupation in Central Alaska, on the islands of the Bering Sea and in the Valley of the MacKenzie, but all known sites to date have been attributed to the Wisconsin or the Recent periods. In the formerly glaciated regions east of the Cordillera and on the high passes this has been easy to understand, for intervening glacial advances could easily have ground away or deeply buried all the evidence. In the Rocky Mountain Trench the same could have been true. Along the Pacific Coast any bones or artifacts would have long since been submerged by the sea, as would any remains of human occupation or passage on the rolling plains of Beringia. But somewhere in the Yukon Basin the broken stones may still be there, waiting to be discovered.

Even if the artifacts of very ancient people have lain on the surface plainly visible for the past century, the chance of their being recognized has been small. Unless they were encountered in a site where later, more obvious artifacts had also been deposited, as at Black's Fork, or were exposed in an excavation overlain by more familiar material, they would almost certainly have gone unnoticed. At Texas Street it was the evidence of repeated fires in the cliff exposure that drew Carter's attention to the broken stones; his work led to my recognition of the artifacts at Buchanan Canyon twenty years later.

But most of the tools of very early man were so crudely made that they have been attributed far too often to simple natural breakage, and since the preferred occupation sites have usually been located near water, thousands of artifacts of these extreme ages must have simply been abraded back down to cobbles again. Skeletal material has been even more vulnerable; humans were too intelligent to wander into bogs or fall into cracks in the ground, and burial was apparently not practiced in very ancient cultures, so that human fossils of great age have been scarce everywhere. Only rarely have soils and sediments been satisfactory for the preservation of bone, even if accidentally buried, and scavengers and rodents have usually made short work of any skeletal material on the surface or even lightly buried.

Although some skeletons had been recovered in North America that could be dated into the Pleistocene, because of their geological association or by radiocarbon testing, these were all placed into the second major phase of the Wisconsin, or less than 30,000 years ago, until Jeffrey Bada's protein racemization dates on the San Diego fossils were released. A possible exception was a human fossil found by a geological survey team near the town of Taber, Alberta, in 1961. Fragments of the skull and other bones of a young child were discovered weathering out of a cutbank on the Oldman River. Deposited in sandy alluvium sixty feet below the level of the prairie and overlain by glacial till attributed to a late advance of the Wisconsin, the remains were estimated to be as old as 60,000 years. Dating was on the basis of a radiocarbon date of 37,000 B.P. obtained on a piece of wood recovered from much higher in the same stratum and considered to have been deposited much later. Even if the estimated age was wrong by 10,000 years it would place humans already south of the continental ice sheet before its formation early in the Wisconsin. They would therefore have had to cross the Bering Bridge during its last previous exposure during the Illinoian more than 125,000 years ago, unless they crossed by boat or over pack ice.

But even without conclusively-dated skeletal remains the evidence for such early human arrival seemed compelling. It appeared to me that the waterworn cleavers collected from the high terraces at Black's Fork, far above the Wisconsin flood plain, could

Early Homo sapiens *hunters as they might have appeared spearing caribou on the tundra of the MacKenzie Valley in Canada during a major interstadial of the Illinoian or Third Glacial period about 150,000 years before the present. Dressed in wrapped-around and sewn strips of caribou hide smeared with fresh caribou dung, they may have lain prone behind screens of Arctic willow along migration routes. When the tough hide of the animal was pierced by a heat-hardened wooden shaft of spruce, perhaps tipped with bone, antler or mammoth ivory, the wounded quarry could have been followed across the open country until it dropped or the spear worked loose. Native hunters in Northern Canada and Alaska still ambush caribou on the tundra, although now they have high-powered rifles. Caribou and reindeer, considered by some naturalists to be different races of the same species, are still the principal bases for native economies in the Arctic regions of both hemispheres. The meat can be preserved indefinitely in ice caves dug into the permafrost, while bone, hide, antler, sinew, gut and tallow all are utilized.*

154

only have been rolled in an earlier glacial stream, meltwater from Illinoian ice at the latest, as no subsequent active stream was possible on those uplifted surfaces. The chipped stones and apparent hearth at Calico were deeply buried under alluvium that appeared almost beyond question to be at least of interglacial age, and far older according to geologists like Vance Haynes of the University of Arizona. The battered bifaces found by Thomas Lee beneath till representing the full Wisconsin could only have been deposited before that glacial advance, and they had not been disputed as the work of man. And evidence of man in the form of broken stones and hearths was found throughout the interglacial deposits at Texas Street. The implication of all these battered, chipped and abraded stones was clear and pointed to the same conclusion: man must have been in America at least since the late Illinoian, or not less than 125,000 years. If the data from Valsequillo Reservoir proved valid after further testing, he had been here 250,000 years.

What could have impelled any ancient people to travel from Asia to Black's Fork, Calico, and ultimately to Texas Street and Buchanan Canyon? Of course they never did; the slow, gradual spread of the human species could hardly be called travel. Movement in any particular direction was controlled by external factors and would have been almost entirely unplanned. Humans simply expanded their ranges, sometimes perhaps no more than a mile a year except in extraordinary situations. Floods, droughts, prairie fires, volcanic eruptions and lava flows, and encroachments by other humans might have moved them completely out of familiar territories at times, but this would have been the exception and they would have traveled no farther than necessary and then settled down again, although they must have been quite mobile within their familiar stretches of countryside. It seems likely that human bands would have left a particular region most reluctantly, since for gatherers of such things as roots, berries and shellfish, knowing exactly where each food resource could be found in season would have been critically important. Hunters would need to know where game watered or bedded down, where it could be easily ambushed or chased over cliffs or into muck holes, where stout poles for shaping into lances grew, where migration routes could be intercepted, and many other bits of information that could make the difference between survival and starvation.

Hunting and foraging was a fulltime occupation for such people; it still is in some remote parts of the world. In the Far North in wintertime it seems doubtful that humans could have survived at all through the long dark months without an intimate knowledge of every food resource in their territories. Even with such knowledge there would have been times when they were reduced to devouring shredded hides and animal droppings gleaned from beneath the snow.

After a very long, gradual expansion during a pre-Wisconsin glacial cycle over the exposed lowlands of Beringia, into the never-glaciated interior of Central Alaska and up the valley of the Yukon River, small bands of human hunters must have gradually sifted south during a long period of temperate climate. Some may have followed the so-called Rocky Mountain Trench and others slowly spread up the valley of the MacKenzie and over the high Canadian prairie. Always few in number and moving like the rings on a quiet pond, over some 5,000 years they could have reached most regions of the continent of North America. The average distance moved along the track by any one individual in his lifetime might have been less than five miles; less distance than a man can see over the countryside.

Few humans would ever have been aware of traveling at all, then. All lived in their own familiar world, and lived far too short a lifespan to be aware of any change in the climate or their surroundings. None knew both the tundra life and the forest of the upper Yukon Valley, although a few intrepid humans must have ventured over the passes of the Richardson Range and down to the plains of the MacKenzie below. But the eastern flanks of the mountains would have been quite similar to the Yukon Basin, so even that transition was gradual.

If the Pacific Coast was indeed a route of dispersal to the south, the movement would have been rather different. Along the beaches deliberate migration would undoubtedly have occurred as shellfish resources were depleted and all the humans in a particular area were forced to move farther down the coast. But these journeys would seldom have needed to be far; a few miles at most and perhaps within sight of the former habitation.

Physical and cultural similarities between very early peoples in Australia and North America have seemed significant. They have seemed to suggest several separate and quite different early dispersals of primitive humans into both continents, people unlike each other in many of their qualities and habits. First and apparently earliest were the most archaic physical types, who seem to have been primarily hunters, in Australia identified by fossil remains. In America their physical characteristics have not been determined, but it is becoming increasingly evident that they left the bifacial tools in the lowest levels of Sheguiandah, on the high terraces at Black's Fork, and deep in the alluvial soils of Calico, Texas Street and Buchanan Canyon.

A quite different people, sedentary shellfish gatherers and later seed-grinders, possibly the distant ancestors of the Ainu still living on Hokaido, Japan, arrived in Australia as early as 40,000 years ago, and much earlier in North America where they were represented by the La Jollans on the Southern California Coast. The individual dated by Bada at 48,000 years old belonged to this group. A much later movement into both continents was typified in America by the Paleo-Indian hunters with their stone projectile points, and Melanesian people similarly equipped moving into Australia.

These latest arrivals were long thought on both continents to have been the first human inhabitants. Many American anthropologists in the early 1970's were still convinced that the Mongoloid makers of sophisticated Folsum and Clovis dart points, thought to have spread into America from Siberia no more than 30,000 years ago, were the earliest humans in the Western Hemisphere.

The shell midden people might have evolved somewhere in Eastern Asia and expanded around the Pacific Basin along the coasts primarily, although they apparently also settled along the shores of Pleistocene inland lakes. Eventually they reached the Atlantic coast region and the Gulf of Mexico, and probably the coasts of South America as well. Carter's observations of artifacts beneath full Wisconsin alluvial cover along the San Diego beaches suggested that they were in America more than 70,000 years ago, and they are now known to have been in Australia by mid-Wisconsin time.

Preceding them by scores of millennia in America and by an unknown interval in Australia, were people more adapted to hunting and perhaps scavenging. These were inland people; gradually they spread over both American continents. Their massive choppers, cleavers and scrapers and their emphasis on blades, completely unlike the tool kits of the shellfish gatherers, suggested a continued major reliance on a meat diet and the working of bone and leather. They undoubtedly availed themselves of shellfish also where these were obtainable, as at Texas Street and Buchanan Canyon and possibly at Calico, but only to a minor degree.

Scientists of the Australian National University have suggested such a dual sequence of early arrivals in that country. The remains of two humans who had been cremated, and their charred bones ritualistically buried at the edge of now-dry Pleistocene Lake Mungo in New South Wales, were found near ancient hearths with mussel shells and crude stone tools. The bones had been daubed with ochre, a natural pigment, and were radiocarbon-dated at 26,000 B.P. Charcoal at one site was dated at 38,000 B.P., while later sites of what appeared to be the same culture had seed-grinding implements, emphasizing even more strongly the relationship to the La Jollans of Southern California. Other skulls found previously in Victoria to the south had features far more archaic than the fairly modern-appearing Lake Mungo skulls, being more suggestive of *Homo erectus*, an earlier human species, even though dated at around 10,000 years, and giving rise to the speculation that these quite different and distinct human types might have co-existed over very long periods of time after separate migrations to the continent.

Apparently at some time after these initial infusions of human stock migrations ceased and Australia received few cultural influences from outside. Clearly the story of the human past in the Americas was very different. The fifteenth and sixteenth century European explorers and colonists found people of enormous diversity living in vastly differing cultures and environments throughout the hemisphere; the Aztecs of Tenochtitlán with their brutal but brilliant civilization, the peaceful Cherokee in their orderly towns and plantations, the bison-hunting Sioux and Cheyenne on the Great Plains, the extremely primitive Pericu isolated at the tip of Baja California.

Great differences in physical characteristics were also apparent. Skull shapes varied from the long, narrow skulls of the Pericu to the more typical round-headed people of the plains. Skin colors came in everything from dark chocolate brown to very light yellowish tans and coppery reds. Some Indians were tall, others extremely short and small-boned. Features varied tremendously from the flat, Mongoloid faces and small noses of the Eskimos to the narrow, hawk-like features and aquiline noses of Comanches and the large, fleshy noses and sloping foreheads and chins of the Classic Maya. Among all these an incredible variety of languages and dialects was spoken, a vast panoply of religious beliefs and customs was cherished, and a multitude of contrasting life styles was followed: swift canoe raids by bloodthirsty and cannibalistic Caribs of the West Indies, the placid life of the sun-drenched pueblos of New Mexico, the patient stalk over the pack ice of the Arctic wastelands.

These contrasts and variations could only have been the result of many complex factors; cultural and even physical adaptations to richly diverse environments over extremely long periods of time; the addition and diffusion of new ideas, customs and changing physical characteristics contributed by later arrivals from outside the hemisphere. Even before the Christian era there may have been junk intrusions by Chinese voyagers along the Pacific Coast and colonists from Japan, and Mediterranean cultural influences and racial stocks brought in by sea by Iberian, North African and Phoenician peoples. Nordic explorers and colonists beached their longboats on the North Atlantic strands and marched inland centuries before the voyages of Columbus. The mix was far too complicated to have yet been appreciated in its entirety and to have been unraveled.

But one observation can be made with some degree of certainty now. The first primitive humans to drift unknowingly across that imaginary dividing line between the Old World and the New did so a very long time ago, in an age far earlier than has previously been recognized and accepted, and they brought with them only the most limited cultural baggage.

They were still nearly 4,000 miles and countless human generations of time away from the campsite below the cliffs near Texas Street and the sheltering walls of Buchanan Canyon.

Bibliography

CHAPTER I.

The glacial and interglacial cycles of the Pleistocene and the mechanics and effects of glaciers are discussed in:

Flint, R. F., 1957. *Glacial and Pleistocene Geology.* Wiley, New York.

Schwarzbach, Martin, 1963. *Climates of the Past.* Van Nostrand, London.

Zeuner, Frederick, 1959. *The Pleistocene Period.* Hutchinson, London.

CHAPTER II.

George F. Carter's attribution of the formation of the sediments in the Texas Street terrace primarily to eustatic rise of sea level and consequent valley filling during an interglacial period, and not to tectonic uplift of the landform, was later solidly supported by independent geological studies of the region reported in:

Allen, C. R., Silver, Leon T., and Stehli, F. G., 1960. *Transverse Structures of Northern Baja California, Mexico.* Bull. Geol. Soc. of America 71, pp. 457-482.

Allen, C. R., Amond, S. T., Richter, C. F., and Nordquist, J. M., 1965. *Relationship Between Seismicity and Geologic Structure in the Southern California Region.* Bull. Seismological Soc. of America 55, pp. 753-797.

Carter's major report on the Texas Street site and his investigation of other very early sites in the area was:

Carter, George F., 1957. *Pleistocene Man at San Diego.* The Johns Hopkins Press, Baltimore.

Early support for recognition of the lithic specimens as evidence of human activity at the Texas Street site was offered in:

Simpson, Ruth D., 1954. *A Friendly Critic Visits Texas Street.* The Masterkey, Vol. 28, No. 5, pp. 174-176.

Witthoft, John, 1955. *Texas Street Artifacts.* New World Antiquity, Vol. 2, No. 9, pp. 132-133.

In addition, ten years after the publication of Carter's book, Sherwood M. Gagliano of Louisiana State University reported on a very early site at which bipolar flaking was practiced, and he specifically refuted the major arguments of critics skeptical of the human origin of the Texas Street cores; namely, that the quartzite cores lacked bulbs of percussion (quartzite often fractures without leaving such bulbs) and that the angles between blade scars and striking platforms did not attain prescribed numerical values and were inconsistent (quartzite flaking permits wide variations in angles). He not only supported the Texas Street artifacts but cited other early sites

where similar bipolar flaking had occurred in:

Gagliano, Sherwood M., 1967. *Occupation Sequence at Avery Island.* Louisiana State University Press, Baton Rouge, pp. 93-95.

Among many critics who seriously questioned Carter's interpretation of the Texas Street site were:

Krieger, Alex D., 1958. *Review of George F. Carter, Pleistocene Man at San Diego.* American Anthropologist, 60, pp. 974-978.

Johnson, Frederick and Miller, John P., 1958. *Review of G. F. Carter, Pleistocene Man at San Diego.* American Antiquity, 24, pp. 206-210.

Wormington, H. M., 1957. *Ancient Man in North America.* Fourth Edition, Denver Museum of Natural History, pp. 222-223.

First reports on Sheguiandah, written before Lee was forced to resign from the National Museum staff, were:

Lee, Thomas E., 1954. *The First Sheguiandah Expedition, Manitoulin Island, Ontario.* American Antiquity, Vol. XX, No. 2, pp. 101-111.

Lee, Thomas E., 1955. *The Second Sheguiandah Expedition, Manitoulin Island, Ontario.* American Antiquity, Vol. XXI, No. 1, pp. 63-71.

Later articles on Sheguiandah were:

Lee, Thomas E., 1964. *Sheguiandah: Workshop or Habitation?* Anthropological Journal of Canada, Vol. 2, No. 3, pp. 16-24.

Sanford, John T., 1971. *Sheguiandah Reviewed.* Anthropological Journal of Canada, Vol. 9, No. 1., pp. 2-15.

Richard S. MacNeish among others was highly skeptical of the antiquity of Sheguiandah. But a decade later he excavated a cave at Ayacucho, Peru, that contained evidence of great antiquity, leading him to change his mind about Sheguiandah and conclude, based on his own findings, "... man may have first arrived in the Western Hemisphere between 40,000 and 100,000 years ago."

MacNeish, Richard S., 1971. *Early Man in the Andes.* Scientific American, Vol. 224, No. 4, pp. 36-46.

In mid-1976 no final and comprehensive report had been published on the results of the Calico archaeological investigation and it was still proceeding. The history and background are well covered in:

Simpson, Ruth D., and Schuiling, Walter C., 1970. *Pleistocene Man at Calico.* The San Bernardino County Museum Association, Redlands, California.

An excellent and unbiased report on the Calico

Conference and the vastly differing views on the lithic specimens, hearth feature and geological dating offered by the various participants is:

Dixon, Keith A., 1970. *Archaeology and Geology in the Calico Mountains: Results of the International Conference on the Calico Project.* Informant, Vol. 1, No. 10, Anthropology Department, California State College at Long Beach, pp. 1-23.

A sympathetic view of the Calico findings is offered in:

Stephenson, Robert L., 1971. *Thoughts on the Calico Mountains Site.* The Institute of Archaeology and Anthropology Notebook, Vol. 3, No. 1, The University of South Carolina, Columbia, pp. 3-9.

An extremely skeptical view of the Calico findings and geological dating, which suggests a non-human origin for the lithic specimens and an age of half a million years for the Yermo Formation, is presented in:

Haynes, Vance, 1973. *The Calico Site, Artifacts or Geofacts?* Science, Vol. 181, No. 4097, pp. 305-310.

Announcement of the critically important microanalyses of use-wear patterns on stone tools from Calico by Clay Singer was made by Ruth D. Simpson, director of the Calico project in a paper presented to the Annual Meeting of the Society for California Archaeology at San Diego, California.

Simpson, Ruth D., 1976. *The Calico Mountains Archaeological Project.* A paper presented to the Society for California Archaeology, April 10, 1976.

CHAPTER III.

In respect to very early sites, an excellent and entertaining book on very early man in America has been written by Louis A. Brennan, who discusses many of the sites mentioned in this book as well as others. However, he seems to have misunderstood the nature of the controversy over dating the Calico site, which has been widely considered to be older than the estimates of Leakey, Simpson and Clements rather than younger as Brennan suggests; too old, it has been claimed, to represent human occupation. He also mistakenly implies that Carter claimed an age of 500,000 years for the Texas Street site when in fact he has never suggested more than 120,000.

Brennan, Louis A., 1970. *American Dawn: A New Model of American Prehistory.* The MacMillan Company, Collier-MacMillan, Ltd., London.

E. B. Renaud's reports of his investigations of the sites in the Black's Fork Basin, Wyoming, and the artifact assemblages collected there were reported in:

Renaud, E. B., 1933. *Archaeological Survey of the High Western Plains, Seventh Report.* Department of Anthropology, the University of Denver, Denver, Colorado.

1938. *Archaeological Survey of the High Western Plains, Tenth Report.* Department of Anthropology, the University of Denver, Denver, Colorado.

1940. *Archaeological Survey of the High Western Plains, Twelfth Report.* Department of Anthropology, the University of Denver, Denver, Colorado.

The question of wind-and-sand erosion versus stream abrasion on stone specimens, and the means of distinguishing between them, is well discussed by Brigham Arnold, who reached conclusions similar to mine in:

Arnold, Brigham A., 1957. *Late Pleistocene and Recent Changes in Land Forms, Climates and Archaeology in Central Baja California.* University of California Publications in Geography, Vol. 10, No. 4, pp. 201-318.

The lower paleolithic stone work of the Old World to which Renaud compared his specimens from Black's Fork is well described and illustrated by Francois Bordes, who appears quite understandably to have been completely unfamiliar with paleolithic industries in the Western Hemisphere:

Bordes, Francois, 1968. *The Old Stone Age.* McGraw-Hill Book Co., New York, Toronto.

The operations at Sheguiandah were reported by Thomas E. Lee, then of the National Museum of Canada, and John T. Sanford of Wayne State University, Detroit, Michigan:

Lee, Thomas E., 1957. *The Antiquity of the Sheguiandah Site,* and

Sanford, John T., 1957. *Geologic Observations at the Sheguiandah Site.* The Canadian Field-Naturalist, Vol. 71, No. 3, pp. 117-148.

CHAPTER IV.

Early Spanish contacts with the Diegueño are well-described in:

Pourade, Richard F., 1960. *The Explorers.* (Volume I of a series *The History of San Diego*), The Union-Tribune Publishing Company, San Diego.

The San Dieguito Complex at the Harris site and the excavations there are described in:

Warren, Claude N. (editor), 1966. *The San Dieguito Type-site: M. J. Rogers' 1938 Excavation on the San Dieguito River.* San Diego Museum Papers, No. 5, San Diego.

Warren, Claude N. and True, D. L., 1961. *The San Dieguito Complex and Its Place in California Prehistory.* U.C.L.A. Archaeological Survey Report, 1960-1961, pp. 246-338, Los Angeles.

An excellent report of the excavation of a typical La Jollan site at San Diego, and the La Jollan culture as deduced from artifactual, skeletal and food refuse remains is:

Shumway, George, Hubbs, Carl L. and Moriarty, James R., 1961. *Scripps Estates Site, San Diego, California: A La Jolla Site Dated 5460 to 7370 Years Before the Present.* Annals of the New York Academy of Sciences, Vol. 93, Article 3, pp. 37-132.

The site at Agua Hedondia Lagoon believed by Moriarty to represent a transition from San Dieguito to La Jollan, a view which he later modified, is described in:

Moriarty, James R., 1967. *Transitional Pre-Desert*

Phase in San Diego County, California. Science, Vol. 155, No. 3762, pp. 553-556.

The best and most complete account of San Diego prehistory, primarily concentrating on the San Dieguito complex is:
Rogers, Malcolm J., 1966. *Ancient Hunters of the Far West.* The Union-Tribune Publishing Company, San Diego.

The Laguna Beach skull, presumed to be La Jollan, was dated by radiocarbon measure at 17,150 ± 1,470 B.P. and reported in:
Berger, Rainer et al., 1971. *Contributions of the Archaeological Research Facility.* No. 12, University of California, pp. 43-44, 47.

Hearth features weathering out of beach cliffs at La Jolla, California, included localized charcoal and burned earth with fragments of bone and shell. Charcoal produced a radiocarbon date of 34,000 B.P. Investigators considered it highly probable that the features represented a hearth and human occupation. Reported in:
Hubbs, Carl L., Bien, George S. and Suess, Hans E., 1962. *La Jolla Natural Radiocarbon Measurements II.* Radiocarbon, Vol. 4, p. 215.

The mano and metates found at Crown Point were reported in CARTER (1957) Op. Cit. pp. 286-290. The storage theory to explain the cleared circles in the desert is offered in:
Carter, George F., 1964. *Stone Circles in the Deserts.* Anthropological Journal of Canada, Vol. 2, No. 3, pp. 2-6.

Dr. H. M. Wormington, in her review of Texas Street, rejected the burned areas as representing man, although pointing out that she had not seen them, and suggested that only definitely prepared hearths would indicate man's presence. Although Texas Street does have basin-shaped hearths, it is clear from many San Dieguito sites that more scattered charcoal also may be typical of occupied sites, particularly temporary camps.
Wormington, H. M. (1957). Op. Cit. p. 223.

CHAPTER V.
Abbé Breuil's comments on the action of streams on quartzite, as well as a great deal more informative material on stone knapping, is contained in:
Breuil, Henri and Lantier, Raymond, 1965. *The Men of the Old Stone Age.* St. Martin's Press, New York. (First published in France, 1959.)

CHAPTER VI.
An overview of discoveries at Choukoutien and numerous other Homo erectus *sites throughout China is in:*
Chang, Kwang-Chih, 1968. *The Archaeology of Ancient China.* Yale University Press, New Haven and London.

The illustration comparing a Buchanan Canyon specimen with an artifact from Choukoutien utilized paleolithic tools illustrated in:
Bordes, Francois (1968), Op. Cit.
The archaeology and Pleistocene environment of

Eastern Siberia, as well as excellent illustrations of paleolithic Siberian artifacts, are well presented in:
Powers, W. R., 1973. *Paleolithic Man in Northeast Asia.* Arctic Anthropology, Vol. X, No. 2, University of Wisconsin Press, Madison (entire issue).

"Skreblos" are described and illustrated in:
Powers, W. R. (1973), Op. Cit.

The experiments in bipolar flaking described in the text are reported fully in:
Minshall, H. L., 1973. *Bipolar Flaking in Quartzite at Buchanan Canyon.* Anthropological Journal of Canada, Vol. 11, No. 1, pp. 20-24.

Further information on bipolar flaking in the San Diego region is offered in:
Minshall, H. L., 1975. A *Lower Paleolithic Bipolar Flaking Complex in the San Diego Region: Technological Implications of Recent Finds.* Pacific Coast Archaeological Society Quarterly, Vol. 11, No. 4, pp. 45-55.

CHAPTER VII.
An analysis of desert patinas and varnishes is well presented in:
Rogers, Malcolm J. (1966), Op. Cit. pp. 31-35.

As early as 1951 George Carter was calling attention to the fact that only minimal desert varnish was found on projectile points in the Mojave, although cruder artifacts like choppers on elevated beaches had coats of varnish as heavy as any on the surrounding rocks. These views were presented in:
Carter, George F., 1951. *Man in America: A Criticism of Scientific Thought.* The Scientific Monthly, Vol. LXXXIII, No. 5, pp. 297-307.

An impressive study of lines of rock cairns and other rock features apparently man-made in the Colorado Desert is:
Begole, Robert S., 1974. *Archaeological Phenomena in the California Desert.* Pacific Coast Archaeological Society Quarterly, Vol. 10, No. 2, pp. 51-70.

The discovery and excavation of Yuha Man, including a description of "ridge-back" artifacts, were reported in:
Childers, W. M., 1974. *Preliminary Report on the Yuha Burial, California.* Anthropological Journal of Canada, Vol. 12, No. 1, pp. 2-9.

CHAPTER VIII.
Very extensive coastal studies were conducted by Peter Birkeland of the University of Colorado and the U. S. Geological Survey. His purpose was to show that elevated terraces both on the beaches and along the stream valley margins could be attributed at least in part to eustatic rise of sea level during the last interglacial, and to date the various levels, demonstrated by their geological features and conformation to be such terraces, by open-system uranium-series dating of shell collected from them:

Birkeland, Peter W., 1972. *Late Quaternary Eustatic*

Sea-level Changes Along the Malibu Coast, Los Angeles County, California. Journal of Geology, Vol. 80, pp. 432-448.

The finding of elongate polyhedral cores similar to those at Texas Street, but in obsidian rather than quartzite, was described by Clyde E. Kuhn (personal communication). The site, in the Mammoth Basin of the eastern Sierra Nevada, was surveyed in 1975, and reported in a paper presented to the Annual Meeting of the Society for California Archaeology at San Diego, California.

Kuhn, Clyde E., and Jersey, Beth, 1976. *An Archaeological Survey in Mono County, 1975.* A descriptive account of an archaeological/cultural resources survey of U.S. Forest Service and Bureau of Land Management Known Geothermal Resources Lands, Mono County, including hypothesis, methodology, results and implications.

CHAPTER IX

Descriptions of early finds of La Jolla fossils are included in Malcolm Rogers' unpublished notes, on file at the San Diego Museum of Man. These are sometimes difficult to interpret; Rogers lacked fluency and writing skills, but his records are invaluable to scholars now.

A reasonably complete summary of human fossil finds in North America up to its time of publication is:

Wormington, H. M. (1957), Op. Cit.

Background material on amino acid racemization and the work of Jeffrey L. Bada is very well presented in:

Alexander, George, 1974. *Fossil-Dating Tool: A New Outlook on Man.* The Los Angeles Times, Vol. XCIII, Aug. 18.

In its issue of September 4, 1972, TIME magazine noted Jeffrey Bada's development of the new "time clock" of amino acid racemization, described the method briefly, and reported that a practical use had now been suggested: it could be used as a geological "clock" to fill important gaps in the earth's fossil records. At that time the dating of human fossils from the San Diego region had not yet been undertaken, and in fact Bada was unaware of the existence of the very ancient skeletal remains collected by Malcolm Rogers more than forty years earlier.

TIME magazine, 1972. *A New Clock.* TIME magazine, September 4, pp. 46-47.

Jeffrey Bada and his development of the racemization technique of dating fossils were featured in a cover story of U. S. News and World Report, which included the following:

"As a result of (Bada's) findings, archaeologists are taking a new look at the length of human history in North America. Growing out of his discovery is the indication that man lived in what is now the San Diego area about 50,000 years ago.

"Previously, it was widely believed that man crossed a northern land bridge from Asia to America about 20,000 to 25,000 years ago. Some experts interpret Mr. Bada's work as a sign that human beings may have made the passage from 70,000 to 100,000 years ago.

"While there are some dissenters, many scientists say the new technique — which links the rate of chemical changes in the amino acids of a substance with its age in years — gives every appearance of being highly accurate."

U. S. News and World Report, 1976. *Young Builders of America; 8 Who Have Made Their Mark.* February 9, pp. 43-44.

The announcement of the dating of the human fossil materials from Del Mar and La Jolla by amino acid racemization analysis appeared in:

Bada, J. L., Scroeder, R. A. and Carter, G. F., 1974. *New Evidence for the Antiquity of Man in North America Deduced from Aspartic Acid Racemization.* Science, Vol. 184, No. 4138, pp. 791-793.

A description and measurements of the Del Mar skull can be found in:

Rogers, Spencer L., 1974. *An Ancient Human Skeleton Found at Del Mar, California.* San Diego Museum Papers, No. 7, San Diego Museum of Man.

A comparative study of other La Jollan skeletons is:

Rogers, Spencer L., 1963. *The Physical Characteristics of the Aboriginal La Jollan Population of Southern California.* San Diego Museum Papers, No. 4, San Diego Museum of Man.

The finding and description of the Utah Lake skull are reported in:

Hansen, G. H., 1934. *Utah Lake Skull.* American Anthropology, N. S., Vol. 36, pp. 135-147.

Dating of the Hueyatlaco site at Valsequillo Reservoir near Puebla, Mexico, is briefly reported in:

Steen-McIntyre, Virginia, Fryxell, Roald and Malde, Harold E., 1973. *Geological Society of America.* Abstracts, 5, (No. 7), p. 820.

The mastodon skull with the flaked tool imbedded in the lower jaw was examined on the site by Ruth D. Simpson (personal communication). Miss Simpson is now at the San Bernardino County Museum, Redlands, California.

CHAPTER X.

Fossil finds of land vertebrates have been rare in the San Diego coastal region. Whether this is because of poor soil conditions for preservation or simply failure to find and recognize such specimens cannot be determined. Only a camel jawbone, some fragments of mammoth bone, a Pleistocene horse skeleton and a few human fossil remains have been reported from widely separated locations in the area. In reconstructing the Pleistocene environments it has been necessary to draw on the rich fossil sites in Orange and Los Angeles counties less than one hundred miles to the north. These contain not only Sangamon and Wisconsin vertebrates but also pollens from which the plant environments have been deduced; the presumption being that San Diego would have been essentially the same. Some source materials are:

Miller, Wade E., 1971. *Pleistocene Vertebrates of the Los Angeles Basin and Vicinity*. Bulletin of the Los Angeles County Museum of Natural History, Science, Number 10.

Stock, Chester, 1963. *Rancho La Brea: A Record of Pleistocene Life in California*. Sixth Edition. Los Angeles County Museum.

Downs, Theodore, 1968. *Fossil Vertebrates of Southern California*. University of California Press, Berkeley, Los Angeles.

Sibley, Gretchen, 1968. *La Brea Story*. The Ward Ritchie Press, Los Angeles.

CHAPTER XI.

For conservative and widely accepted views of the occupation of North America, the following are considered representative and are suggested:

MacGowan, Kenneth, 1950. *Early Man in the New World*. The MacMillan Company, New York.

Willey, Gordon R., 1966. *An Introduction to American Archaeology, Vol. I, North and Middle America*. Prentice-Hall, Englewood Cliffs, New Jersey.

Wormington, H. M., (1957), Op. Cit.

Studies of the Bering Bridge in many disciplines and by scholars of many nations are included in:

Hopkins, David M. (Editor), 1967. *The Bering Land Bridge*. Stanford University Press, Stanford, Calif.

The work in the Old Crow Basin of the Porcupine drainage was reported in:

Irving, W. N. and Harington, C. R., 1973. *Upper Pleistocene Radiocarbon-Dated Artefacts from the Northern Yukon*. Science, Vol. 179, No. 4071. pp. 335-340.

The dating of the apparent kill-sites of dwarf mammoths, implying human presence on Santa Rosa Island about 30,000 years ago, is documented in:

Orr, Phil C., 1956. *Radiocarbon Dates from Santa Rosa Island, I*. Santa Barbara Museum of Natural History, Anthropology. Bulletin 2.

Raymond M. Gilmore's early conclusion that man might have entered North America across an exposed "Amerasia" and survived during glacial cycles, to move into the interior of the continent during the interglacials, was stated in:

Gilmore, Raymond M., 1942. *Review of Microtus Voles of the Subgenus Stenocranius (Mammalia: Rodentia: Muidae), with Special Discussion of the Bering Strait Region*. Abstract of Theses, Cornell University for 1942, 1943. Cornell University Press, Ithica, New York, p. 292.

The finding of human skeletal remains near the Oldman River, Alberta, estimated to be 60,000 years old, was reported in:

Stalker, A Mac S., 1969. *Geology and Age of the Early Man Site at Taber, Alberta*. American Antiquity, Vol. 34, No. 4.

The Lake Mungo finds in Australia of very early man sites including fossil human bone, shell and artifacts are reported in:

Bransdon, Terry, 1974. *Evidence Suggests First Modern Man Also Occupied World's Oldest Continent*. Australian Information Service, P.O. Box 12, Canberra.

An excellent overview of Australian archaeology is offered in:

Tindale, Norman B., 1974. *Aboriginal Tribes of Australia*. University of California Press, Berkeley, Calif.

Acknowledgements

For their generous help in critical reading of sections of this book manuscript and other valuable assistance, I am greatly indebted to the following: Dr. George F. Carter of Texas A & M University; Ruth De Ette Simpson of the San Bernardino County Museum, Redlands, California; Professor Thomas E. Lee of the Centre d'Études Nordiques, Université Laval, Quebec, Canada; Dr. James R. Moriarty of the University of San Diego; George Miller, paleontologist, and Morlin Childers, archaeologist, of the Imperial Valley College Museum, El Centro, California; Dr. Raymond M. Gilmore of the San Diego Museum of Natural History; Dr. Jeffrey Bada, Scripps Institution of Oceanography, the University of California at San Diego; and Dr. Spencer Rogers and the staff of the San Diego Museum of Man. All opinions expressed, interpretations of the evidence and conclusions drawn are my own, and do not necessarily reflect the views of the above scholars and institutions.

Index